T0243262

Praise for

Practical Optimism

"Sue Varma has given us an approachable and well-researched book that integrates the best of science and experience. Given the shortage of mental health professionals, this singular and approachable resource is a great place to start for many."

—Ken Duckworth, MD, CMO of the National Alliance on Mental Illness and author of the national bestseller *You Are Not Alone*

"Get ready to feel inspired as you learn how to overcome obstacles, build genuine relationships, and create a future filled with hope and possibility."

—Kimberly Rae Miller, bestselling author of *Coming Clean*

"*Practical Optimism* is an exceptional guide to moving through the trauma of life and relationships. Deeply wise, and rooted in Dr. Varma's clinical work, her own personal experience, and the latest research, it is an essential and inspiring resource to help us all build a critical resource: our inner strength."

—Eric Manheimer, MD, clinical professor at NYU School of Medicine, writer, producer, and author of *Twelve Patients*

"Theory makes little difference without accompanying action, and *Practical Optimism* powerfully bridges that gap—giving us both the resources *and* the tools to navigate challenges and help us find a sense of peace, balance, and hope. Practical Optimism teaches us that things won't always be perfect, but they can be better."

—Sara Blanchard, author of *Flex Mom*

Practical Optimism

The Art, Science, and Practice of Exceptional Well-Being

Sue Varma, MD

AVERY
an imprint of Penguin Random House
New York

AVERY

an imprint of Penguin Random House LLC
penguinrandomhouse.com

Most Avery books are available at special quantity discounts for bulk
purchase for sales promotions, premiums, fundraising, and educational needs.
Special books or book excerpts also can be created to fit specific needs.
For details, write SpecialMarkets@penguinrandomhouse.com.

Library of Congress Cataloging-in-Publication Data

Title: Practical optimism: the art, science, and practice of
exceptional well-being / Sue Varma, MD.
Description: New York: Avery, [2024] | Includes index.
Identifiers: LCCN 2023030992 (print) | LCCN 2023030993 (ebook) |
ISBN 9780593418949 (hardcover) | ISBN 9780593418956 (epub)
Subjects: LCSH: Optimism. | Attitude (Psychology) | Well-being.
Classification: LCC BF698.35.O57 V37 2024 (print) |
LCC BF698.35.O57 (ebook) |
DDC 149/.5—dc23/eng/20230928
LC record available at https://lccn.loc.gov/2023030992
LC ebook record available at https://lccn.loc.gov/2023030993

Printed in the United States of America
1st Printing

Book design by Patrice Sheridan

To my patients: your courage and commitment to optimal living inspire me. You are my greatest teachers.

For you—the reader, my friend and fellow Practical Optimist—I hope this book serves as the wellspring from which you refill your glass each and every day.

To my family: your love and belief in me replenish my glass with an abundance that allows me to pour for others.

And to the footprints in the sand—my own Practical Optimism journey—you've taught me that it doesn't matter whether the glass is half full or half empty. It is always refillable.

Contents

Author's Note

ix

Introduction

Kintsugi: Beauty from What Is Broken

1

Chapter 1

Why Practical Optimism?

19

Chapter 2

Purpose: Connecting to What Energizes and Inspires You

41

Chapter 3

Processing Emotions: Name, Claim, Tame (and Reframe) Them

66

Chapter 4

Problem-Solving: Moving Toward Action

94

Chapter 5

Pride: A Deep Knowing of Your Self-Worth

122

Chapter 6

Proficiency: Believing You Can Achieve

158

Chapter 7

Present: Being Here Now

189

Chapter 8

People: Creating Nourishing Relationships

220

Chapter 9

Practicing Healthy Habits: Automating Good Daily Decisions

260

Epilogue

303

Acknowledgments

309

Index

313

Author's Note

The principles of Practical Optimism (PO) go beyond simply reducing or helping us withstand stress. Together, they add up to the ultimate PO goal: a secure, level-headed sense of self-worth, resulting in more confidence in ourselves and our abilities, helping us unleash our natural strengths and talents and build a life of meaning, purpose, connection, and joy.

I hope this book will be deeply useful to you. However, please bear in mind that this book is not meant to be a manual on mental health disorders and their treatments. And while suicide, grief, anxiety, depression, loss, peripartum disorders, burnout, pandemic losses, discrimination and bias, social and political uncertainty, trauma, exceptional longevity, chronic illness, exercise, sleep, habit formation, workplace wellness, interpersonal relationships, couple dynamics, and other topics are discussed on varying levels, this book isn't intended to be an exhaustive or comprehensive discussion of these topics.

The cases in this book are composites to ensure confidentiality and to be reflective of a variety of experiences, and they are used to illustrate key points in each Pillar of Practical Optimism. Some of the cases may feel more relatable than others. I'm deeply indebted to my patients, from whom I have learned so much and whom I deeply respect. I am also indebted to all those pioneers, named and unnamed, whose work, research, insights, and philosophies have informed and influenced my thinking over the years and as this book has taken shape. Our scientific understanding of health and well-being is ever-evolving. I've drawn on what is known to this point, and I look forward to the evolution and application of Practical Optimism as we continue to learn more.

Case composites have been condensed and don't reflect the process of mental health treatment. No book, no matter how helpful, can replace the careful and thorough evaluation and examination of an experienced and qualified trained mental health professional. There is no substitute for the work done in psychotherapy (be it group, family, couples, or individual), nor for the benefits from thoughtfully and carefully combining medications or other important treatment modalities as part of an individualized and comprehensive treatment plan, when needed/deemed essential by you and your treatment provider. The progress is often in the process, and the process unfolds over time.

As much as this book is about Practical Optimism, there are some obstacles—such as racism, discrimination, bias, sexism, victimization, neglect, inequity, barriers, healthcare disparities, flawed or broken systems, to name only some—that can make the practicality of achieving optimism (either in philosophy or practice) feel insurmountable. This book's message, its positive outlook, its tangible tips and strategies, are not meant to minimize or negate anyone's lived experience. PO is about trying to figure out what works best for you, given your own unique circumstances, background, experiences, goals, and resources. Sometimes it's not so clear what we need. PO helps you try to figure out what you need and then helps you get it—whether it's time, perspective, acceptance, concrete know-how, rest, self-soothing, feeling understood by others, material resources, or otherwise. PO aims to help remind you of your choices and expand your repertoire of choices, skills, and mindset, so you feel empowered through considering numerous possibilities and options. Don't get disheartened if things don't unfold neatly or according to a certain specific timeline or your expectations. The goal is to show you how Practical Optimism worked in my life, and I wholeheartedly hope it will help in yours.

Depending upon your life experiences, some of the topics discussed could trigger distressing emotions. *You can skip ahead if the topic feels too triggering or stick around longer if you feel up to it.*

It's also important to keep in mind that many life transitions or other important life changes and choices might also bring about periods of struggle and challenge—and that too would be totally within the realm of normal. For example, in chapter 3, "Processing Emotions," pregnancy, childbirth, and motherhood are discussed. The transitions accompanying these life stages can bring about unanticipated feelings—from stressed and overwhelmed to sad and anxious (in addition to wonderful moments). Even if your life change is one that you very much welcome, if these feelings persist, interfere with your daily life, or impact your functioning, my suggestion is to seek help. I usually tell mothers and those supporting mothers to understand that perinatal mood and anxiety disorders are common and treatable.

Regardless of your life situation, *if you are struggling, please seek help.*

In crisis, please call 988 for the Suicide and Crisis Lifeline (within the U.S.) or use the chat at 988lifeline.org.

Kintsugi

Beauty from What Is Broken

I neatly hung up my white coat, took off my scrubs, and slipped into a hospital gown. Settling onto the examination table in the neurology department, I made a mental note to remember how cold I felt, how vulnerable. It would help me relate to my patients, I thought.

As a resident, I spent numerous hours a week in this hospital, but I'd never been a patient here before. I'd made an appointment with one of the hospital's finest neurologists after I started feeling weakness in my legs—literally becoming weak in the knees. At first it was only while I was walking or exercising, but within a week or two I started feeling regularly on the verge of collapse. I'd position myself against a wall or sit during exams, hoping my patients took it as a sign of intimacy, not infirmity.

When the constant headaches started, I knew I had to make an appointment. Was it Guillain-Barré syndrome—a rare autoimmune disorder—or multiple sclerosis? If twelve years of medical education had given me anything, it was an exhaustive list of possible diagnoses to freak out over.

Before my wardrobe change, I'd been answering intake questions I was used to being on the other end of.

"Any stress?" the doctor asked—but then her once-over answered that: My white coat had seen better days and was permanently ink-stained, pockets bulging with discharge papers, EKG reports, protein bars, and pocket-sized medical handbooks.

"I see they're keeping you busy," she said. That was certainly true, but there was more. While I was in the midst of the most grueling work schedule of my life, my mother had been diagnosed with stage 3 breast cancer. The recommendations were surgery, radiation, and chemotherapy. But because of underlying heart problems (she'd undergone a quadruple bypass), she wouldn't be able to withstand the heart toxicity of chemo. When I wasn't at my hospital, I was at hers, taking her to specialist after specialist in search of a treatment plan that could save her.

"Yes," I said. "A little stressed."

"We'll do some tests," she said, and I was ushered to the room where I waited now.

The doctor explained she'd be putting some needles in my legs, performing an electromyogram (EMG) to test the electrical activity (in response to nerve stimulation) of my muscles. Some pinching, prodding, and waiting later, she gave me my results.

"You're fine," she said.

"But I'm not fine." Obviously I wasn't—I couldn't even stand anymore. "I have these symptoms."

"Sorry, but I'm not finding any neurological abnormalities in your exam and testing," she said.

I left feeling an uncomfortable mix of relief and frustration. If I didn't have a debilitating neurological condition, what did I have?

It seemed I was back to square one. The metaphor of my physical problems mirroring my life situation—being literally unable to stand what I was going through—wasn't lost on me. Sometimes the body expresses what the mind cannot. But I didn't have time for an inner odyssey. I just needed to push through, as I always had. Somehow.

I don't believe in coincidences, only synchronicity. Besides which, admittedly, I was getting desperate. So soon thereafter when a guest lecturer spoke to my department about cognitive behavioral therapy (CBT), I took it as a sign.

Much of my medical education and training so far had focused on psychopharmacology and psychoanalysis. I'd found wisdom in both. But I was fascinated by CBT: a proactive, systematic, effective, evidence-based mental health approach, with practices people could use to solve problems in real time, so maybe, just maybe, they wouldn't happen again. Insight about the problem, coupled with real-time solutions? That was an idea I could get behind.

In the first year of my psychiatry residency, two years earlier, it had been suggested (though not required) that we engage in our own psychotherapy. Many of my fellow residents signed up immediately, mostly with psychoanalysts. I was reluctant. The program neither paid for nor allowed time for it. Medical school plus living in New York City was expensive, and my residency consumed most of my life. What little downtime I had was reserved for my family and self-care: exercise, meeting friends, seeing a movie or Broadway show. I even acted in one (well, an off-off-Broadway show). While I strongly believed in the power of psychiatry and psychoanalysis—I was, after all, making a career out of it—I wanted at least some small part of my life to not involve therapy. The thought of spending money and time I didn't have to dredge up old memories of how my (mostly well-intentioned) parents did me wrong wasn't too appealing. There was the time, of course, when they uprooted us from our comfortable New York suburban life and plunked us down in their homeland of India, where we lived for two years in a house with dodgy electricity (read: intermittent fans in 105-degree heat) and squat toilets (I tried and quickly failed to hold it until we returned to the United States). On our first morning, we woke up to a house flooded up to our ankles, which led to my father pulling open a drain on the veranda, causing an army of ten thousand angry cockroaches to swarm everywhere as I frantically whacked them with a *jhadoo,* a dried-grass broom.

But the India Roach Fiasco had become family folklore, something we laughed about during my weekend visits to my parents outside the city. Did I want to spend one of my handful of free hours a week swatting old memories with a metaphorical jhadoo? So I put therapy off. And put it off . . .

Now life had finally pushed me to my limit. I needed to find peace and purpose in what was happening to me personally and professionally and to get a handle on my unexplained physical symptoms. After the lecture, I approached the speaker for a referral. I was a therapist finally ready for therapy.

After just a few months of therapy and learning how to practice CBT, I felt more empowered than I'd ever felt in my life. That feeling only increased as I applied what I was learning to manage work stresses and navigate my mother's health crisis. These were techniques I could rely on. And the strange physical symptoms? They were suddenly . . . gone.

I had learned to take care of my wellness before it became my illness.

But the practitioner in me wanted to dig deeper. I wanted to understand how to manage my stress so it didn't escalate to manifesting as physical symptoms. And I wanted to use these methods to help my patients.

My Path to Practical Optimism

On September 10, 2001, I was a trainee at a New York City hospital. The next day, September 11, my world, along with everyone else's, changed forever. Suddenly I was responsible for the care of my fellow New Yorkers—many rescue, recovery, and support workers—while we all struggled to make sense of life after the largest terrorist attack on American soil.

I immersed myself in trauma therapy training so I could be the psychiatrist the people in my care needed. My work eventually led to a leadership role a few years later as the first medical director and attending psychiatrist at the World Trade Center Mental Health Program (WTCMHP) at the World Trade Center Healthcare Center at what was then called NYU Medical Center/Bellevue Hospitals. And while all this was happening around me, I was caring for very ill patients while my mother navigated severe cardiac disease and cancer.

The directorship was a transformative challenge that also gave me a unique vantage point professionally. As the only psychiatrist attending to both the civilian and first-responder program at the hospital at the time, I met people on every point of the stress and trauma continuum. Some, I noticed, had serious exposure to all the life-threatening aspects of that horrific day, but never met the criteria for a mental health disorder. The question began nagging at me: How do some people survive, even thrive, despite profound challenges? And how can we maximize and optimize the things we have control over while buffering ourselves from stress?

While CBT could help people address symptoms of stress, anxiety, and depression, could we prevent those symptoms from happening in the first place? Wouldn't it be wonderful if doctors could not only help their patients move from a dysfunctional state to a functional one—an important and worthy achievement in itself—but also enable them to take the extra step of going from a functional state to an optimal one?

I found myself in uncharted territory as a physician. But from my personal experience as a patient getting poked and prodded for unexplained leg weakness and as a daughter taking my mother to her medical appointments, I felt something was missing from what many patients were receiving—at least, from my perspective of being on both sides of the examining table.

It would be several years before I could pinpoint that my Western medical and psychiatric training prepared me for what we call a *deficits model*—to fix what's broken and to focus on pathologies. In contrast, a *strengths-based model* seeks to maximize our strengths, resources, and assets to not only assist in recovery but also help us go beyond just returning to our baseline. And when we focus on what's best in a person, we're more likely to bring out what's best.

As I sought answers—through my experiences with patients and by immersing myself in the literature—all roads led me to optimism. But what did that translate to on the ground? And was there a way to marry a deficits model (in which I was well trained already) with a strengths-based model (which I was determined to learn) so we could help people—optimists or not—not only to be resilient but also to have the means to flourish? While resilience is important, flourishing is even better.

PO Pearls

Flourishing is more than bouncing back from adversity. It's thriving in the face of it.

The next phase of my professional life—first as medical director of the World Trade Center Mental Health Program and later as a private practitioner—would be focused on learning from people who'd made it against the odds. In the next chapter, we'll look at the foundations of Practical Optimism (PO) in more detail, but suffice it to say that PO evolved from multiple threads of my work coming together. My work with 9/11 survivors, grieving families, and first responders, alongside my years of work with hundreds of patients, including survivors of domestic violence, women without housing, people in prison, and others in painful circumstances, has given me a window on just how difficult daily life can be, as well as on the courage and perseverance it takes to steer a steady emotional course, particularly in the face of emotional distress.

In addition, my work as a medical contributor and media advisor and consultant on issues ranging from mass shootings to natural disasters to pandemic parenting gave me the opportunity to interact with the public through radio, TV, social media, and public talks. I saw how eager people were for clear, practical, compassionate information about how to make sense of a tragedy and how to cope. The overwhelming response I've received from media projects to reduce stigma around mental health further reinforced my conviction that we must make it easier to help ourselves and our loved ones. Furthermore, teaching medical students, residents, and therapists in training over the last two decades has helped me appreciate that clinicians might benefit from more robust training in the formation of healthy habits, emotional regulation, and coping skills so our patients could turn to us not just in sickness, but also to help promote their health and wellness—and that we, too, needed to learn how to heal and remain healthy so we could be the best versions of ourselves for others. I've sought to combine these understandings with the best science gleaned from hundreds of research studies published over the years into a workable, tangible, accessible framework.

My quest to create Practical Optimism reached far and wide. So imagine my surprise when I realized that in many ways, the model for the insights I was seeking had been in front of me all along.

Practical Optimism Personified

If you asked my dad, a successful New York psychiatrist, to tell you of his beginnings in India, he'd say he was born with more than enough of the essentials—love, kindness, and lots of books! But anyone looking at his early life might see he was born with very little. Despite his humble beginnings, my dad had a vivid and vibrant childhood filled with exotic camel rides, monsoon dance parties, desert nights, candlelit family dinners, ghost stories around the fire (there was no electricity—only hurricane lamps), and rooftop slumber parties under the stars with his five siblings and his parents. All my life, my dad has smiled with nostalgic fondness every time we speak about it. "We were never poor in what mattered, Sue: love, education, laughter, and vision."

What is that vision, Dad? "Simple living and high thinking."

What else, Dad? I probe, like any good psychiatrist would. "That you *see* the best in everything, you *make* the best of everything, and everything that has happened has also happened *in the best possible way for you*."

My dad doesn't deny he had struggles. He tells of flunking out and having to repeat the fifth grade. Of making do with what was broken, insufficient, or nonexistent, from toys to furnishings to appliances. Of not getting into medical school when he first applied. But those challenges were learning grounds for persistence and problem-solving: not giving up in grade school; making his own toys with his siblings by stitching rope onto a ball for a soccer ball and playing cricket with branches for wickets and pieces of wood for bats; becoming a wizard at repairing or making makeshift appliances and furnishings—like the time he, to my mother's chagrin, rigged up blackout curtains for my bedroom with thumbtacks, packing tape, and black plastic garbage bags. As for applying to medical school, he kept at it and got accepted the following year at the state medical school—the only medical school (at the time) in one of the most populated states in India, with a large number of applicants (approximately four thousand per year) and one of the lowest acceptance rates in India (only about eighty seats). My dad admits there were kids a lot smarter than he who didn't make it.

This wasn't sunny-skies positivity or bouncing back from a setback or two. This was a focused, intentional, time-tested, in-the-trenches kind of optimism and resilience—the kind you glued together from life's broken pieces. This was flourishing at its finest.

Dad, were you born this way? "No. But what choice did I have? I could laugh or I could cry," he tells me, cracking himself up as he often does, with a mischievous but grounded gleam in his eyes.

With respect to his mindset, I think he did have a choice. So do I. So do you. That possibility, that dignity of choice is what Practical Optimism helps me find and provide for myself and for my patients, time and again. This is what I want to share with you.

Practical Optimism in a Nutshell

Practical Optimism is a unique mindset, skill set, and action set that equips you with evidence-based tools and techniques to help you reach your career, financial, fitness, personal, and relationship goals more quickly and sustain momentum toward your future goals, wherever you are on your life path.

Practical Optimism draws its power from uniting what many might consider to be two opposing ideas. The *optimism* part is about cultivating a mindset grounded in a belief in the boundless positive potential in yourself and others. The *practical* part is about implementing the key behavioral skills that will give you access to the most reasonable, rational course of action among all possible courses of action. It also refers to the fact that PO is a *practice*—yes, optimism can be learned and implemented—no different from learning and practicing anything you want to get better at, be it a musical instrument, a work skill, a language, or a sport. Practical Optimism is concrete and becomes more natural with time.

Chapter by chapter, we'll delve into the principles and practices I've distilled into what I call the 8 Pillars of Practical Optimism:

Pillar 1—Purpose. Identify and invest in authentic goals that energize and inspire you.

Pillar 2—Processing Emotions. Deepen your emotional wisdom and awareness.

Pillar 3—Problem-Solving. Marry intuition, logic, and emotional regulation and become a masterful problem solver.

Pillar 4—Pride. Challenge negative thoughts and behaviors and use self-compassion to develop a stable, intrinsic sense of self-worth.

Pillar 5—Proficiency. Build confidence in your abilities and improve on them.

Pillar 6—Present. Cut mental clutter, ward off worry, and take back your time.

Pillar 7—People. Develop a relationship practice with yourself and others to reduce loneliness and cultivate belonging and connection.

Pillar 8—Practicing Healthy Habits. Use Practical Optimism and other science-backed hacks to create and sustain new habits.

The principles underlying Practical Optimism are founded on years of scientific research and approaches to everything from treating depression and anxiety to coping with distress and managing everyday stressors and challenges. They form a multidisciplinary approach that integrates best practices and evidence-based therapies with mindfulness, distress coping skills, exercise, and more into an accessible model for living an optimal life. They've been battle-tested by me and by my patients, but they're also rooted in years of research and theory by scientists and researchers, authors and practitioners, whose shoulders I'm grateful to stand on and whose work I diligently researched throughout my career and in the writing of this book. Together, they can provide a mindset for living wisely that can help stabilize you in stormy waters or guide you during smooth sailing.

The Pillars can also double as an eight-step action plan—starting with having a vision, goal, idea, or intention (Purpose), ending with making it a reality (Practicing Healthy Habits), and navigating whatever may come along in between, from emotional processing to problem-solving; from gaining proficiency to cultivating relationships with people who get and support you, and more. Whether you want to change careers, go back to school, start a family, get healthy, or pursue any life path important to you, Practical Optimism helps you establish the vision; summon dedication, perseverance, and support; develop an action plan; and then automate that action plan, steadfast in the face of obstacles.

Unprecedented Times Call
for Unprecedented Coping Skills

When I ask my patients of all ages what's on their mind, they share that not only are they contending with day-to-day stress, but they're also experiencing pandemic fatigue, climate fatigue, political fatigue, and financial exhaustion. These last few years, world events have challenged us all. Now more than ever, we're collectively looking to emerge from a stressful period equipped with skills to protect and safeguard our health, happiness, and capacity for resilience. Consider just a few telling findings:

- According to the annual Stress in America Survey,[1] Americans are feeling battered by a multitude of stressors that they experience as being outside their control, including political divisiveness, economic instability, racial climate, and concern for violence. Survey participants reported notable physical symptoms related to their emotional distress, including headache, fatigue, insomnia, and nervousness.
- Gallup's 2019 Global Emotions report included results of interviews with the more than 150,000 individuals surveyed from 140 countries worldwide. It found that 55 percent of Americans said they experienced stress "a lot of the day," compared with only 35 percent globally. (Americans' stress, worry, and anger had intensified according to the report, and this was *before* the social isolation, job loss, financial strain, loss of loved ones, and

[1] Further details of this October 2022 survey can be found at the American Psychological Association press release "Stress in America 2022: Concerned for the Future, Beset by Inflation," https://www.apa.org/news/press/releases/stress/2022/concerned-future-inflation, or more specifically, the American Psychological Association press release "Stress in America October 2022 Topline Data," https://www.apa.org/news/press/releases/stress/2022/october-2022-topline-data.pdf.

other stressors of the COVID-19 pandemic, not to mention its potential long-term consequences.)

- According to the World Health Organization (WHO), one in four people in the world will be affected by a mental or neurological condition at some point in their life, with many women experiencing anywhere from a two to four times increased risk for mental disorders—thought to be due in part to the increasing number of roles they juggle inside and outside the home.

- There was a 65 percent increase in antidepressant use between 1999 and 2014. Researchers in this study found that one in eight Americans over the age of twelve had taken an antidepressant in the last month.[2]

- Despite the availability of numerous treatment options, WHO cites depression as the leading cause of ill health and disability worldwide.

- Depression has been found to raise our risk of early death. A large long-term study showed that having at least one major depressive episode is linked to increased mortality for both men and women. Those with a history of depression saw as much as a 50 percent rise in risk of death by any cause, reducing the projected lifespan of sufferers by ten to twelve years on average.

- Current evidence indicates that the quality of our relationships is declining, and more and more people report not having any true confidants in their lives.

---

[2] Increased antidepressant use may be connected to multiple factors—some positive; some negative. It may signal a rise in awareness: more people are getting diagnosed and treated, with less stigma and secrecy surrounding mental health issues (positives). It may also signal a rise in rates of depression, and even perhaps in overdiagnosis (negatives). It's hard to pinpoint the exact reasons for the rise. But what is clear is that people are languishing or suffering, and they need help—better assessments by physicians and trained behavioral health specialists, more mental health services, and better coping skills and improved relationships. To me, all prove the need for an empowering framework like Practical Optimism.

How (and When) to Use This Book

Have you ever thought:

- *Could I be doing something just a little differently so that I would be happier?*
- *What are my goals, and how can I achieve them? What will make me really and truly fulfilled?*
- *Some days I feel like I'm just going through the motions.*
- *It's been one crisis after another. How can I keep an even keel?*
- *My life's in transition [new school/job, new parent, newly single, starting a serious relationship, empty nester, caregiver, etc.] and I'm overwhelmed. I need to level up my coping skills.*
- *I want to do something about the injustices and suffering in the world, but it's hard to keep momentum, or even know where to start.*

If you can relate to any of these statements, I hope you'll let Practical Optimism help. Each person will come to Practical Optimism at different seasons and for different reasons. You can customize it to your own pace and needs, whether you are coping with emotions through a difficult time, want to find more productive approaches in your relationships or at work, are looking to make some fundamental life changes, yearn to enjoy life more, or want to be your best self and contribute your best to the world. The techniques in the 8 Pillars can be transformative for those who are languishing—not living with a specific mental health disorder, but feeling dissatisfied with how their life is going. Think of it as the ultimate form of self-care, helping us handle problems in real time so that they don't become unmanageable chronic stressors.

I also encourage you to familiarize yourself with the roles of exercise, sleep, nutrition, and a host of other modalities that could be used to maximize your mental wellness. While you are reading this book, I ask that you consider: *What new skills out there can I learn and use?*

If you are under extreme stress, this book will still be of help—though it doesn't hurt to also consider getting additional mental health support and treatment.

You will bring your unique strengths to Practical Optimism. Maybe you're good at problem-solving but struggle with being fully present in each moment. Or you're full of passion and purpose but have let your health practices fall by the wayside. I encourage you to read through each chapter and take what serves you. Practical Optimism can serve as both a mirror and a window: a chance to reflect and gain insight into your journey, and to look outward for ideas, strategies, and skills that can help you make the most of your life path.

I tell my patients that when it's possible, you'll find it best to learn new coping skills in the calmer stretches of life, so those skills, like life preservers on a boat, are on board and ready to use when rough seas come. Take your time absorbing the ideas and practicing the tools. Any skill we learn takes practice to incorporate and be of real help. If your experience is anything like mine, your daily life will present multiple opportunities to practice Practical Optimism. It's here for you.

Bottom line: The path and practice of Practical Optimism is as individual as you are. I welcome you on this journey, as I continue to take each and every step, every day, with you.

Kintsugi

As I look back, I realize that I've had a front-row seat to Practical Optimism my entire life. My dad was my earliest case study in the benefits of being guided by the 8 Ps. I didn't know it was anything special growing up. I just saw that he and my mom were both driven by a sense of purpose: to serve others—their family of origin, their patients (for Dad) and students and colleagues (for Mom), their children, and each other—in sickness and in health.

Dad was one of the first trained child psychiatrists in Northern India and an advocate for children's rights. He had completed his psychiatry training in the United States and had a flourishing career in New York but returned to India regularly to volunteer his time teaching doctors, teachers, social workers, and childcare workers how to care for children with physical or learning disabilities, attention deficit or behavioral problems—children who up until then were considered a community burden and were punished harshly or sent away. It was challenging work that could be done only by someone who could problem-solve like nobody's business.

While resourcefulness, creativity, flexibility, and openness in his thinking appear to be Dad's default settings, I came to see that he works every day to develop his inner resources. When he experiences challenges and obstacles, he processes his emotions so he remains calm, patient, and pleasant. In an era of multitasking and innumerable distractions, he's unashamedly old-school and has mastered an uncanny ability to stay in the present moment, doing things one at a time. People know they have his undivided attention because he listens, remembers, and follows up on what's important to them—things they don't even recall sharing—with a phone call, a card, a visit, or an email.

He has never forgotten a birthday, an anniversary, or an excuse to celebrate and give and receive the positive energy that comes from being with others. He's a favorite guest at cocktail parties, minus the cocktails (he doesn't drink!); is the belle of his medical school alumni class chat group; and reconnected after five decades with old medical colleagues in Vancouver Island, Heidelberg, and Udaipur. His daily practice of healthy habits for as long as I've known him—meditating, yoga, strength training, daily walking, and more—has been in part responsible for his exceptional longevity and, equally important, a life of exceptional health. Not only does he still take care of himself in his late eighties, but he continues to take care of all of us. He cuts fruits and vegetables for me every time I see him!

And in the hard times, when my mother's cancer brought me almost literally to my knees, my father used all of the capacities of the 8 Pillars of Practical Optimism to stay present, emotionally connected, and able to face the difficult truths while waiting on my mother hand and foot as this strong-minded, super-capable woman—a noted educator and holder of four bachelor's degrees, four master's degrees, and a PhD, whose accomplishments in India had won national attention and who made significant contributions to education and child mental health in the United States—came to terms with her painful reality and said goodbye to this life.

I've learned from my dad that an optimist is what an optimist does. This union of positivity and pragmatism forms the cornerstone of Practical Optimism.

In my dad's living room is a beautiful ceramic he brought back from Japan. Kintsugi, he told me when I was a kid, is the Japanese art of creating beauty from broken ceramics. The idea of putting something fractured back together and in the process restoring it to something beyond its original glory appealed to me. As I now realize, it is the very essence of Practical Optimism. I knew early on in my years as a psychiatrist that when I saw patients who described themselves as "broken," I wasn't interested in just helping them put their life together again. "Better, but not well" wasn't good enough. I wanted to be a coconspirator in helping them create something radically more durable and radiant than they'd dared to hope. Practical Optimism allows you the ability to work with your life and all its ups and downs—imperfections, cracks, and breaks; promise and potential—by employing patience, practicality, creativity, resourcefulness, skill, and love in applying the golden glue of joinery that results in an even more beautifully adorned and fortified creation.

This book is a labor of love for me, a distillation of the years I've spent helping patients live healthier, happier lives through the practices in these pages. It is research- and fact-based, with clear takeaways and useful action steps. Practical Optimism helped me to not only survive but thrive in the hardest times of my life. It has improved the lives of my patients over my two decades in practice. It has changed my life. And it can change yours.

To view the scientific references cited in this chapter,
please visit doctorsuevarma.com/book.

CHAPTER 1

Why Practical Optimism?

The pessimist complains about the wind; the optimist expects it to change; the realist (Practical Optimist) adjusts the sails.

—WILLIAM ARTHUR WARD
(AS MODIFIED BY THE AUTHOR)

When people walk into my office for the first time, they have a problem they want to solve. Some may be navigating one of the darkest times of their life. Others simply can't catch their breath in the waves of trials and traumas that come with being human. Either way, telling them to look on the bright side wouldn't be an effective treatment. They'd probably nod politely (or not so politely!) and never return—because I'd discounted the gravity of what they were dealing with. That's not optimism, that's denial.

That's precisely where Practical Optimism comes in. It incorporates the resilient positivity optimists are very good at, without the denial that can sometimes land overly sunny optimists in trouble—*plus* the proactive life steps that lead to flourishing. Practical Optimists squarely face and fix what's broken, but they don't stop there. They improve on it.

Practical Optimism combines a mindset of affirmation, agency, and conviction that we can make a positive difference in our own and others' lives with a clear-eyed acceptance—appreciation, even—of the fundamental uncertainty and the unknowableness of existence. Whether you're using it to cope with the harshest of realities, to better manage your daily life challenges, or to push toward your dreams and goals, Practical Optimism taps into your natural resilience and boosts the heck out of it.

Practical Optimists Are Made, Not Born

I'm not sure I'd consider myself a natural-born optimist, but I try to think and act like one. The term *optimist* usually refers to a person who tends to look at a given situation positively, anticipating a favorable outcome. We might even conceptualize optimists as having a naturally cheerful disposition, given their positive skew on things. And while optimists might be born with a greater tendency to experience positive affect due to their more generous interpretations of situations, they are not happier "just because" or cheerful "no matter what." Optimists have ebbs and flows in their mood in response to what is happening in their lives and in the world around them, just like everyone else. But what allows optimists to experience greater well-being and happiness and a generally good mood is their attitude—specifically, which aspects of a situation they home in on and their interpretations of what is happening around them. Optimists tend to focus on the positives of a given situation and focus on areas within their control, which allows them to experience greater self-confidence around navigating life's challenges. They also tend to take responsibility for their part in a situation, and let the rest go. In addition, their proactive capacity to deploy key coping strategies when perceiving themselves to be under attack (instead of resorting to shame or blame) allows them not only to be able to withstand stress better than pessimists, but also to return to this higher mood set point following adversity or setbacks. They naturally have access to these high-value psychological resources. Optimists persist in the face of failure and regularly engage in trying to see things from a more open, flexible, and hopeful point of view—all of which allows them to remain persistent and proactive in the face of potential obstacles.

But, you might ask, how is it that they are naturally able to do this? Well, through my work, I've learned that optimism isn't just a feel-good term. Optimism has a neural basis in the brain. Boosting activity in the left hemisphere of the brain can be correlated with promoting optimism, a sense of calm and agency, and proactive thinking and behavior. And while both hemispheres of the brain, right and left, work together to create a seamless experience of ourselves and the world, knowing that each hemisphere plays a specific role can help us hack our way to better outlooks and outcomes in our lives. (For example, increased activity in the right hemisphere—the part of the brain that scans the environment for threat and danger—is associated with pessimism, depression, passivity, and avoidance.) Each of the 8 Pillars of Practical Optimism and the associated tangible exercises are shown to enhance optimism on a neurophysiological level, leading to the positive, hopeful, and proactive stance that optimists are more readily able to tap into, and that we can all learn to practice, regardless of our natural skew or predispositions. Optimists may be born, but Practical Optimists are made.

––––

Optimists also live longer, are healthier, recover from stress, injury, and illness faster, and sleep longer and better. In the September 2019 *JAMA Network Open*, one of the most highly respected peer-reviewed publications in the world, researchers reported that not only is optimism associated with a lower risk of cardiovascular events, but it can also decrease death by all causes. Combining the results of over fifteen different studies, the authors were able to analyze data on more than two hundred thousand individuals to reach this conclusion. A meta-analysis of eighty-three studies on optimism showed optimism to be associated with beneficial outcomes in immune functioning, cardio-vascular health, cancer, pregnancy, physical symptoms, and pain.

In addition, optimists are more successful and report greater in-comes and job satisfaction, have better health habits (have a better diet, more consistently engage in physical activity, are less likely to be smokers), have stronger relationships, report greater life satisfaction, and—most importantly—are happier.

But here's a surprising fact: research shows that while optimism is to some extent genetic, only 25 percent of one's proclivity toward op-timism is inherited. When it comes to our psychological health, genes may predict our destiny, but they alone don't determine it.

So whether you were born with optimism is . . . rather irrelevant.

More and more studies are examining how to use optimism as an intervention instead of viewing it as a trait you either are or are not born with. Some of these interventions ask us to envision positive future outcomes, such as what life would look like if everything we worked toward came through for us.

While I'm all for these mood-boosting, hope-enhancing exercises, the results can be temporary. For lasting change, we have to change not only how we see the world but also how we interact with it.

Indeed, optimists might benefit from taking a page from the Prac-tical Optimism playbook. As mentioned, unrealistic optimists can get into trouble. They may be masters of the ostrich effect: a tendency to bury their head in the sand, ignoring information that's uncomfortable or contrary to their beliefs, pretending everything is (or will be) okay. Or they may use this attitude to abdicate responsibility—for example, by engaging in risky behavior, not getting preventive medical care, or underestimating danger and overestimating their ability to handle it.

Practical Optimism does more than encourage us to envision

positive outcomes. It equips us with a mindset, skill set, and action set for achieving them—and the ability to apply these capacities when they may not come naturally to us, especially during challenge and adversity.

Can Practical Optimism Reduce Pessimism?

Martin Seligman, PhD, a pioneer in the field of positive psychology and the study of optimism, found that while optimists and pessimists experience roughly the same number of adverse life events, pessimists engaged in the three Ps in regard to negative thinking: personal, pervasive, and permanent. When something bad happened to them, they predominantly blamed themselves for it (taking things personally), believed all aspects of their lives were at risk (pervasive), and viewed it as a permanent loss. I might add a fourth P: remaining passive in the face of obstacles.

Here again, genetics is part of the story. In 2011, UCLA researchers found that optimism was associated with the oxytocin receptor gene, or the OXTR gene, and that this gene was also related to having good psychological resources. What are these resources? The UCLA researchers defined them as optimism, mastery, a sense of control and agency, and a sense of self-worth.

Oxytocin is popularly understood as a cuddle and bonding hormone, secreted when a mother is bonding with her baby, during childbirth and breastfeeding, and during sexual activity. But oxytocin also functions as a neurotransmitter in the brain that increases in response to stress and is associated with prosocial skills such as empathy, trust, relationship building, and enjoying the company of others. In addition, it's now believed to be linked to having key psychological resources that can make the difference between experiencing temporary disappointment and sadness and falling into a prolonged depression.

It turns out there are variations of this OXTR gene. An individual with the A (adenine) variant—with either one or two copies—has a higher likelihood of stress sensitivity, reduced social skills, and worse mental health outcomes.

I won't kid you. Pessimism's pitfalls aren't great for health. Pessimists tend to ruminate about the past and are thus more predisposed to depression. They also worry about the future, putting them more at risk for anxiety. Either way, they're rarely living in the present, which makes it hard for them to fully relax and enjoy the joyous moments, and subject to following old, outdated, or unproductive scripts from the past in their daily life, where they may struggle with assertiveness and problem-solving.

Those who show characteristics of pessimism may have a few things in common. Negative beliefs may sometimes get in the way of forming close and trusting relationships, or they may perceive intimate relationships as exhausting for various reasons, including often feeling hurt or rejected. They may hold themselves and others to very high (sometimes arbitrary or unrealistic) standards, making it hard for them to give themselves and others credit for positive outcomes. Their brains and bodies are exposed to high levels of stress hormones such as cortisol, norepinephrine, and epinephrine. Exposure to chronically high levels of these hormones leads to increased inflammation and damage of blood vessels, atherosclerosis, and elevation of the risk for everything from depression to strokes, heart disease, vascular dementia, and beyond.

But here's the good news: your OXTR gene isn't the lone determinant of your capacity for emotional resiliency. Most of us can, with some awareness and skills training, strengthen our protective psychological resources for stress buffering as well as flourishing. The UCLA researchers suggest that through cognitive behavioral therapy (CBT), study participants could employ these psychological resources to buffer themselves against stress, depression, and anxiety.

What Is Cognitive Behavioral Therapy (CBT)?

Cognitive behavioral therapy (CBT) is a heavily researched and supported form of psychological treatment shown to be effective for a wide range of problems including depression, anxiety disorders, substance abuse, marital problems, eating disorders, and severe mental illness.[3] Although informed by a patient's past, CBT focuses on and has been shown to improve functioning and quality of life in the present.

CBT is based on the premise that our interpretations concerning people, events, our future, the world, and even ourselves matter, and psychological problems are often a result of faulty thinking, maladaptive or unhelpful behavioral patterns (perhaps based on old, outdated, or distorted ways of thinking, sometimes called scripts), and persistently negative emotions. When these aren't aligned with reality, they can lead to distorted thinking, rumination, and excessive worry, and eventually even result in impairment in functioning—enter anxiety and depression.

Learning to recognize these unhelpful thought patterns and challenge them with more accurate, realistic, and logical thinking helps us feel like we're in the driver's seat. People who work on CBT techniques in collaboration with their therapist will build upon and test

[3] The work of Aaron T. Beck, MD, in the area of cognitive therapy and cognitive behavioral therapy is globally renowned; this type of therapy is now used to treat a wide range of mental health disorders. Blending cognitive- and behavior-based elements and building upon the research on behaviorism and behavioral psychology, cognitive behavioral therapy is not only known as a therapy but also now used as an umbrella term for all cognitive-based psychotherapies. This includes but is not limited to rational emotive behavior therapy, cognitive therapy, acceptance and commitment therapy, and EMDR (Eye Movement Desensitization and Reprocessing). The works of Albert Ellis, B. F. Skinner, Joseph Wolpe, Claire Weekes, and many other giants in the field have all played important roles in our current understanding of these therapies. Cognitive therapy's roots can be traced back to ancient philosophies, including Stoicism.

what's discussed in sessions by doing "homework" outside of sessions. Gradually they expand their coping skills to include a wide variety of positive and proactive techniques, including relaxation, assertiveness, and reengagement with people and activities instead of avoidance. They may use thought logs—exercises that prompt us to uncover and challenge distorted thinking, distressing emotions, maladaptive behavior patterns, and the events that trigger them. Worry journals in CBT can help us become aware of the cyclic nature of our worries. The truth is, many of the situations we worry about aren't as bad as we fear they'll turn out to be, and we're often much more capable of handling them than we give ourselves credit for.

The science of optimism has caught the attention of researchers in nearly every field of medicine, from psychiatry to immunology, cardiology, and surgery. The 8 Pillars of Practical Optimism are grounded in evidence-based approaches and best practices in multiple areas, including internal medicine, psychiatry, neuroscience, behavioral and positive psychology, social science, positive psychiatry, neurobiology, yoga and mindfulness, and even philosophy. They're formulated to help you build your psychological reserves and serve as skills you can rely on in times of need. Think of them as emotional shock absorbers, cushioning you against life's inevitable speed bumps and (sometimes ginormous) potholes.

Optimist or Pessimist? It's Usually a Mix— One You Can Influence

Most people show qualities of both optimism and pessimism. They'll feel optimistic about some areas of their lives, more pessimistic about others, and sometimes both at once. For example, if you're the only hardworking person on the team at your job and your bonus depends on the whole team's performance, you may feel pessimism about your relationships with your coworkers and about your work future, but have a high sense of self-efficacy in your own life. This doesn't make you a pessimist—just someone in touch with reality.

Bottom line: Optimism and pessimism can coexist. Which is why it's totally normal to want to believe in and hope for the best possible outcome, while also experiencing fear and doubt. The key is being able to accept fear and doubt while maintaining a constructive outlook, applying strong coping skills, and doing your level best to make positive differences in the areas of your life that need a boost.

Perhaps you're familiar with the story "The Two Wolves." There are different versions of the story, but in the one I know, a Cherokee elder is teaching his grandson about life. "A fight is going on inside me," he says to the boy. "It is a terrible fight, and it is between two wolves. One is evil—he is anger, envy, sorrow, regret, greed, arrogance, self-pity, guilt, resentment, inferiority, lies, false pride, superiority, and ego."

He continues: "The other is good—he is joy, peace, love, hope, serenity, humility, kindness, benevolence, empathy, generosity, truth, compassion, and faith. The same fight is going on inside you—and inside every other person, too."

The grandson thinks about it for a minute and then asks his grandfather, "Which wolf will win?"

The Cherokee elder replies simply, "The one you feed."

This is a story about the connection between personal accountability and human potential. According to a study published in *Psychology and Aging* on the role of optimism and pessimism in breast cancer recovery, it was more important not to be a pessimist than to be an optimist. This is an important finding, because as we've said, pessimism and optimism are actually two pathways that often coexist. Which pathway you choose, like which wolf you feed, is up to you.

From Languishing to Flourishing

"The Two Wolves" holds true for us as a society, too. We could be taking better care of ourselves and each other on many levels.

Wellness is more than just the absence of illness. The World Health Organization (WHO) defines mental health as a state of well-being in which an individual realizes their own abilities, can cope with the normal stresses of life, can work productively, and can make a contribution to their community.

We're falling far short of this, and it has led to a culture of pessimism. In 2023 the United States ranked nineteenth in the World Happiness Index. Also, as we know, the odds of achieving and maintaining optimal physical and mental health are often stacked against many people. The social determinants of illness include all the consequences of poverty and discrimination: limited access to education, jobs, and medical and prenatal care, and a higher association of incarceration, violence, mental health disorders, substance abuse, and mortality. The chronic stress associated with these issues undermines our ability for good decision-making, goal-setting, and problem-solving.

As we entered 2020, we simultaneously saw a rise in loneliness, suicide rates, and opiate use disorder—and this was before the COVID-19 pandemic (a period I nostalgically refer to as BC). The unimaginable events and pressures of the pandemic escalated the medical, emotional, social, and economic suffering of the human family to the point where the Stress in America Survey 2022 showed that 65 to 80 percent of people are stressed out about a wide range of factors—economic and financial uncertainty, political strife and warfare, health, and more.

Depression and mental health disorders are a leading cause of disability worldwide and cost the United States approximately $250 billion per year. In the U.S., over half (54.7 percent) of adults with a mental illness do not receive treatment.

Those seeking help for mental health issues may find that as life-changing and lifesaving as our mental health treatment options are for many people, medications may not always work optimally for everyone, although research continues. What we do know is that the insights built in therapy can stay with us for years and create lasting changes in our lives and even in our brain circuitry—creating new learning patterns and promoting thought restructuring and behavior modification. Which is why, when I (thoughtfully, carefully, deliberately) prescribe medication in collaboration (i.e., discussion/participation) with my patients, it is often in concert with therapy.

For me, the essence of my therapy was the skills I came away with that I could use for the rest of my life: greater self-awareness, self-compassion, and emotional regulation; flexible and diverse coping strategies; and a more attuned and mindful awareness of the world as it is. While no book can replace the individualized work of and rapport built in therapy, I believe it's important that we all learn key life skills like these. When diligently practiced, these skills can change how we view ourselves, others, and our world in a positive way, to achieve positive results. Key psychological resources such as these can serve as a stress-buffering reservoir and wellspring for positive emotions and coping skills by helping us connect with our purpose, process our emotions, problem-solve, benefit from present-moment awareness, and hone our people skills. This forms the heart of Practical Optimism.

The beauty of PO is that it's proactive, not reactive. PO doesn't suggest, "Let's wait for something bad to happen. Then let's fix it and we are done." Think of an injury you've had—maybe a broken arm. The cast allows the bone to heal, but when the cast comes off, is your arm maximally functioning? More is needed for that. Similarly, treating a mental illness promotes healing but doesn't automatically confer wellness. It means you're better, but not well. While one in five people might be diagnosed with a mental illness in their lifetime, five out of five—all of us—have the potential to create a life of meaning, mastery, joy, and purpose. For any of us, achieving a high quality of life depends on a variety of factors, including our health, our support system, our treatment team, our lifestyle habits, and, frankly, our outlook.

Too many of us are languishing—a term professionals use to describe the lower end of the mental wellness spectrum, or making do with moderate mental wellness—when the goal should be flourishing, or peak mental wellness.

Languishing comes with its own set of costs, including cardiovascular problems, days missed from work, less productivity, a decreased quality of life, and increased risks for anxiety and depression. Languishing, while not meeting a mental health disorder criterion but still not functioning optimally—feeling bored, hollow, empty, stuck in a rut, stagnant—often flies under the radar.

What does flourishing look like? Flourishing is fully experiencing meaning, pleasure, self-acceptance, and mastery in our lives. It's taking on challenges, growing as people, and reveling in our relationships. It's creating a life of joy and purpose, enhancing the positive aspects while taking steps to reduce the negative. It's feeling that we matter, both in the world and to others. And it's seeking to do what has import, both for ourselves and for others. That's feeding the good wolf. Flourishing and resilience, along with the tangible steps for practicing both, are the very essence of PO.

Clearly as a society we need to fix our tactics on many fronts—but the most immediate benefit will come from a multipronged approach to mental health and general well-being, including doing what we can to develop an accessible, flexible wellness practice for ourselves. Practical Optimism was created to help bridge the gaps between illness and wellness by providing one singular approach combining techniques that can serve everyone and anyone, whether you need coping mechanisms during a crisis, fuel for flourishing, or a way to take your life to the next level.

The Power of Practical Optimism:
Living Fully and Joyfully in an Imperfect World

The 8 Pillars of Practical Optimism are based on many of the evidence-based techniques we use to address and reduce symptoms of anxiety and depression through effective stress management and coping skills. PO can help you cope with stress and tough times so the lows aren't so low: you'll be able to take them in stride and work to prevent the lows next time.

But as mentioned, preventing the lows is only part of the equation.

Practical Optimism combines a strengths-based model of health with the traditional Western medical deficits and disease model in a wellness practice designed to meet you where you are wellness-wise and to empower you to go beyond simply reducing discomfort, helping you to release your natural strengths and talents and to build a life full of meaning, purpose, joy, and connection.

As a Practical Optimist, you'll be training yourself not to dwell in adversity or a "water your weeds" mindset—thus sidestepping rumination, a key risk factor for depression and anxiety. Instead, you'll adopt the healthier habit of dwelling in possibility.

Practical Optimism gives you the self-awareness tools not only to address what isn't working in your life, but to develop more productive thought patterns, more compassionate emotional responses, and more effective behavioral strategies. It also invigorates your sense of purpose. It's not magical thinking, but a concrete philosophy and skill set rooted in best practices.

Practical Optimists are resourceful, realistic, thoughtful problem solvers. Like chefs assembling the ingredients and tools they need to make their work go smoothly, they take a deliberate approach to problem-solving. They're able to decipher precisely what a situation needs because they're self-aware and know what they need, can discern what others need from them, are confident in their abilities, and are able to admit what they don't know and learn what they need to know to live a better life.

The authentic positivity of Practical Optimists is positively infectious. They attract good people and good opportunities. People see them as success magnets. Practical Optimists don't wait for the silver lining to appear. They create their own silver linings: spotting positives in everyday events, looking for ways to turn negative events around, and making good situations even better. They have the courage to walk away from opportunities that don't serve them or allow them to grow, no matter how enticing. They've mastered the liberating power of knowing how to direct their energy to where it's most needed, valued, and deserved. They possess something of rare value: the inner resources to live fully and joyfully in an imperfect world.

Exercise: Practical Optimism and You

The exercise below is designed to help you make optimal use of the 8 Pillars of Practical Optimism by taking a friendly life "selfie"— one you'll share only with yourself—about areas in your life that are working pretty well, just okay, or maybe not as well as you'd like. Through nonjudgmental reflection, we can arrive at a clearer sense of where we need to focus our efforts.

You may want to take a moment now to begin keeping a journal or notes dedicated to your practice of PO, where you can write your answers to this and later exercises, record insights along the way, and track your progress, if you wish. Bear in mind that this exercise isn't meant to provide a diagnosis.[4] Think of it as a low-pressure sit-down with yourself to assess areas of your life that need your

---

[4] This exercise is meant to bring attention to your level of Practical Optimism and is not meant to replace a mental health evaluation by a trained clinician.

attention, to identify sources of imbalance, and to get a sense of how you feel in each domain of Practical Optimism.

———

For each statement below, write *yes* to indicate it's mostly true for you, or *no* if your answer would be no most of the time. There are no right or wrong answers. Consider this an opportunity for some quiet reflection, a gift of attention to your needs and truths in your heart of hearts.

1. I rarely feel bored.
2. I am generally upbeat and positive in the morning as I anticipate the day ahead.
3. I feel energized, satisfied, and fulfilled by the activities in my life, and I have at least one activity where I feel a sense of flow or like I'm in the zone.
4. I have a sense of direction in my life and look forward to the future.
5. I feel like I'm making a contribution in my own way.
6. I am introspective and able to name and identify my feelings.
7. I can usually point to a trigger or antecedent for strong positive or negative emotions.
8. Even when my negative emotions feel uncomfortable, I can examine and accept them without becoming self-destructive or using unhealthy coping mechanisms.
9. I am able to express my feelings appropriately to family, friends, and coworkers.
10. I don't experience too many unexplained medical symptoms— i.e., my doctor has thoroughly checked me out and ruled out symptoms (such as headaches, heart palpitations, weakness, fatigue, etc.) as not being solely stress-related.
11. When I'm tasked with a problem, I'm able to generate a few possible solutions fairly easily.

12. Once I've generated solutions and options, I'm able to narrow them down and able to make many decisions with ease.

13. Through regulating my emotions in a healthy way, I'm able to recover from setbacks and disappointments so that they don't interfere with my day-to-day tasks or relationships.

14. When I'm unable to change a situation that is causing me upset, I try to find a way to change my attitude toward it. This shift in perspective allows me to reframe what would've been an otherwise unpleasant situation for me and turn it into a more tolerable (and maybe even pleasant!) experience.

15. I will persist until I see a task through—I'm of the belief that "where there's a will, there's a way."

16. When I make mistakes, I don't beat myself up too much, nor do I spend a lot of time thinking about what I "should" have done.

17. It gives me great pleasure to see other people succeed, and I'm easily able to give credit where credit is due. Verbal praise and open acknowledgment of others' success come easily to me.

18. I don't play the blame game with myself or others, nor do I internalize or take personally other people's bad behavior.

19. I stand up for myself in a respectful way, because I feel I deserve a seat at the table or am worth it.

20. I get the self-care I need and don't feel like I need others' permission or approval to rest.

21. I know what my skills are and feel confident about them.

22. If I feel just so-so at something or if I've set a new goal for myself, I feel capable and confident in my abilities to learn the necessary skills in order to see the goal or activity through and even succeed at it.

23. I don't let my fears, worries, or regrets hold me back from pursuing dreams or goals, but choose to see/use setbacks and challenges as learning opportunities and am proactive about trying again.

24. I'm not afraid to ask for feedback or seek advice from role models and mentors when I want to achieve something.

25. I feel that I am in control over my environment, including my ability to regulate my emotions in the midst of distressing or challenging situations.

26. I limit distractions and interruptions—i.e., I regularly turn off social media, silence my cell phone, and set limits on when I answer messages. I resist multitasking and rushing.

27. I am not consumed by the fear of missing out and am able to immerse myself in the activities I have chosen—and in the people in front of me.

28. I rarely compare myself to others.

29. I don't feel weighed down by past regrets.

30. I'm not worn down by worries about the future.

31. I feel satisfied with the quality and quantity of my friendships/ important relationships. I feel understood by the important people in my life and can rely on them for support.

32. I can balance the enjoyment of other people's company with meaningful time alone.

33. I am intentional about making and maintaining new friendships (especially when I feel lonely) and can do this with ease.

34. I am able to balance self-soothing with reliance on others for emotional comfort.

35. In relationships, I'm proactive about resolving conflict and providing support and emotional comfort to (or for) others. Others seek me out as a source of emotional comfort.

36. I plan to (or already am finding ways to) meet many of my health and wellness goals—and regular movement is one of them.

37. I do my best to get the medical care and health screenings I need.

38. I try to be intentional about setting new goals and pursuing the habits needed to attain them.

39. I try to be open to learning new things.

40. I make time for quiet time and reflection.

While I suggest reading this book in its entirety, it may be helpful to know up front which areas may warrant more attention. To that end, each statement in the exercise correlates with a particular PO principle, as follows:

1–5—Purpose
6–10—Processing Emotions
11–15—Problem-Solving
16–20—Pride
21–25—Proficiency
26–30—Present
31–35—People
36–40—Practicing Healthy Habits

The point of these statements is simply to help you understand any particular areas of interest for you as you approach the Pillars. You may find some areas that are working pretty well, but you may have lost sight of others. Or you may identify an area where you're overperforming—say, you're performing well at work, but working way too much—while underperforming in another—such as building relationships with family and friends. (Chapter 7, "Present," and chapter 8, "People," may help!) The Pillars work synergistically, so the areas where you're strong will help you navigate the areas that need tune-ups.

Everyone, no matter how capable, has vulnerabilities and blind spots. I know I do. So even if you feel as if you've "mastered" a particular area, I hope you'll decide to read the book in its entirety as I've suggested. As you read the chapters and practice the techniques, return to this exercise as often as you need to to gauge how you're feeling about the core ideas being explored.

Many of these might feel like far-reaching ideals, particularly in times of stress. And that would be totally normal. Or if you can't relate to some of these statements, not to worry!

PO isn't a crash course or a quick fix, but rather a steady companion and wellness approach for life that you can customize to your needs. If these questions ignite your curiosity to dig deeper, including considering doing so in an individualized setting with a mental health professional, I hope you'll find PO useful in that journey.

I encourage you to read the book in sequence, because the Pillars do build on one another, starting with considering your sense of purpose and ending with practicing the healthy habits that will help you fulfill your purpose—with the Pillars in between serving as scaffolds for building emotional awareness, problem-solving capacities, a healthy sense of personal pride, proficiency in the skills you need and want, a steadying awareness of life's wonders, and a buoying sense of belonging. If you feel you must jump to a specific Pillar, go for it, but remember to come back to the others, because they all work together to support the unique, beautiful edifice that is YOU.

You can also revisit specific Pillars if you feel stuck or are struggling. Ask yourself, "Which Pillar do I need right now?" Processing can help if emotions are overwhelming. Turn to chapter 4, "Problem-Solving," for a refresher if you're grappling with a challenge. Don't be disheartened. Look for areas of strength in your life. They're always there in each one of us.

The 8 Pillars of Practical Optimism
And here they are! Take a look at these fuller descriptions of the Pillars that you met in the Introduction. Then we'll dive in.

Pillar 1: **Purpose.** Deliberate, intentional thinking can solve almost any problem—including the age-old question "What is my purpose?" We'll look at how to connect with your purpose and come up with authentic goals that energize and inspire you. And I'll let you in on a secret that Practical Optimists (POs) know: you don't always have to find or search for meaning in life. You can *create* it.

Pillar 2:   **Processing Emotions.** Identifying, expressing, and releasing emotions skillfully can increase energy, mood, memory, concentration, and overall health. When it comes to powerful emotions, we'll talk about how to name them, claim them, and tame them! You'll deepen your emotional wisdom and awareness, learn how to cope with painful or negative emotions and maximize positive ones, and (best of all) let them work for you instead of against you.

Pillar 3:   **Problem-Solving.** I will introduce you to the 5 Rs of Emotional Regulation and Real-World Problem-Solving to help you marry intuition and logic and become a master problem solver, turning obstacles into opportunities, engaging in proactive problem-solving, making better decisions . . . and learning to let go—because not everything and everyone deserves your energy.

Pillar 4:   **Pride.** I will show you how to challenge negative, self-destructive thoughts and behaviors and use self-compassion to develop a healthy sense of self-worth that stays steady regardless of life's ups and downs. Result: a happier and more authentic and fulfilling life.

Pillar 5:   **Proficiency.** Practical Optimists know how to go from "I want to do this" to "I did it!" We'll explore why your belief in your abilities is just as (if not more) important as your actual ability, and how to build confidence in your abilities and improve on them.

Pillar 6:   **Present.** Here we'll explore the power of focus to cut mental clutter, ward off worry, let go of ruminations and past regrets, destroy distractions, and combat comparisons. We'll work on the tools necessary to take back your time in the here and now, develop a healthier relationship with technology and social media, and keep depression and anxiety at bay.

Pillar 7:   **People.** I'll share ways to develop a relationship practice (with yourself and others) to reduce loneliness, create new friendships, solidify existing bonds, and cultivate a sense of belonging, greater joy, and satisfaction in our connections with loved ones and at work (hint: emotional attunement is the secret sauce).

Pillar 8:   **Practicing Healthy Habits.** We'll delve into why optimists are healthier and have exceptional longevity, and how to use PO to create new habits. I'll share the 4 Ms of Mental Health (mastery, movement, meaningful engagement, and mindfulness) as science-backed habits for illness treatment and prevention, and why automaticity is the secret to longevity.

In the coming chapters, we'll delve deeper into each of the 8 Pillars of Practical Optimism. I'll introduce you to patients (whose names and identifying details have been changed as part of case composites) who've utilized these principles to change their outlook and their lives: Sam, a burned-out executive who fears his prime is past and his marriage is in trouble; Nicole, a working mom struggling with work/family decisions; Lina, who deserves a seat at the table at work but is struggling to demand it; Shelly, who came to me describing herself as "broken" by trauma; and others. I'll share more of my own story as I sought to reconcile my dharma—my duty to family, society, and patients—with the feeling that I deserved the same compassion I was extending to others. In the process, you'll learn ways to make Practical Optimism a regular practice in *your* life.

Practical Optimism is an attitude, a choice, and a practice, and one that I work at every day. Some days it's just a five-minute "PO workout," and other days it's a bit longer. One thing I know: it's a muscle worth exercising. While incorporating Practical Optimism training into my medical practice has been an integral part of my treatment plan with a number of my patients, it has also been transformative in my own life. It has helped me to take chances, persist despite obstacles, and enjoy successes that at one time I didn't think were possible for me. May Practical Optimism help you to light up your corner of the world.

As you read the chapters and practice the Pillars, please know that everything in this book is a suggestion: If it doesn't work for you, move on. If it speaks to you, try it! You may find some of the Pillars resonate more over time. My great hope is that this book will serve as a companion and reference. Maybe others will be inspired by your example. It takes only one person to change the world. I hope that person is you, my Practical Optimist friend!

To view the scientific references cited in this chapter,
please visit doctorsuevarma.com/book.

CHAPTER 2

Purpose

Connecting to What Energizes and Inspires You

If a man knows not to which port he sails, no wind is favorable.

—SENECA

There is a brief discussion of suicide in this section. You can skip ahead if the topic feels too triggering or stick around longer if you feel up to it. While this chapter focuses on the role of purpose as an essential Pillar in the PO program, it also discusses what happens when we don't feel like we have a purpose.

Sam, a forty-seven-year-old marketing executive, came to see me at his wife's insistence. He was losing his temper with her and the kids, and she was tired of it all. In many ways, so was he.

When I asked him what made him happy, what got him out of bed each morning, he said, "Dr. Varma, I feel like I've lost my direction. My work hours are long and strenuous—plus there's my daily two-and-a-half-hour commute. But I'm not getting the recognition I deserve. I feel like I'm going through the motions, just putting more money in the company's pockets. This isn't what I envisioned for myself at forty-seven."

I asked Sam if he felt similarly discouraged at home. "I'm more irritable," he replied. "My wife complains I'm distant. She goes to bed earlier than me, partly to avoid me, I think. I sometimes fall asleep in my home office. I can't recall the last time we had a date night or I had any fun. But with three kids, we're both pretty beat by day's end."

Despite his fatigue and signs of burnout, something *was* preoccupying Sam: "There's this younger, attractive coworker paying me a lot of attention. I don't want to be unfaithful. I love my wife, but honestly, I'm eating it up. This woman and I have had drinks a few times—always with coworkers. I'm also drinking more."

Sam's words were providing clues about multiple issues in his life that needed to be addressed, including an inner struggle I often hear: he felt disconnected from his sense of purpose.

The quest for meaning, purpose, depth, or direction is a universal human longing. It's a theme in mythology, sacred texts, and popular literature—proving that many of us aren't born knowing our purpose. If you don't feel as if you have a clearly defined purpose, rest assured you're not alone.

Sam was also missing opportunities for joy and fun. Joy *plus* purpose leads to flourishing—a key goal for Practical Optimists. Pursuing purpose at the expense of joy can come to feel like drudgery even if what you're doing is worthwhile and meaningful, be it working, parenting, caring for a loved one, or serving your community. Pursuing happiness without purpose can ultimately feel somewhat superficial. Lacking both—Sam's situation—leads to languishing, even misery. If this state is prolonged, it can make a person lose hope and any sense of agency. When that happens, depression is a real risk.

I've noticed it's when purpose and joy dim that people come in to speak with me. I think that's what finally got me into therapy. I had tons of purpose in my service to others. What I didn't have so much training for was seeking out joy. I was good at giving. I wasn't as good at taking what I needed so I could continue to give.

What does having both purpose and joy feel like? It's enjoying our relationships (most of the time!), finding ways to make our work meaningful (possibly through a role remake—more on that later), and pursuing activities where we feel what's known as a state of flow.

Flow, described by Mihaly Csikszentmihalyi in 1975, is the experience of people engaging in activities for pleasure, even when they are not extrinsically rewarded (i.e., with money or fame). Flow involves being deeply engaged, immersed in something that offers both enjoyment and challenge. Here, awareness and action meet: we are absorbed, alert, energized—and nothing else seems to matter. Our skill level and the challenge of the task are almost perfectly aligned. It feels like the ultimate state of mastery and of being in the zone—you're learning, growing, *and* enjoying. Flow feels like the perfect marriage of purpose and joy.

The key to achieving a life of meaning, joy, and flow is to be purposeful in pursuing them. I'll share how to develop your personal road map to purpose through a concrete three-step plan I call the Three Pathways to Reigniting Your Purpose. They distill down to the handy (and appropriate) acronym AIM (see page 53).

Pinning Down Purpose

I define *purpose* as a way of becoming very intentional and thoughtful about what you want to do. Purpose is what gets you up in the morning. It motivates, excites, and positively pushes you. When you're excited by something that benefits others and when the pursuit of that goal is also beneficial to your health and well-being, that's when you know you have a sense of purpose.

When we live purposefully, other things tend to fall into place. It's easier to make decisions (*Does this align with my purpose?*) and say no—something many have a hard time doing. Purpose is a buffer against envy, comparisons, and FOMO—the fear of missing out. Purpose is our first Pillar because it is both the vision board for mapping out your life and the scaffold for building it as a Practical Optimist.

Lack of purpose can manifest in various ways. Like Sam, we may feel like we're going through the motions. Uncertainty, doubt, and irritability may be our daily companions. Distraction or escape behaviors—like Sam's attraction to his coworker or his tendency to drink too much—can be signals of a flagging purpose compounded by a lack of joy, made manifest in certain behaviors that may contradict our core values.

With my patients, I listen for key phrases. They'll tell me, their friends, or their partners things like "I used to be excited about what I'm doing, but I'm not learning/growing/enjoying it/fulfilled anymore . . . I'm avoiding or procrastinating . . . I feel lost, bored, cynical, constantly irritated, unappreciated."

Sometimes these comments are part of a larger constellation of symptoms signaling depression and/or work burnout (particularly the constellation of cynicism, lack of self-efficacy, work dread, and physical and mental exhaustion), which is why a careful evaluation is necessary. For Sam, his work was one of several stressors. He was now worrying that things weren't going to improve in multiple areas. These factors, and the way they were starting to impair his functioning and quality of life, were suggesting depression.

Sam confessed there was a brief moment when he even questioned his purpose in living—wondering whether his family would be better off without him. He told me he wasn't actively thinking of or planning to end his life, nor did it ever come to that point. After he reassured me he had no intent or plan to harm himself, I asked more in-depth questions about these thoughts (and would continue to assess and monitor these with specific questions throughout the course of our work together, ready to address them with appropriate treatment as needed).

Science is still working to improve our proficiency in early detection and prevention of suicide,[5] particularly because one core feature is impulsivity. So while we did a thorough risk assessment, as I'd do for any patient, and while I assessed Sam's risk for suicide was low, I also knew that something in his life needed to change to keep it that way. The line between risk levels can sometimes change and can be preceded by a sense of worthlessness and feeling like a burden to others. I knew that as part of depression, severe feelings of guilt and shame can take over and add to the person's feelings of helplessness and hopelessness. Having a clear plan in place can be crucial when risk level changes, and Sam and I discussed one.

When I asked Sam whether he had felt this way a year or more ago, he said, "Not at all. I was actually looking forward to turning fifty." He looked down, tears welling in his eyes. Sam was depressed, and from what he was telling me, he was feeling purposeless. I was concerned that this could soon turn into hopelessness, which could lead to a further downward trajectory for his mental health.

It can be hard to tease apart depression and a sense of purposelessness. A person can be doing meaningful work yet fighting the drag of depression—which shows that you can't just "purpose" your way out of a medical disorder like depression. Conversely, depression can obscure your sense of purpose. Lack of purpose can feel depressing. And having purpose without joy can make life feel empty or devoid of meaning or substance. This is why I work carefully with patients like Sam using a whole-person approach, which includes a thorough

---

[5] What you are learning about Sam is a condensed version of his story. I am of necessity selecting aspects of his case and treatment relevant to the points in this chapter, which focuses on the importance of connecting with or creating purpose, joy, flow, or meaning in our lives. Each individual's journey is unique. It's not my intention to suggest or attempt to present a comprehensive discussion of depression, burnout, marital issues, employee mental health and workplace dynamics, suicide risk factors, or available mental health and/or medical treatments (nor suggest that they are widely available to all individuals, given the disparities in healthcare and society in general). It's important to discuss your unique concerns with your healthcare provider.

medical workup and risk assessment and, when indicated, medications alongside therapy and lifestyle interventions.

I've shared this not to alarm you, but to emphasize the importance of not brushing aside these feelings. Cultivating a sense of meaning or purpose is vital to mental health and can be protective against mental health symptoms or, in conjunction with other evidence-based treatments, can at least lessen their burden and help steady us while we address a mental health disorder with a therapist, as needed.

Generally, though, in the absence of other warning signs, dissatisfaction, persistent procrastination, or a sense of stagnation or languishing tells me my patients need to rededicate themselves to their purpose and see if there's a way to get more pleasure while they're doing it. It might be as subtle as parents volunteering at their child's school as a way to be more involved in their child's life, plus adding a parents' night out after the meetings. I've seen this purpose/pleasure combo take the form of a fundraising exercise session followed by a communal dinner. Or someone whose work is consuming their nights and weekends deciding to reclaim their time and give back by volunteering in a community garden on Saturdays. The effort doesn't have to be big. It just has to address this key question:

> How can I bring value to others through my innate talents and interests while also investing in myself to enhance my joy along the way?

Sometimes our longings to find purpose in our lives take the form of an interest in or a desire to try something new, a yearning for something deeper, or a desire to contribute in a meaningful way—to make our world a little better and brighter.

External forces play a role, too. We see people doing inspiring things. Maybe our new boss sets an example of purpose wedded to profession. World events can spur us to action. For many people, the COVID-19 pandemic shifted their purpose and priorities.

Family and cultural roots can influence our purpose. My parents had thriving careers in the United States, but they always believed that their purpose, work, and the community they were meant to serve were in India. To Hindus, the word *dharma*, rooted in Sanskrit, is the belief in righteousness, including everything from ethical, religious, and moral conduct to what one considers the right way of living. Dharma calls on us to carry out this righteousness. Only then will we have fulfilled our aim in life. My parents believed each person has a dharma to fulfill. My family's dharma was to learn humility and offer service. My parents felt that giving back to the world—looking for great need and seeking to meet it in ways that aligned with their natural interests, talents, and proclivities—brought them alive and enlivened those around them.

In India, they pursued their mission to bring children's mental health to the fore, ensuring that learning disability evaluation and treatment would be available in the school systems through a strengths-based model in which children, regardless of disabilities or disorders, were given the same academic, arts, and cultural opportunities through integrated, not separate, classrooms. This was revolutionary, given the significant stigma and discrimination these children had previously experienced.

When we returned to New York, to fill the void created by leaving our purpose-focused activities in India, my mother established the Indian Cultural Institute, where she taught Hindi, Indian culture, and Indian drama to children in our community. She'd written one of her research papers on the learning advantages of bilingual children and believed a strong sense of identity, community, and belonging were important to a child's self-esteem. Her institute combined these philosophies to improve the lives of children in our community. She continued her work as a supervisor of a New York City school-based support team, as well as performing educational testing with students to assess their learning needs. She also advocated for educational testing in children's primary languages. When I was a preteen, she encouraged me to teach children only slightly younger than I was, as in

India I'd absorbed Indian culture and history and learned to speak, read, and write in Hindi fluently. I've had many jobs since—retail; food services; educational, healthcare, and community organizations. My parents' example and my early memories of working for the betterment of others helped me find meaning and satisfaction in my jobs, knowing I was bringing comfort and help to those I served.

Perhaps reading this is giving you ideas about the life influences that connect to your purpose. The self-assessment questions later in this chapter will help you do a deeper dive.

Three Misconceptions About Purpose
There are three misconceptions about purpose I believe can derail us from pursuing our purpose:

Misconception 1: Purpose should come through our job.
New Conception 1: Purpose is more than a paycheck.

Purpose can come from many aspects of life, including hobbies, interests, and relationships. It's wonderful if your sense of purpose is fulfilled through your job, but if your work situation changes (or you do—more on that shortly), your sense of purpose can take a hit.

While it was his relationship with his wife that brought Sam to see me, his troubles started with work stress and burnout that affected his self-esteem. Born to Greek parents who worked tirelessly on behalf of their kids, Sam was the first in his family to obtain a graduate degree and was reminded frequently not to "waste" it. "Work satisfaction just wasn't part of my parents' thinking. It was about paving the way for the next generation's quality of life and giving them opportunities previous generations didn't have: 'Go to school; get the good, stable job; keep the job.'" Sam derived much of his self-worth and identity from his work. When work wasn't going well, it impacted his home life. He started feeling helpless and hopeless about his work situation, and then started questioning his sense of self-worth.

Remembering your purpose is portable and not dependent on your paycheck can help you stay in touch with your purpose no matter what's happening on the job. We increase our opportunities for flourishing when we seek meaning and purpose from a variety of sources, including our relationships (with a partner, our kids, our friends, and coworkers) and our hobbies and interests.

So if, as is true with many of us, your job is "just a job," don't worry. Purpose doesn't have to be paid.[6]

Misconception 2: Purpose means doing something "big" and "important" (or that it should have the approval/buy-in of others).
New Conception 2: Our purpose doesn't have to be big, glamorous, or approved by anyone.

Your purpose needn't be glamorous or a thing on social media. It doesn't need to keep up with the Joneses (or the Kardashians). It needn't align with what others think you should be doing.

Sam had been conditioned to do what he had to in order to support his family, no matter how unrewarding. Any time he considered starting his own business, the thought was quickly shot down by his parents and extended family, with whom he was very close: "They don't want me to struggle like they did."

"Am I being self-indulgent in wanting something different?" he asked. "I'm doing this to make my family happy, but it's having quite the opposite effect."

---

[6] That said, beware of assuming that just because it's paid, work can't bring a sense of enjoyment or purpose. In his 1975 book *Beyond Boredom and Anxiety*, Mihaly Csikszentmihalyi writes that we've become conditioned to think that "what one must do cannot be enjoyable. So we learned to make a distinction between work and leisure: the former is what we have to do most of the time, against our desire; the latter is what we like to do although it is useless. We therefore feel bored and frustrated at our jobs, and guilty when we are at leisure."

Your purpose is yours to conceive and carry out. It needs to feel important only to you.

Misconception 3: True purpose lasts a lifetime.
New Conception 3: Our sense of purpose may change with time.

Purpose can change and grow, as we do. After our return from India, my mother translated her sense of purpose into our life in the U.S. by founding the Indian Cultural Institute, working as an educational evaluator in the public school system, and advocating for South Asian teachers through an organization she created with my dad. Realigning her purpose with our New York life yielded a rich new vein of good she could do.

Your purpose at age eighteen will be different from your purpose at eighty. It's only natural. A longitudinal study published in *Psychology and Aging* looking at folks over a sixty-three-year span showed that while personality changes only gradually throughout life, when you get older, your personality may be markedly different from your personality in childhood.

Awareness of your changing needs can help you better align with your purpose. I like to think of it as updating your software. I often see people getting stuck, thinking they've lost a sense of purpose. In reality, they're holding on to a purpose that just doesn't fit anymore.

Purpose Is Good for You:
The Science of Giving Back

Living a purposeful life can improve every aspect of our life, from our personal health to our educational, career, and community success.

In a study published in *The Lancet*, study participants who'd expressed a sense of meaning and purpose were 30 percent less likely to die during the average eight-and-a-half-year follow-up period than those with the least well-being.

A 2013 study published in the *Journal of Behavioral Medicine* showed that for every 1-point increase on a 6-point scale measuring purpose in life, adults with heart disease had a 27 percent decreased risk of having a heart attack over a two-year period. And per the *Journal of Psychosomatic Research*, for older adults, a 1-point difference in purpose meant a 22 percent decreased risk of having a stroke! Studies have also shown that physical pain will decrease through altruism.

A sense of purpose increases your lifespan! Did you know that volunteering at least two hours a week was found to increase longevity and improve mental health? According to a study published in the *American Journal of Preventive Medicine*, in a large, diverse prospective and nationally representative sample of close to thirteen thousand participants over the age of fifty known as the Health and Retirement Study, those who volunteered one hundred hours a year or more for others' betterment had a 44 percent lower risk of dying than those who didn't volunteer—and they reported a higher positive affect, a greater sense of purpose, more optimism, and less hopelessness, depression, and loneliness.

Getting adolescents to volunteer also benefits their health. A randomized study published in *JAMA Pediatrics* showed that teens who volunteered weekly (in this study, it was helping elementary school children with homework, arts and crafts, cooking, and sports) reduced their risk for cardiovascular disease—specifically, less inflammation, lowered cholesterol, and a lessened incidence of obesity. Studies are showing that giving support might even be more beneficial to our mortality than receiving support! (Though I think both are equally important for our well-being and relationships.)

Connecting to a bigger vision and worldview can help us manage life's inevitable ups and downs. People with purpose have low amounts of the stress-related hormones cortisol and epinephrine in their urine, showing that having purpose translates into having lower stress levels. Having a sense of purpose also buffers us against depression, anxiety, pessimism, and work burnout, allowing us to experience joy and pleasure more fully. Having a sense of purpose is associated with better sleep, a lower risk of dementia, and a greater likelihood of engaging in preventive health measures like getting the flu shot, mammograms, and colonoscopies.

Stress causes changes on a cellular level, and sometimes excessive stress can cause damage such that your biological age is greater than your chronological age (i.e., you're fifty but have the health of someone much older). We know one sign of biological aging is a shortening of our telomeres—the end caps on genes that naturally tend to shorten as we age. Telomere shortening can also signal aging due to psychological stress.

But one study of highly stressed mothers who participated in meditation showed that they actually prevented the shortening of their telomeres—and their meditation practice was linked to supporting, renewing, or helping them to identify with a sense of purpose! As we'll see in chapter 3, meditation is more than sitting quietly and clearing our mind. It can be a reflective process that helps guide our actions.

Having a sense of purpose creates better educational and work habits. For example, students encouraged to consider education as relevant to their life are more likely to try harder in classes they find boring or hard. Having enrolled in a challenging premed program at sixteen while working full time to pay for it, I can attest that my connection to my sense of purpose was a driving force for my education.

Purpose is good for business. According to Gallup's annual State of the American Workplace report, businesses that put purpose before profits tend to be more enjoyable and financially successful places for their employees in the long run. Companies with a sense of purpose are able to create more engaging environments for employees, which means better mental health, greater productivity, more prosperity, career longevity, and less absenteeism and "presenteeism" (when the employee is showing up to work but is unable to be productive or is making a lot of mistakes).

While having purpose is good for us as individuals, it's also collectively beneficial. Our purpose-driven actions bring us closer to those served by them. Researchers found that hospital workers were 45 percent more inclined to use good handwashing hygiene if they were told it helped prevent patients from catching diseases than if told it helped only them. Connecting their habits to a service-oriented purpose inspired better behavior. Having a purpose, and one with an altruistic bent, is linked to an overall improved sense of well-being. As I learned from my various early jobs, when we reframe our everyday work or actions in terms of how they benefit others, it's amazing how many parts of the day that seem humdrum can take on a satisfying, purposeful glow.

So, with the health benefits of purpose in mind, let's step onto the Three Pathways to Reigniting Your Purpose.

Taking AIM at Purpose:
The Three Pathways to Reigniting Your Purpose

Aim: It's a noun and a verb. Something you have; something you do. As a noun, it describes your intention, goal, purpose, or desired outcome. As a verb, it's about choosing a direction, a target, or an objective. *Aim* is apt for framing human life: we are what we think and what we do. It's apt for framing our search for purpose, which is shaped internally by what we feel, think, and decide; externally by what we do. "Finding our aim" means asking: "Where do I want to go, and how do I want to get there?"

In my Three Pathways, AIM stands for:

Acknowledge: Acknowledge your life decisions, including those that brought you to where you are right now. While you might have regrets and dissatisfactions, reflect on what these have taught you and how they've prepared you for this moment. When you acknowledge where you are right now, you free up key mental resources to go from here to where you want to be—despite the ambivalence or sadness that sometimes accompanies exchanging the old for the new.

Identify: Identify what's working and what's not, what brings you meaning and joy, and what needs to happen to add more of both to your life.

Move forward: Take active steps toward feeling a sense of meaning—from mining your past for ideas to consulting your mentors, role models, and friends to celebrating each step and experiencing joy and enthusiasm for your shift in trajectory.

Knowing your aim allows you to be deliberate about what you take on. It allows you to take responsibility for your past choices: "I chose this path and not the other one" (notice I didn't say *better*—because maybe that road helped bring you to the path you're choosing now).

Knowing your aim means realizing that purpose doesn't always follow a linear path. Some of the most interesting, wisest people we know are those who've had many twists and turns along the way—and who can appreciate it as all part of the beautiful ride. It lets you make the most of those twists and turns, glean lessons from them, choose new trajectories, and let go of those that no longer serve you.

As you read each section and complete the self-assessments below, I hope you'll feel your AIM coming into sharper focus.

Pathway 1: Acknowledge

Most people's lives are so busy that personal development goes on the back burner. When Sam started his job, he delivered 200 percent of himself—and burned out. He rose in the ranks fairly quickly, but at the expense of missing out on a lot of family time and activities, hobbies, and recreation that would have refreshed his energy and added dimension and joy. Lacking in both joy and purpose, Sam was miserable, but he now realized he was also making his family miserable, taking on the role of martyr and working himself to the bone in an unrewarding job. His wife pushed back, saying, in effect, "I never expected you to make yourself unhappy. I thought you wanted this." Sam realized he'd thought he wanted it, too. But now it just wasn't enough.

Sam's breakthrough was in taking ownership of his life. Instead of blaming the job and his family, he was able to acknowledge, in essence, "These were the choices I made. It was good for a while and I'm glad I did it. I gained a lot from this job." Sam came to appreciate the opportunity, experience, professional leverage, and financial stability afforded by his hard work and his job. But he also came to acknowledge what was lost: making memories and celebrating milestones with family and friends. He needed to grieve those losses while taking stock and moving forward.

Acknowledging what has happened isn't about beating ourselves up with blame or trying to "fix it." Sometimes no one's to blame. Sometimes we can't fix it. We can only learn the lessons and be intentional about where we go from here.

With these ideas in mind, consider these questions:

- Are there some situations in my life that I need to take more responsibility for?
- What was my contribution to my current situation?
- What circumstances made me choose the path I'm on? [Here are some examples: It was what I wanted then, but not anymore; it was the only choice I had/could afford; my family wanted me to; it was the best option at the time.]
- Could there have been some benefit in taking the road that led me here, maybe even people or opportunities I can feel grateful for, even if I no longer want to be here?
- What do I need to accept about my life in order to be able to change it?

A Word to the Wise

Purpose and Burnout

You may be so busy achieving that other areas of your life are suffering. Even purpose-driven achievements can exact a price, as shown by Sam's story (and mine!).

As is true with our bodies, overdeveloped muscles in some aspects of life (hypertrophy) can lead to underdeveloped or neglected capacities (atrophy) in others. That imbalance can create problems over time. Sometimes we're too invested in our purpose—work, service—and not enough in our joy.

When our work, including our important work in our families and households, starts to feel burdensome, it could mean a variety of things. While it might signal our need to reconnect with purpose (i.e., see the value in what we're already doing), it might also signal the beginnings of burnout that, if unaddressed, may lead to languishing, even depression.

Burnout includes feelings of energy depletion and exhaustion, feeling cynical and negative about our work, and being less effective and productive as a result.

While getting in touch with what gives your life purpose, meaning, and joy can buffer you from burnout, no one is immune from burnout. You can have strong purpose and feel deep satisfaction, even joy, in your work, and still be vulnerable to burnout. If there are factors beyond your control—for example, menial tasks, red tape, or bureaucracy soaking up your time; constant frustrating roadblocks; discrimination; unrelenting overwork; patterns of unfairness, of lack of support, or of not being recognized, valued, or appropriately compensated; or other factors that come between you and the meaningful parts of your work or make meaningful work unsustainable—burnout can take hold and, if unchecked, can lead to pessimism and depression. Here's a prime example: the burnout among health professionals from the unrelenting stresses of the COVID-19 pandemic, atop the already existing strains in our healthcare system.

Having frequent check-ins with yourself, your family, and your place of employment, where appropriate, are key. While preventing burnout sometimes requires change in larger, systemic factors, at the same time, on a smaller scale, feeling recognized, valued, and appreciated for your efforts can go a long way. Actively seeking opportunities to grow and add value (in multiple areas of your life) so that you're seen as—and feel—valuable is also important. Feeling recognized and appreciated for your efforts—on the job, in the community, or in your daily life—is essential to burnout prevention. Also, look for opportunities to recognize someone else's efforts and, where appropriate, let them know the positive impact they've had at work or at home. In later Pillars, you'll find strategies and self-compassion practices to help with easing up on too many obligations, or "dharma overdrive" (chapter 5, "Pride"), and with slowing down to soak up the moment (chapter 7, "Present"). You'll also find a personal favorite of mine for self-care, the 4 Ms (chapter 9, "Practicing Healthy Habits").

Pathway 2: Identify

Often my patients are surprised to find we examine the interplay between many aspects of their lives as part of their treatment. When Sam did this, he was staggered by the domino effect he saw. His job dissatisfaction was creating tension at home and vice versa, and both were (further) fueling his attraction to his coworker. His long commute left no time for fun, making the coworker and evening drinks more alluring. He wasn't making time for his health, which further sapped his energy, adding to his feeling of being past his prime as the Big Five-Oh approached. While Sam was grateful for his financial security, he was startled to realize he was really struggling in multiple other areas of his life.

Hindsight is the benefit of a life well lived. And a life well lived should, in my opinion, include at least a regret or two. I say that only half in jest. After all, if you have no regrets, have you really lived? We often make the best decisions we can, given the knowledge and tools we have at the time.

So take gentle inventory with these questions:

- Has my family or cultural background influenced my sense of purpose?
- Does my current path still serve me? Or do I need/want to make a change? What might that change look like? [Here are some examples: letting go of unhealthy relationships, of roles you've outgrown, or of outdated expectations, or investing in other relationships.]
- Knowing what I know now, which path will I *choose* this time [italics intentional!]?
- What am I risking and or/giving up by aiming differently?
- What might I gain or learn?
- What help would I need for what's next?
- If I visualize an old-fashioned balance scale, with my life purpose on one plate and my life joy on the other, is the scale balanced, or does it tip to one side or the other?
- What activities do I love, feel excited about, or find satisfying or rewarding? When was the last time I did them?
- Whom would I like to serve or give back to?
- When and where (and/or with whom) do I experience a state of flow? Of learning? Of growth? Of inspiration? [*Note:* Your list of inspiring people might include those living or not, as well as fictional or historical characters.] Why do these places, activities, and/or people inspire me?

If you're struggling with these questions, take a breath and a break. Then return at your own pace to the task at hand.

PO Pearls
- It's okay to express gratitude, even for things you no longer want, and to grieve the loss of things you once chose. Grief and gratitude can coexist.
- It's okay to take a different path from the life you've built and are vested in.
- It's okay to choose a path different from the path of people around you, or a path no one but you understands.
- It's okay to take time for both joy and meaning—serving others needn't come at the expense of your well-being.
- It's okay to take your time.

Pathway 3: Move Forward

Once Sam had a clearer idea of his situation, feelings, and needs, we looked at what he could do to bring greater meaning and satisfaction to his life.

Since Sam's sense of self was highly informed by his professional life, he wanted to start by becoming proactive about trying to create a sense of purpose at his current job. While receiving fair compensation was still a priority for Sam, there was an additional priority: he wanted to feel as if his work helped others and had impact. He asked his boss about managing brands focused on sustainability, education, or health messaging, or that had a charitable arm, which resonated with his values.

As he saw that the projects he worked on were doing good in the world, Sam's sense of purpose began to coalesce around contributing to something bigger than himself. That led to looking at how his actions could positively affect others, which helped counter his previous tendency to focus on how others' actions were affecting him.

As Sam connected with a sense of purpose, his attitude started to shift. His irritability lessened. He no longer felt resentful that no one was applauding his efforts or worried that people were wondering what value he'd be adding as "younger, fresher" people joined the company at half his salary. His attitude changed as we discussed how his perceptions of aging were interfering with his finding his purpose. When he made a conscious effort to be kinder and more patient, to give praise to others, and to make himself available as a mentor to the younger, newer account executives he'd once seen as competition, he was recognized for helping to develop junior colleagues.

I also worked with Sam to help him develop a more meaningful life at home, improving his communication with his wife (instead of investing in the coworker), increasing their intimacy, and expanding his network of friendships. All these actions added positive deposits in the joy bucket and nothing to the drudgery drawer! We also worked to help him create time for relaxation, learning, and exercise. As he felt more rested, he could participate more in his children's activities. He started volunteering at their school and assisting with their sports teams.

By committing to the process and taking things a little at a time, Sam made big shifts toward leading a more purposeful, joyful life. The joy was having lunch with colleagues at work, engaging in date nights with his wife, and goofing around with his kids.

Some actions you'll take will be internal—as when Sam challenged his negative assumptions about aging or tuned into his irritability (more on emotion management in chapters 3 and 4, "Processing Emotions" and "Problem-Solving"). Some will be external—as when Sam asked for work aligned with his sense of purpose, took better care of his health so he could be more present and patient with his family, and sought out ways to mentor at work.

Your next step is to develop a "purpose in motion" plan. This is the actionable component of purpose. Purpose belongs to you, but it's also up to you. What will you do to promote purpose in your life? When negative things happen, what will you learn, decide, and do to make constructive meaning from them?

Don't pressure yourself to figure out your purpose right away. The journey itself often turns up clues. Just start! Below are some ideas. Try to commit a few minutes daily to one or two of these purpose-promoting activities. I hope they help you explore the many ways to find meaning and joy through curiosity, learning, service, connection, movement, and time in nature, to name just a few!

1. **Cultivate curiosity** through books, documentary films, podcasts, journals, or articles. Keep a list of friends' recommendations. Track what you read and view—what interests continually crop up?

2. **Find more flow through challenges of choice.** Curiosity and a small amount of challenge help us build excitement, combat complacency, and serve as an antidote to languishing and burnout. Enroll in a class or training. Build your skills and apply for that promotion. Improve at a language or a sport. This is the personal growth/learning/mastering part of purpose.

3. **Try a tip called behavioral activation.** If you aren't sure what purpose to choose, put the cart before the horse: let purposeful action lead you toward purpose. Start populating your calendar with activities you think might spark and nurture motivation, energy, meaning, and interest, even if in the moment you aren't feeling quite up to it. Are you interested in spending a summer abroad but aren't sure where to start? While you research options, sign up for some language classes that will help you communicate once you get there. This smaller step could prepare you for more down the road.

4. **Connect with awe.** Reminding ourselves that we're part of something bigger can help us connect with a desire to contribute to that great web of life we're part of. Try the practices in chapter 7, "Present," particularly for savoring and awe.

5. **Get a mentor, be a mentor.** Ask three people who know you well what they think you do best. Sometimes we need help to stay

accountable to our goals. Ask a few folks who have your best interests at heart to help you stay on your game. Earlier you listed people who inspire you. What thought patterns and/or actions would bring you closer to the ideals they represent? What abilities and passions of yours could benefit others?

6. **Could you find more meaning by seeking a role remake at work?** Perhaps it's talking with your boss about adding work that feels new and fresh—a process known as task crafting—and transferring some duties to someone else, or investigating another division or department where the work would be more rewarding. Sometimes it's about seeing or doing the same job in a different way—maybe taking on a company initiative, project, or social role that would be fun/meaningful to you or aligns with your values—or reminding yourself how your job already helps others (a process called cognitive crafting). You might also try taking an online test to define your strengths.

7. **Find a purpose together.** Join a networking group, Rotary club, meet-up group, or book club—or host or create one yourself.

8. **Turn your pain into purpose.** Has your own pain led to insights or transformed your thinking in a way that could be helpful to others? I know people whose extreme life experiences have required them to cope with loss, trauma, and hardship—and sharing what they learned became an important part of their own healing journey. We know that altruism can be therapeutic for those who've experienced severe stress. Several of my patients have expressed interest in the areas of grief counseling, rehabilitation, and therapy—from helping others with physical injuries to substance use disorders as a result of their own experiences, losses, trials, and triumphs. If it feels like giving back is a tall order, especially in the midst of your pain, that's okay, too. If or when you feel ready, realize that what you give needn't be a large gesture or deplete you. Many of my patients in the WTC Mental Health Program simply accompanied others to

their medical appointments at the center. Their presence was the greatest gift to their fellow humans.

9. **Start a "movement for purpose" practice.** It's true! Exercise helps us generate more purpose—and having purpose promotes exercise and movement (see The Movement-Purpose Connection on page 64). Dedicate time at least three days a week to an exercise of your choosing. Journal about how movement impacts your mood, memory, concentration, and motivation. Does it help you create goals elsewhere in your life?

10. **Jump-start your joy practice.** Edit out tasks that drag you down; add tasks that lift you up. This will require you to ask for help, maybe at work (see number 6 above), from your partner, or from others. Purpose is about reclaiming what's important to us— including your time and focus through self-care, some fun, and the reduction of constant interruptions (including our own multitasking or distraction habits). You can increase your purpose by slowing down and appreciating the nuances and value of the tasks you're engaged in, your conversations, and your effect in the world (more on this in chapter 7, "Present"). Being in nature revives my energy and joyfulness. On busy days, my joy practice can be as simple as getting out for a quick morning coffee or a lunch between meetings, working on my laptop outside, or bringing the outside in with a plant or fresh flowers on my desk. Tracking your time in your journal, noticing the emotional peaks and valleys, and paying close attention to the contexts and activities that brought you the greatest joy can reveal clues to possible wellsprings of purpose.

Bigger-Picture Thinking

- Envision your life one year, five years, and ten years from now. What does a meaningful, well-lived life look like to you at those milestones?

- What do you love so much that you'd do it for free? (You don't actually have to do this for free, but it helps in the brainstorming process.)
- What does the world need or what could it use right now?

The Movement-Purpose Connection

I'm fascinated by—and sold on—the purpose-promoting power of exercise. I often tell my patients to think of exercise as a natural antidepressant. Once they get into it, they swear by it.

Exercise is an antidote to procrastination and a purpose promoter. As part of the Health and Retirement Study mentioned earlier, a project involving about thirteen thousand adults over fifty, participants were asked questions to evaluate their sense of purpose in life and the amount of physical activity they regularly engaged in. The authors defined a sense of purpose as "having goals and aims that give life direction and meaning."

Having a sense of purpose led to greater physical activity, and in general, those with greater physical activity showed a stronger sense of purpose!

Exercise provides structure, meaning, and a sense of accomplishment, and it improves our sense of self-worth and proficiency. It boosts mood, memory, concentration, information processing, and creativity—making us feel more open to possibilities. By increasing our motivation, it creates a virtuous cycle: it helps us complete the tasks we set out to do, enhancing our commitment to our goals, which strengthens our purpose. Bonus: Exercise and a sense of purpose both contribute to exceptional longevity.

Be Flexible in Your Path, but Firm in Your Purpose

In his book *Man's Search for Meaning*, renowned Austrian psychiatrist Viktor Frankl talks about what he learned as a survivor of the Auschwitz concentration camps—the importance of having purpose in life: "Woe to him who saw no more sense in his life, no aim, no purpose in carrying on. He was soon lost."

While most of us will never experience or witness the horrific hardship of a concentration camp, having a driving sense of purpose is a vital element in safeguarding our health, happiness, and relationships. Philosopher Daniel Dennett once said, "Find something more important than you are and dedicate your life to it."

I hope this chapter has put you on an intriguing path to seek what nourishes your soul, confirmed or revitalized a driving purpose, and connected you with sources of joy to nourish purpose. Taking ownership of your present and future in this way is the essence of Practical Optimism.

The research shows unequivocally that we need a sense of purpose in order to live a long, healthy, meaningful life. Let your quest for purpose be one that energizes and nourishes you. Trust that when you find and feel that special surge of energy, that glow of soul satisfaction, you'll know it. There's really no other feeling like it.

To view the scientific references cited in this chapter,
please visit doctorsuevarma.com/book.

CHAPTER 3

Processing Emotions

Name, Claim, Tame (and Reframe) Them

Anything that's human is mentionable, and anything that is mentionable can be more manageable.

—FRED ROGERS

"'Sleep when the baby's sleeping' is nice advice . . ." Nicole told me during our first session, now several years back, "but it's probably coming from someone who's never actually seen a baby."

I smiled. If only my patients knew how well I could sometimes relate to their experiences.

Nicole was someone who somehow could manage both a tear and a twinkle in her eye at the same time. She'd first come to me when experiencing anxiety and depression after her first child was born. We'd talked about the transition to motherhood—the shifts in her identity and her body after delivering her first baby; how she felt surprisingly unprepared for it all—and the consuming mix of love, worry, and concern for her baby that had preoccupied her and kept her from "sleeping while the baby was sleeping."

We worked together until her second child was a year old, when Nicole was able to continue practicing the skills she'd learned in therapy on her own, and we mutually agreed the time felt right to end therapy, with the understanding that she would be in touch in the future if needed.

Nicole had been in a good place and ready to "fully get back into the game with work and friendships" when we ended therapy. Then some time later, I received a message that she and her husband (whom I'd met during our previous work together) had had their third baby several months ago: "We need to talk."

Now Nicole was a working mom of three kids under six. She'd recently enrolled her eight-month-old, Emma, in day care and returned to work full time after maternity leave.

"I feel overwhelmed, but it's different from the postpartum depression," she told me. "Now I know what's bothering me, but I still don't know what to do. I feel a heaviness, like an elephant sitting on my chest."

With her first two kids, Nicole said, she and her husband had managed the daily juggle of school, sports, and playdates. With three kids, their skillful juggling act was more like a bunch of dropped balls. Emma was prone to ear infections, requiring Nicole or her husband—but mostly Nicole—to take time off from work for doctors' appointments and home care. After Emma had gone through several rounds of medications, the doctors thought ear tube surgery might decrease her infections. In a last-ditch effort to avoid surgery, Emma's pediatrician suggested keeping her at home for two months. Without exposure to other kids at day care, her ears might recover more fully.

This felt like a punch to Nicole's gut. As the lower earner, she'd be the one sacrificing her job to stay with Emma.

I knew Nicole preferred day care to in-home babysitting, citing its structure and socialization as childcare priorities. Now I learned there were more layers to this.

Nicole understood that hiring in-home help for Emma would allow her to keep her job while reducing her daughter's exposure. Fortunately, too, the family could afford it. But something was keeping Nicole stuck: "This voice inside says I'm not a good mom if I hire help."

Peripartum mental health disorders (i.e., those occurring before or after childbirth) are complex and occur within a broader social context. While Nicole was actively using her work in therapy to keep those symptoms at bay, sometimes even the best coping skills can seem insufficient when we don't feel supported, especially in the face of larger (systemic) barriers.

Nicole and I would discuss the challenges and generally limited support many mothers and young families experience in our society, including how the salary gender gap translates into career setbacks for many women, who may give up their lower-paying job for family caregiving. Add the unrealistic expectation that women be perfectly pulled together as professional, parent, and partner, and you have an impossible standard coupled with galling trade-offs.

But while there can be comfort in knowing that we're not alone, that what we're experiencing is part of a larger social construct mostly outside our control or responsibility, often some variables are in our control. It's important to maximize our perception that we have options. Sometimes knowing we have choices (even if they are limited) promotes a sense of agency in our situation, helping us combat the helplessness that can take us down a downward path (as in depression).

I was sensitive to the social context yet saw that some emotional processing was in order. It was important for us to look at why Nicole didn't feel as if she could act in a situation where she knew intellectually that she had some potential solutions. Possibilities and solutions lay on the other side of the dam she'd erected against some of the strong emotions this situation was evoking, which were threatening to overflow.

If I had to capture Practical Optimism's essence, it would be manage your emotions, or they will manage you. Put simply, managing emotion is about being able to name it, claim it, tame it, and then reframe it so our emotions can work for us as valuable feedback, helping us solve problems and enhance our relationships. There are two main ways to do this: emotional processing and emotional regulation.

Emotional processing, as we'll explore here, entails being aware of what we're feeling and how our emotions connect with past experiences.

Emotional regulation, which we'll discuss in the next chapter as part of problem-solving, entails accurately sensing and managing our emotions from moment to moment in real-time situations. Emotional processing and emotional regulation are distinct but related Pillars of Practical Optimism. You need both in order to be fully effective.

If we don't process our emotions, we're at their mercy, reflexively reacting to life out of our intense feelings, unmet needs, outdated scripts, and fears. We may have a hard time choosing the most rational response to situations. Or, like Nicole, we may become so mired in our emotions that we feel incapable of action. This Pillar focuses on understanding our emotions so that we can be better, more effective problem solvers and advocates for ourselves, working as effectively as we are able within the circumstances at hand—and realizing that sometimes we just might have a tad more control than we think, even if it's only our reaction to a situation.

In this chapter, we'll look at how to befriend your emotions, recognize, respect, and understand them, and work with them.

The Iceberg Effect

There's an old saying: "It took me fifteen years to become an overnight success." Smart marketing and social media can make success look easy. But when we look at someone we consider to be inspiring and highly effective, we're seeing the tip of the iceberg: someone who's calm, confident, resourceful, decisive, and empathetic. We're drawn to their positive energy and actions. We don't see the inner work they do to elevate their own and others' potential.

That's the work of emotional processing. Unhindered by intense and painful emotions, these individuals can make decisions with clarity and have a strong positive influence over others.

Nicole was brilliant and highly capable. At work, she constantly put out fires for others. But what about the combustion within that can prevent us from feeling and doing our best? Are we assessing situations accurately, not projecting past grievances and traumas onto our present life? Are our responses appropriate, aligned with our values and intended goals? I have patients who say, "I want to be closer to my partner, but I'm upsetting them with my words. What's going on?"

If you're not in touch with your emotions, you can't respond appropriately because your emotions, like it or not, are in there clouding your judgment. Managing you.

True success requires not only tangible skills but also the ability to skillfully manage the biggest intangible of all: our own mind. That's the inner game of emotional processing.

Tools of the Trade: How Emotions Help Us

The word *emotion* comes from the French *emouvoir*, meaning "a (social) moving, stirring, or a physical disturbance," encompassing mental states previously characterized as appetites, passions, affections, or sentiments.

Historically, emotions were seen as intrusions no self-respecting, self-restraining individual would want anything to do with. Science reveals a different story.

While scientists are still working out how emotions arise and interface with our conscious awareness, we can think of emotions as short, intense, spontaneous biological experiences occurring when our reaction to something in our environment correlates with a physiological process in our brain and body. Some emotions, like fear, typically last seconds to minutes. Others, like sadness, can last up to two hours (or much longer). Emotions lingering for hours or days are called moods.

Contrary to historic belief, emotions serve a purpose. They're intimately connected to our motivation and drives. Drives can mobilize our emotions to effect a particular outcome through promoting specific behaviors. Charles Darwin believed emotions were adaptations allowing humans and animals to survive and reproduce. Fear can motivate us to flee a threat; anger may motivate us to confront it. Motivated by love or the desire to feel it, one might seek a mate and reproduce. Our emotions help us prioritize, plan, and focus on what needs our attention by influencing our thought processes. Thus, emotions serve to maximize our chances of survival by permitting us to avoid danger, thrive by taking opportune and appropriate risks, and finally pass on this accumulation of wealth, wisdom, and knowledge to future generations. An astonishing seven-thousand-plus different facial movement combinations have been found to be comprised from the forty-six unique facial movements discerned by experts Paul Ekman and Wallace Friesen. It seems clear we wouldn't have such an astounding array of expressive capacities if emotions had no positive role to play.

From an evolutionary perspective, our survival depends on our community relationships. Emotions can promote group cohesion by helping us understand each other.

Despite commonalities in how we experience emotions, there

might be cross-cultural differences in how we express them—societal norms we internalize as children. In one classic experiment, researchers secretly observed Japanese and American participants viewing gruesome, violent images and videos, including amputations and surgeries. People from both backgrounds showed similar facial expressions, grimacing and conveying disgust.

However, when a scientist was in the room while participants viewed these scenes, the Japanese participants were more likely to mask their feelings with smiles. In Japanese culture, it's typically considered less acceptable to display strong negative emotions in front of others (especially if those others might be seen as authority figures or someone with a formal title) than in American culture. By masking their expressions, the Japanese viewers were adhering to the (traditional) emotional expression rules of their culture. So while many expressions of emotion are innate, social pressures, cultural influences, and past experience all shape our emotional expression.

If emotions serve all these positive purposes, why can they be so disruptive? We have more neurons in our cerebral cortex than any other animal. And we can thank our cerebral cortex for our sophisticated capacities—self-awareness, language, problem-solving, abstract thinking, executive functioning, and visual-spatial abilities, among others. But with all these talents comes a downside: the ability to worry, perseverate, and project into the future things that will most likely never happen.

PO Pearls
Our brains are meant to keep us alive—not necessarily always happy.

Practical Optimism helps us maximize our brain's positive capacities, while setting boundaries around our less productive thought processes. You might think worry helps, but there's a difference between the concern that leads to planning and the prevention of problems and the treadmill of excessive worry.

As mentioned, most emotions are brief—but if a negative situation is important, the emotion will likely persist. Sadness might persist considerably longer because it's often related to prolonged or changing life circumstances like loss or bereavement. Emotions can persist around events tied to our identity, or perhaps around a situation that's forced us to question what we believe to be true, or, conversely, one that confirms it.

It's important to appreciate the fleeting nature of emotions so we don't get bogged down by them or fear opening the emotional floodgates. Think of emotions as visitors: let them come and go. We're one of the only species that can act contrary to our emotions. We possess the rapid-fire feedback of emotional awareness *and* the measured ballast of rational thought. Often, emotions will subside within minutes if we simply observe the thoughts, feelings, and body sensations occurring and don't engage. I'll share exercises for doing this.

I feel that emotions provide valuable information and can help us make decisions—IF (a) we're in touch with them, and (b) we can regulate them. Think of your emotional range like a piano keyboard. A piano has eighty-eight keys spanning seven-plus octaves, providing unique expressive power. You can play high and low notes, even simultaneously. Our goal is to be emotionally versatile, like a beautifully tuned piano.

How Unprocessed Emotions Can Hinder Us

Unprocessed emotions can dominate to the point that they no longer protect or connect us, but rather can hurt us and others. The grief of loss; the churn of chronic anxiety; and the shame, fear, and anger that are the toxic legacy of trauma—left unprocessed, these put us at risk for myriad physical and mental health problems. I learned this firsthand when my legs literally wouldn't support me during the stress/sadness overload of medical training combined with my mother's illness.

Below are some patterns I commonly see that tell me emotions need processing.

Overestimating the Threat; Underestimating Our Ability to Handle It

When we overestimate the threat and underestimate our ability to handle it, we may respond with anxiety, fear, withdrawal, or avoidance, none of which rectifies the problem or helps us handle our distress.

People vulnerable to this emotional response may be more sensitive to nuances and outside influences and more likely to consider a number of potential outcomes of situations. The potential ramifications of situations may loom large for them. Even neutral or low-threat stimuli might be seen as more dangerous than they are, which puts these individuals at higher risk for anxiety and depression.

Examples abound. I've heard countless reasons why people fear asking for a raise: "I'll be told I don't deserve it/it's too soon/I'm lucky to have a job." They jump to worst-case outcomes, discounting the evidence I remind them of: "You've held the department together for the past year . . . You were praised and thanked only last week . . . You're actually quite capable of asking for what you need." Nicole feared negotiating a childcare provider's salary, wondering how to put a price on caring for one's child. I reminded her she'd worked in HR for years, negotiating salary and job responsibilities. While this felt like an entirely different situation, Nicole had the capabilities. She just didn't give herself credit for them. (In the next chapter, you'll learn to address the distorted thought processes that keep this cycle going.)

Too Much Stress Versus Just Enough

Small amounts of controllable stress are good for us, actually leading to neuronal growth, or neurogenesis, in the hippocampus. Examples might be a side hustle, a hobby, or a project you willingly took on, or a new baby. But even positive challenges become problematic when they outweigh our ability to respond and recover. Uncontrollable chronic stress causes a decline in neurogenesis in the hippocampus that's associated with depression and memory problems. In fact, the very definition of stress is external demands and expectations that overwhelm our inner capacity and resources to handle them.

Yet refusing challenges because we fear they'll "stress us out" can keep us from pursuing goals and dreams. Many have internalized the idea that our emotions are "too much." But it's not the presence or absence of emotion that predicts success. It's whether they're in a manageable amount.

Anxiety in small quantities—just enough to motivate you, not paralyze you—can be helpful. Low levels of epinephrine or adrenaline (think: a bit of excitement) lead to a cascade of biological responses, culminating in brain levels of norepinephrine that facilitate memory and learning. Manageable stress levels counter boredom and motivate us, fostering peak performance and productivity. In contrast, significant amounts of stress do quite the opposite, actually impeding memory retention. An interesting experiment with college students studying for an exam found that, in small quantities, increasing anxiety levels correlated with increases in test performance, up to a point. After this point, any additional outside stress or pressure resulted in increased anxiety, leading to diminishing output or performance.

Emotional processing is about harnessing the power of pressure situations so the conditions are favorable for you to do your best. Like Goldilocks in the house of the three bears, looking for the porridge, chair, and bed that were "just right," we need to find the "just right" level of stimulating challenge.

But here's a PO secret: Stress isn't really the issue. The problem is actually our perception of it. If we perceive something to be manageable, it likely will be. Think of how powerful that is! It starts with knowing how much anxiety is the right amount for us. We develop this awareness not by avoiding, but by learning to sit with and process our feelings in controlled, compassionate ways. Then we can harness and use our anxiety to propel ourselves forward.

So when patients say they don't want to do something because it makes them anxious, I respect their feelings, but we also explore: "Is there value in doing this?" If there's something to be gained, then we look at their anxiety level. If it's mild discomfort, but it's pushing them toward growth, then doing the activity might be worthwhile.

"Emotional Loops": Rumination

While emotions are generally short-lived, there are some notable exceptions. Negative emotions especially are associated with rumination, a repetitive thought process that replays events and the associated negative emotions. Let's say you failed a big exam or didn't get an important promotion. You've been in the dumps for days. That's an emotional loop. The driving thought might be something like *I can't do anything right.*

Sometimes we feel the distress of these loops. Other times, we barely notice them until emotional processing attunes us to the mental static we've been putting up with. I sensed some long-standing emotional loops were playing under Nicole's paralyzing anxiety around hiring care for Emma.

Like many women, Nicole felt tremendous pressure to breastfeed her children. "Among my friends and my healthcare providers, 'breast is best,' and I believe that," she said. But Nicole said her job hadn't done much to support her pumping schedule post–maternity leave. When she could steal twenty minutes from her meeting-packed schedule to pump, there was no designated space for it. She often pumped in the supply closet, leaning against the door and hoping no one would come looking for pens. Her irregular pumping schedule and stress levels caused a considerable drop in her milk supply, exacerbating her anxiety: "I couldn't nurse Emma as long as I did the other two—maybe she missed out on the immune system benefits of breast milk."

Nicole also came from a family background that harshly judged women who hired outside help. Her family and friends stigmatized day care—but her family's perception was that having full-time in-home childcare was for privileged women who didn't want to be bothered raising their own children. The women in her family, Nicole said, had appeared to "do it all, all by themselves."

Many women blame themselves for struggling with motherhood rather than realizing it really does take a village to parent a child. A woman's ability to nurse her baby while working requires support. Childcare decisions are stressful—and everyone, it seems, has an opinion. It's easy to start an emotional loop of: "I'm not doing this right. I'm not doing enough. I'm not a good mom."

The Little Engine That Couldn't: Learned Helplessness

Learned helplessness occurs when we feel helpless to prevent negative outcomes. Experiments conducted in several animal species—with rats, dogs, and humans among those most well studied—have demonstrated the phenomenon. In 1967, American psychologists J. Bruce Overmier, PhD, and Martin Seligman, PhD, described learned helplessness based on experiments that found that dogs who received electrical shocks that they could not control later failed to learn to escape shocks in a different situation where escape was possible. Soon after, Seligman and Steven F. Maier, PhD, would conduct experiments that confirmed their hypothesis that the dogs' passivity was due to the uncontrollable and inescapable nature of the original shocks.

While these experiments laid important groundwork on the relationship between pessimism and passivity to anxiety and depression, fifty-plus years of research in neuroscience have given us a more nuanced and updated understanding. In fact, Seligman and Maier write in a paper titled "Learned Helplessness at Fifty: Insights from Neuroscience" that their team had gotten the theory backward. Five decades later, they explain that passivity and anxiety in response to shock is not learned (as they'd previously thought)—but rather is our default mammalian response to prolonged adverse conditions. What we learn, therefore, is not our helplessness, but rather our control. We can override our default setting of passivity through tapping into our agency and perception of control.

How does this happen in the brain? The activity of the ventromedial prefrontal cortex (vmPFC), involved with the perception and detection of control, is crucial in inhibiting the serotonergic activity in our dorsal raphe nucleus (DRN) that gives rise to the anxiety and passivity ensuing from unrelenting aversive events. It's as if our more rational forebrain (evolved later) is saying to our more reactive brain stem (evolved earlier), in Maier's words, "Cool it, brain stem, we have the situation under control." Training our brains to activate the vmPFC to enhance our perception of control quiets and encourages us to exit this default "helpless" position that assumes stress is uncontrollable. Enter PO—which helps us detect and promote a sense of control through many modalities. Through problem-solving, promoting proficiency, challenging distortions, and reframing negative thoughts, PO activates our "hope circuitry."

When life experiences condition us to believe there's nothing we can do about situations, we may become passive spectators of our lives. When life constantly kicks us to the curb, interfering with our ability to regain our footing and catch our breath, we become skeptical, even pessimistic, about our prospects for changing our future. We start feeling sad, hopeless, helpless, stuck in self-doubt, questioning our self-worth and sometimes even the purpose of our existence: "Life won't get better/it can only get worse." That's when I know I need to intervene fast, since depression can take hold and suicide risk can elevate quickly.

Cognitive Dissonance: Us Versus the World

"I want to keep my job," Nicole told me. "I've worked too hard to get to this point." She also understood most families need dual incomes. Yet she struggled to hire help at home "because of the expectations I've been raised with."

According to Nicole, "good" moms could wake up at five A.M. and squeeze in a workout and sex with their husband before pulling together runway-worthy hair, makeup, and outfits, then whipping up gluten-free breakfast pancakes from scratch and packing social-media-worthy bento boxes for school lunches by seven A.M., when they'd take their children to school and get to their desk (remote or on-site) in time for an eight A.M. meeting. All without outside help or breaking a sweat.

We all know women like this—at least on social media. We rarely see the story behind the story. In fact, Nicole's the kind of mom others might put on a pedestal—vibrant, sexy, fit, stylish—when in fact she's a human being vulnerable to the doubts and insecurities we all have. Which just goes to show that it's best not to compare our insides to other people's outsides.

When we feel torn, as Nicole did, between current life challenges and conditioned roles and expectations, the result is called cognitive dissonance. Even when we don't fully buy into society's expectations, we still, on some level, may strive to achieve them.

According to economists Rakesh Sarin and Manel Baucells, understanding and managing our expectations is a fundamental question of well-being. In their book *Engineering Happiness*, they share this equation: Happiness = Reality − Expectations. This equation maximizes for happiness in one of two ways: if your reality turns out better than you expected, or if your expectations were tempered (by you or by someone else).

Nicole expected herself to measure up to society's unattainable standards, but I wondered whether she kept her expectations of others low as a survival technique, to stay happy. "Don't expect too much and they can't let you down," she'd say.

Nicole had a complicated relationship with her mother, who "drank too much alcohol and was mean when she did." She experienced her mother as critical (especially when she'd had too much to drink) and judgmental of her childcare decisions without actually helping. Nicole's relationship with her father was equally complicated.

There was no one in her extended family she could ask for caregiving help. And her husband, she said, "already does so much," working long hours like her and sharing childcare responsibilities: "He makes more money, his job is more high pressure. I can't ask for more." Any adjustment to her own work schedule, she felt, would result in her being taken less seriously professionally—they'd already begrudged her taking a six-month maternity leave.

It seemed Nicole's reality had fallen below even her minimum standard. Yet her expectations of herself were as unrelenting as ever. An unfulfilling reality, with a sense of limited support from family and her employer, alongside extremely high expectations of herself—which she felt she wasn't meeting—equated to net unhappiness. This type of thinking is a slippery slope to depression and pessimism. It produces another kind of cognitive dissonance . . .

Cognitive Dissonance: Us Versus Us

Sometimes the biggest stressors come from a clash between our own values. Nicole values handling things herself, BUT she needs help. She values women speaking up, BUT as a middle child who played the role of peacekeeper and people pleaser in her family, she finds it hard to rock the boat. These competing agendas zeroed in on core aspects of Nicole's identity: "I want to do X, but there will be the costs and consequences, and it also clashes against other values of mine." Nicole needed to update her software to work with her current reality: she needed to set boundaries and ask for help. It was as if "old Nicole" were in a boxing match with "new Nicole"—and depending on what day you asked her, a different Nicole would win.

Cognitive dissonance—whether Us Versus the World or Us Versus Us—is uncomfortable and can arouse powerful emotions. Nicole's cognitive dissonance caused considerable anxiety. She'd freeze up and cry. Wanting things and not feeling able to ask for them can lead to resentment and anger. The energy it takes to suppress those emotions had a high cost: Nicole felt their weight like an elephant on her chest.

Name It, Claim It, Tame It, Reframe It:
Four Steps to Self-Awareness

I often find myself reassuring successful women like Nicole that "complaining" (Nicole's word) about their lives or their experiences as mothers doesn't mean they love their lives or their kids any less. It means they're rational human beings in touch with themselves. I try to validate and empathize with them—but I'm careful not to provide too much reassurance. That can interfere with people's innate need and ability or tendency to process uncomfortable emotions. I want individuals to know their experiences are normal, but I also want to give them the tools to process their emotions and face new challenges. Self-awareness is the first step.

Self-awareness starts with being able to pay attention to our emotions without needing to respond or change things. As Rumi wrote, "Do you pay regular visits to yourself?" Often we cut ourselves off from our feelings through numbness, distraction, or self-medication. This sends our brain the message that emotions are to be avoided instead of understood, processed, and regulated. We end up instead with headaches, leg weakness, anxiety, depression, insomnia, gastritis, high blood pressure, chronic pain and inflammation, autoimmune disease, and heart disease.

We all have ways of avoiding dealing with strong emotions. In fact, I sometimes joke, "How can I avoid my emotions? Let me count the ways!"

Our avoidance responses tend to be tactics we developed in the past that might not be healthy for us and sometimes for others, then or now. Often they're ingrained from having to adapt to situations we felt powerless to deal with.

We might suppress our emotions, like Nicole, taking their weight within. We might take refuge in destructive behaviors—overeating, drinking, and more. We might become irritable and lash out, as we saw with Sam in chapter 2.

What do you do with big feelings? Here's a four-step approach to help you tune into your emotional patterns and process emotions, rather than bottling them up or lashing out: Name It, Tame It, Claim It, and Reframe It.

Step 1: Name It

Emotions can be recognized as physical sensations. Allowing your mind and body to experience emotions and then labeling them lowers your fear response by reducing activity levels in the amygdala, our fear center. When you speak about things, you lessen their power over you. Affect labeling, as it's called, can be incredibly liberating.

Holding feelings back takes energy, requiring an active process of inhibition. According to one study, this taxing effort is associated with increased disease, autonomic dysfunction (the fight-or-flight response going haywire), and decreased immune function. When people enter psychotherapy, we also see that their medical visits for physical health concerns decrease. Talking or writing about painful or traumatic experiences not only relieves the burden associated with the inciting events but also lets us assimilate or make sense or meaning out of what happened to us.

Labeling emotions can feel awkward at first, and be prepared for some strong bodily sensations, as happened with Nicole when I asked her to label some of her emotions.

"I'm sad," she said.

I nodded sympathetically, and we sat quietly. "Nicole, I'm wondering whether you'd be open to exploring those feelings a bit? Is there anything else that's coming up for you right now?"

I could see she was struggling, so I asked, "Can I tell you what I'm hearing?"

She nodded.

"Nicole, I hear a lot of sadness. I also hear notes of rejection, disappointment, betrayal, frustration, and anger in what you've shared today and in other sessions, but also compassion toward your family."

"They're good people," she said, tears streaming.

"Of course, Nicole, and they're your parents and you love them. And you're also angry at them. I get it—this feels hard right now. I appreciate your sharing and that you're connecting to your emotions. This is a huge and important step for you."

When you can name your emotions and not do anything with them, you're in charge. You can feel furious at someone but be able to say, "I'm really angry at so-and-so," and not have to immediately call them up and yell at them. That's freeing! Now you can move to real problem-solving: "What will best serve the situation?" It builds in an all-important *pause*—something we'll explore in the next chapter—so we can bypass a reflexive, almost always destructive reaction and *choose* our response: not sending that knee-jerk email, giving ourselves a time-out with our partner or kids, or simmering down during a tense meeting.

Exercise: Naming Your Emotions

Sit quietly. When you feel ready, think of a situation or person that brings up some negative emotions—for starters, choose something that brings up medium-level feelings.

Do you feel sensations in your body? Tight chest? Jumpy stomach? Clenched jaw? Tense hands or feet?

Can you find some language around the emotion you're feeling? See if you can label this emotion.

Sit a bit with this label. Are there facets to this emotion? Try saying to yourself, "Tell me more." For example, if you're feeling angry, "Tell me more" may bring details: "I feel I've been treated unfairly. I feel misunderstood. I feel humiliated."

Continue until you feel complete in how you've named these particular emotions.

Next, reflect on or complete the statements below. What do you feel, and where do you feel it, including bodily sensations?

- When I feel powerful sadness, I _____.
- When I feel powerful hurt, I _____.
- When I feel powerful fear, I _____.
- When I feel powerful anger, I _____.

Step 2: Claim It

This step digs deeper into root causes and triggers of our emotions. Studies show that the more "granular" we are in labeling, differentiating between and knowing what triggered our emotions, the better we are at managing them and succeeding in the external world. You're moving from an amorphous "feeling bad" to connecting specific emotions to situations: "When he did/said X, I felt humiliated."

Once you understand your emotions and what triggered them, then you have control over what situations you're vulnerable to, and you can reconcile past with present and make a plan for the future.

Exercise: Claiming Your Emotions

Write your responses to the following:

- Are there some emotions that are more difficult or "forbidden" for you to feel than others?
- Are there situations that feel overwhelming or that you're afraid will stress you out?
- What are some emotional loops you tend to get caught in?
- How often do you feel powerless or helpless to change a situation?
- What are your expectations of yourself? What are your expectations of others? How do you think your life "should" look? How do you feel when your expectations of yourself, others, or your life aren't met?
- Zen master Thích Nhất Hạnh said, "Let your anger be the compost for your garden." What does this statement mean to you?

• What do you think your strong emotions might be trying to tell you?

Remember the strength that got you here—where you can choose to do things differently.

Step 3: Tame It

There are various ways to "tame your emotions." These are my four go-to practices for building emotional processing muscles:

1. Disrupt unhealthy emotional patterns with the 4 Cs of Healthy Coping.
2. Break negative emotional loops with decentering.
3. Befriend your mind and body.
4. Empty your anxiety spam folder into a worry journal.

Let's unpack each.

Disrupt Unhealthy Emotional Patterns with the 4 Cs of Healthy Coping

A key emotion-taming tactic is having some healthy, flexible coping mechanisms to help you work with your emotions, not avoid them.

An effective coping mechanism should make you feel better, not worse. It should pass this little test and be:

1. **Compassionate.** An effective coping mechanism is gentle. (Self-flagellation, begone!)
2. **Corrective.** It should address the underlying problem, or at least not worsen it. Avoidance behaviors (binge eating; cutting; substance abuse; numbing out with gaming, media bingeing, or scrolling; excessive shopping; gambling, etc.) only lead to shame,

more emotional distress, or problems atop the underlying problem.

A corrective coping strategy can be an insight. Insight helped Nicole counter her guilt over getting childcare: "I don't think these outdated values ever really served anyone in my family. When I was growing up, there was no need for babysitting. Two of my aunts lived nearby. Older cousins were around. When my mom wasn't home, I took care of my brothers. It wasn't like she was watching us 24/7. The whole neighborhood was looking out for us."

3. **Calming**. A healthy coping mechanism should create calming distance from anger, anxiety, or aggression so you can problem-solve. A habitual anger response is a sign that someone isn't able to process or regulate their emotions, often because they weren't taught how or learned through early experiences that anger and aggression were the only ways to be seen and heard. Conversely, stuffing down emotions, as Nicole was doing, doesn't make them go away. Developing a simple but regular breathing practice, mindfulness practice, meditation practice, or journaling practice can help us regain calm. Some turn to nature, exercise, yoga, cooking, or gardening. Just make sure your chosen activity is in moderate doses and isn't an unhealthy distraction. And of course, seek professional help if you are in distress.

4. **Connective**. Ideally, our coping mechanisms seek to connect us better, leading to improved communication with people we want or need to interact with (think boss, coworker, or family member).

Break Negative Emotional Loops with Decentering
We get stuck in emotional loops by holding on to an emotion and adding our own spin or interpretations. If we simply observe and don't engage, the physiological response often subsides.

Decentering is a fundamental change strategy of Mindfulness-Based Cognitive Therapy (MBCT)[7] that entails stepping outside of our mental experiences and seeing them from a neutral, nonjudgmental stance. We allow our negative emotions and thoughts to be experienced as passing mental events (or visitors) rather than holding on to them, personalizing them, or seeing them as reflections of ourselves or of external reality. In cognitive therapy, we then dispute irrational thoughts (sometimes called cognitive distortions). In mindfulness practice, thoughts are nonjudgmentally noticed and let go.

PO Pearls
You don't have to believe all your thoughts.

Let's return to an earlier example: You failed an exam or didn't get that promotion. You're caught in an emotional loop of anger and shame.

In MBCT, you identify the thought behind those feelings—maybe *I can't do anything right.* With practice, you learn to limit its scope: *I had trouble with this one thing. It's not accurate to say I can't do anything right. Look how well I'm doing in these other aspects of my life. I have strong feelings because this is important to me, as it would be to most people. With practice and help, I can do better.*

---

[7] MBCT, an approach to psychotherapy that uses cognitive behavioral therapy (CBT) methods in collaboration with mindfulness meditative practices, was first developed as a method for depression relapse prevention. It interrupts the cycle of self-criticism, rumination, and low moods that typically give rise to the negative thought patterns and downward spirals that trigger subsequent depressive episodes in chronic depression. MBCT can be used in group or individual therapy settings and can be used for a wide variety of mental health disorders, including addiction, chronic medical ailments, and chronic stress. Mindfulness-based stress reduction (MBSR), though similar, is used as a more general approach to stress reduction, not necessarily for mental health disorders, and is often used for pain, addiction, and prenatal programs across the board (though without the psychotherapy piece that MBCT offers). Many of my patients have received immense relief through both programs. *The Mindful Way Through Depression*, authored by the pioneers in this field, Mark Williams, John Teasdale, Zindel Segal, and Jon Kabat-Zinn, is a must-read if you are interested in learning more. The goal in MBCT is to interrupt the automatic cognitive processes that take us down a rabbit hole of negativity and to observe, pay attention, accept, and, hopefully, let go.

Befriend Your Mind and Body

In this step of taming, we actually make room for our emotions—as if inviting them to dinner or tea, welcoming them, paying attention to them nonjudgmentally.

Nicole was pushing down her anger about her situation, funneling all that energy into anxiety. It was like playing one key repeatedly on her emotional piano. My job was to help her welcome her full range of emotions—including anger, a feeling she had a hard time accepting and expressing—and know she could accommodate them all. Only then could she begin playing a different tune.

These Befriending exercises can be done anytime—in the morning to set the tone for your day, before an important meeting, to unwind after work, or before bed. Or try them before or after a stressful situation.

Doing these exercises regularly, not just when you're feeling down, helps you strengthen your moment-to-moment awareness of emotions—important for regulating your emotions in real time in the world.

If you're experiencing significant or acute distress or trauma, you may want to do some of these under the guidance of a therapist. They're not meant to trigger anyone, but sometimes when we have significant wounds, we may need a little extra help and support during this journey.

Exercise: Befriending Your Breath

Find a quiet space. Sit back in your chair, both feet relaxed on the floor. Let your shoulders softly shrug and drop naturally.

Gently close your eyes. Inhale slowly through your nose to the count of five, then exhale slowly through your mouth to the count of five. If you'd like, place one hand on your abdomen, feeling it expand as you inhale. This encourages deeper, diaphragmatic breathing (breathing that starts in the belly, not in the chest).

And that's it. There's no right or wrong way to experience this exercise.

Exercise: Befriending Your Body

Start with the Befriending Your Breath exercise, above. When you feel ready, bring your attention to your body. Do you notice any sensations? In your head, arms, legs, feet, or stomach, do you notice any tightness, tension, weakness, or pain? What do you notice about your heartbeat (fast or slow)? Your breathing (shallow or deep)? Are you sweating? Simply notice.

Notice any feelings that may be coming up: sadness, worry, anger, calm. Create space for them all as you continue to breathe.

There's no right or wrong way to do this. You're working on acknowledging these sensations but not dwelling on them. Notice . . . let go.

Empty Your Anxiety Spam Folder into a Worry Journal
Our self-confidence takes a beating when anxiety flares up. Releasing our fears by writing them in a worry journal, an exercise used in cognitive behavioral therapy (CBT), is one of the healthiest ways to tame emotions. Believe it or not, students who got all their worries out were found to do better on a math test, including strong math performers. If you're facing a test, performance, or anything of consequence, take ten minutes just before to write about any aspect of the event that worries you.[8]

Why spend time worrying when you're trying to *stop* worrying? Because:

- **It's a relief.** Like lifting the lid off a boiling pot lets off steam. It takes more energy to hold things in than to let them out.

---

[8] Journaling may have more general benefits: a 2013 study published in *Psychosomatic Medicine* showed that journaling for twenty minutes, three times per week, led to faster wound healing after a medically necessary biopsy.

- **You reach an important realization.** Much of the time, the things we worry about don't happen. But when they do, we're better equipped to handle them, because writing them down helps desensitize us to them over time. It's called exposure therapy.
- **You see patterns.** Our emotions are less likely to blindside us when we see the patterns: "There's that worry about failure again (even though I'm always prepared). There's that worry about looking needy (even though people are glad to help)."
- **You can park your worries.** Once out of your head and on the page, they have less power over you.

Step 4: Reframe It

This final step in emotional processing is one you continue to practice and get better at with time. You might say it's part of a long-term project called living.

Essentially, reframing is seeking to understand or view something from a different angle. It's trying to see from another's perspective or to seek a positive takeaway—a silver lining, a lesson learned, a bullet dodged, a crisis averted.

Reframing uses empathy and compassionate understanding of ourselves and others to release negative emotions that keep us trapped. It allows us to open our minds to a plethora of possibilities and ideas we might never have found from our former vantage. It makes us more adaptable, better problem solvers, and more able to heal from hardship. Reframing is the hardest emotion-taming task to do, but science shows it's the most powerful, sophisticated, and enduring.

As we practice emotional processing, we may see how our interpersonal conflicts sometimes stem from others' unprocessed emotions. Nicole came to see that the "elephant" on her chest (her physician had given her a clean bill of health) was her own unexpressed anger at, among other things, how her mother's unresolved emotional issues affected Nicole and the family. While it seemed that women of her mother's generation prioritized family and did it well, Nicole realized it came at a cost. Nicole suspected her mother had lived with undiagnosed/untreated postpartum depression and anxiety. This, combined with Nicole's understanding of the social pressures back then, helped her reframe her mother's unprocessed anger and limitations (and the unhealthy ways it manifested—i.e., drinking and critical behavior): *Maybe if she hadn't felt the pressure to work so hard to conform to society's expectations, she wouldn't have been so angry all the time. I can relate to that. I feel society's pressures, too. It wasn't all her fault.*

Nicole, too, had issues with anger. She bottled it up: "I don't do anger very well. I just end up crying." She was also angry about the self-sacrificial role women are still too often pressured to play, and she resented how hard she'd worked to live up to a flawed standard: women are expected to work like they aren't parents and parent like they don't work.

Learning to express her needs in a healthy way rather than let them fester into a deep anger that she would then suppress would be key to Nicole's success. She needed just enough anger to help her set boundaries and hold others accountable. She needed her support system to actually support her, including her mother (instead of being judgmental and not helping), her husband (who needed to take a more proactive role alongside her in childcare and childcare decisions and respect her ambivalence about in-home childcare, even if he was in favor of it), and her employer.

As she processed her unacknowledged anger and needs, Nicole was able to reframe her view of her mother. She saw that her mother, when she drank, sometimes to excess, was self-medicating. Nicole's mother had been tasked with managing a family of multiple children—some with special needs—and she had to do it mostly alone because Nicole's father traveled frequently for work. Nicole was able to regard her mother with empathy.

But Nicole's biggest reframe? She could be in the driver's seat. She realized she'd been waiting for permission to do what she knew she needed to—like hiring help and asking her husband to initiate a bit more in his involvement at home, so the default assumption wasn't that these things were her job to do or delegate—and that she was holding on to things she no longer needed (like other people's approval). She stopped overestimating the risk (losing others' respect and approval by standing her ground and asking for help) and underestimating her ability to cope. She was a healthy coper and an excellent juggler—after all, even masterful jugglers drop a ball now and then. She knew she wasn't alone in her struggles and that she was doing the best she could. Her reframing went from *I'm a bad mom* to *I'm a mom who's doing the best she can, given the circumstances. I'm actually doing a great job, even when I don't feel I am. I have a right to ask for help. I have a right to feel better. It's not feasible (or even advisable) for me to continually try to meet other people's expectations. Their expectations are a by-product of their own thinking and circumstances. It's not serving me. This can be a moment of breakthrough for me.* Processing her emotions lightened Nicole's load. "That pressure, that elephant on my chest . . ." she would later tell me, "it's gone."

The Work of Wisdom

Finding this balance between empathy for others and empathy for ourselves is the work of wisdom. In our individual ways, we're all here together, equally subject to life's dealings. As part of my own emotional processing, I try to remember these principles:

Share in our common humanity. No one is perfect.
Extend empathy. Each person walks through life with their own struggles.
Acknowledge your own hurt and feelings and allow yourself to grieve a resolution you will most likely not have.
Practice compassion. Offer forgiveness, if only in your own mind.

Let go. Release your pain in any form that feels right to you (i.e., writing a letter that you never send).

Adjust expectations. Accept that this person can't give you what you need.

Let go of self-blame. Whatever happened, you can learn something from it.

In the next chapter, we'll look at how Nicole problem-solved her day-to-day challenges, including asserting herself to ask for what she needed. Her emotional processing practices helped her stay grounded. She regularly practiced deep breathing and connecting with her body's experience of worry. When stressed, she used the 4 Cs of healthy coping, with yoga as her calming practice. Labeling her emotions before, during, and after stressful situations helped her validate her feelings and stay level-headed when asking for help and accommodations at work and home.

Emotional processing was Nicole's first imperative step in making peace with a past she couldn't change and finding empowerment in her strength to change her story. I hope it will empower you in shaping yours.

To view the scientific references cited in this chapter, please visit doctorsuevarma.com/book.

CHAPTER 4

Problem-Solving

Moving Toward Action

Everything can be taken from a man but one thing: the last of the human freedoms—to choose one's attitude in any given set of circumstances, to choose one's own way.

—VIKTOR E. FRANKL, *MAN'S SEARCH FOR MEANING*

None of us lives in a vacuum. The outside world is constantly calling upon us. There are changes, challenges, opportunities, messes. Problem-solving is what we do with what the world throws at us.

When we think of problem-solving, we tend to think of concrete solutions. In truth, we problem-solve internally and externally simultaneously. Indeed, the majority of problem-solving is internal. The instant it recognizes a problem, our mind sets to work determining what actions we need to take.

This often happens outside our conscious thought and awareness. But problem-solving prowess has everything to do with our *conscious* thought process. Can we consciously manage our emotions minute to minute in real time? Can we distinguish feeling from fact, then choose wise action based on what both reveal? Blending our cognitive skills with our psychological and emotional resources is called emotional regulation. It's the problem-solving machinery of our mind.

In chapter 3, we discussed how we can't manage our emotions if we don't know what they are. Emotional recognition is essential for emotional regulation. But naming and claiming our feelings is only half the battle. Problem-solving is how skillfully we regulate our emotions and then act when confronted with reality.

Emotional regulation in problem-solving allows us to

- pause,
- check in with how we're *feeling*,
- pay attention to what we're *thinking*, and
- rationally assess a situation so we can *respond*, not simply *react*.

And all of this happens in seconds.

This internal aspect of problem-solving is crucial because it determines our outlook on the problem. And if I've learned anything as a doctor, it's that one of the most important steps in addressing a problem is to accurately assess before you address. The safety and efficacy of your solutions depend on it.

Emotional regulation isn't about overriding our feelings (or suppressing them). That can be as (or more) harmful than overreacting. Our responses should match the situations we're in. The goal is not just to manage stress and survive, but to use our emotional wisdom to thrive.

In this chapter, I'll share a tool kit of techniques for problem-solving as Practical Optimists do. You'll discern your problem-solving persona and the cognitive distortions that hinder thoughtful solutions. I'll share powerful strategies that I call the 5 Rs of Emotional Regulation and Real-World Problem-Solving, and four guidelines for problem-solving with others. Finally, I'll share a quick, question-based method I developed from helping my patients get to the heart of a problem. I'll include examples of these tools in action, including how Nicole, whom you met in chapter 3, resolved her childcare challenges coupled with a super-busy job and a rocky relationship with her mother.

With these tools, I don't mean to imply quick fixes. Human relationships are deeply complex, and we can never presume to understand each person's unique situation. If you're struggling with significant life challenges, I hope this chapter provides useful options. You may also find them helpful to try with support from a therapist.

Your Problem-Solving Persona

Many of my patients tell me they know what to do about a problem but struggle to do it (the "intention to automation" gap—more on this in chapter 9, "Practicing Healthy Habits"). Most of us engage in some form of problem avoidance at times. We frequently get stuck worrying about potential obstacles, often without analyzing things objectively. It may feel as if worrying accomplishes something, but all we're doing is avoiding uncomfortable feelings—which can cause physical and mental health symptoms.

The chart below details common problem-solving practices of Practical Optimists and optimists, compared to pessimists and the over-optimistic. (Let's call this last group Ostrich Optimists, for their tendency to avoid problems/deny/take a passive approach by sticking their head in the sand.)

Problem-Solving Practices of Practical Optimists	Problem-Solving Practices of Pessimists/Ostrich Optimists
Acknowledge the problem and their thoughts around it: "There's something important that needs my attention right now."	**Deny the problem/Engage in projection:** "What problem?" "I don't have a problem." "Maybe you're the one with a problem."

Problem-Solving Practices of Practical Optimists	Problem-Solving Practices of Pessimists/Ostrich Optimists
Make efforts to understand the problem: "I want more information. When did it start? What's causing the issue? What makes it better/worse?"	**Avoid facing the problem, minimizing or magnifying it:** "It'll be okay. Things will work out." "It's not as bad as all that." "It's hopeless, we're doomed."
Lay out next steps and the potential upside, based on realistic assessment. Be self-compassionate but clear about their own responsibilities: "If I can get some information, I might be able to make a viable decision, but I need to get cracking."	**Passively wait for things to work themselves out/Worry about the worst-case scenario/Ask for information but reject it:** "There's nothing that can be done." "I don't believe what they're saying."
Take a proactive approach: • Brainstorm a variety of solutions creatively to explore all viable solutions (i.e., divergent thinking). • Do research, ask for advice. **Create an action plan that addresses obstacles via multiple if-then scenarios.**	**Unhealthy coping (distraction, procrastination, rumination, blame/shame):** "If you had/hadn't done X, this wouldn't have happened." "If I had/hadn't done X, this wouldn't have happened."
Assess all available options, narrow them down to the most viable, make a decision based on the relevant information (i.e., convergent thinking).	**Indecision or decisions that don't solve the underlying problem:** • Paralysis by analysis. • Anger- or fear-based decisions. **Hasty/superficial "research":** Talks to one person who already agrees with their opinion. **Snap decisions:** "So-and-so said X, so that's what I'm doing." **Tune out:** "I don't trust anyone who suggests that."

Problem-Solving Practices of Practical Optimists	Problem-Solving Practices of Pessimists/Ostrich Optimists
Proactive decision-making, follow-through, and acceptance. "Here's what I've decided." "Is it working? If not, why not?" "What can I change? What can I not change? What have I learned?"	**Rage, deflection of responsibility, withdrawal, resignation.** **Lack of action, or action based on cursory research.** **Possible unhappiness with what happens but resigns themselves to the results and/or has a hard time admitting they were wrong:** "I guess there was nothing I could've done." "This would've happened anyway."

Do you notice how these responses to problems are rooted in our comfort level with the underlying emotions (e.g., anger, fear) stirred up by the situation? How we deal with our emotional responses directly affects our problem-solving effectiveness.

Which column do you tend to fall into? What aspects of your problem-solving approach do you think work well for you? Are there aspects you could do better with?

Exercise: Are You a Maximizer or a Satisficer?

Pop quiz! Answer yes or no to the following questions:

1. Do you perseverate over details when making decisions?
2. Does it take you a long time to come to that "one right decision"?
3. Do loved ones get upset about how long it takes you to decide?
4. Do you easily get flustered when presented with too many options?
5. Do you avoid decisions because you don't have time to collect the data?

6. Does the thought of a big purchase—car, home, new appliances, technology—make you anxious, anticipating all the research involved?

7. Do you frequently regret decisions, especially when new information surfaces after the fact?

8. Do you often experience buyer's remorse, thinking that something better exists out there or that what you bought seems less interesting once you bought it?

9. Have there been consequences of inaction in your life?

10. Does "good enough" feel like settling to you?

If you answered yes to many of these, you may be a maximizer.

Maximizer and *satisficer* are words used to encapsulate two predominant decision-making styles. Satisficing (a blend of *satisfy* and *suffice*) is characterized by accepting an option as satisfactory for one's needs, given the best available options at the time. Maximizing is characterized by the wish to explore all possible options, glean all information, before deciding.

Satisficers are able to reach decisions fairly quickly. Maximizers tend to insist that all options, regardless of their importance or their relevance to what's actually needed, be considered before deciding. By searching for perfection, maximizers can lose sight of the good or the good enough, perhaps to their own detriment, as this approach can delay—even paralyze—decision-making and lead to post-decision regret.

What's important isn't which camp you're in, but whether you can be flexible to what the situation calls for.

Although my mom rarely experienced post-decision regret, her maximizer tendencies—in everything from buying tomato sauce to buying a car—were family legend. She dragged us from dealership to dealership, feverishly taking notes on horsepower and mileage. Did she need a moonroof? No. But if a similarly priced car didn't have one, there'd better be a good reason why. She needed to make the "best decision," taking into consideration elements that might or might not be relevant to her actual needs.

It was the same with her cancer treatment search. Yes, the decision was complex: trying to maintain her heart health in the context of the cardiac risks and side effects of chemotherapy. But as we searched and searched in her quest for the "perfect" medical team, I realized her cancer was at risk of spreading and we needed to shift into satisficer mode.

While they may assess things more accurately, the risk for maximizers is their instinct to delay necessary and important decisions when there isn't a perfect option. Satisficers make decisions based on reasonable expectations. They're willing to adjust their expectations and negotiate on less important details in order to ensure their basic needs are met.

Practical Optimists are versatile decision makers, able to toggle between the modalities of brisk Satisficer and more deliberate Maximizer, depending on the situation and the stakes. They can reach quick conclusions if the situation calls for that, and they're able to accept the choices they make without looking back and ruminating. In a time crunch, depending on the importance of the decision, POs may use what I call the Rule of Threes: give themselves three days; ask no more than three trusted people for input; narrow the choices to three. Their decision-making style is characterized by one of my favorite African proverbs: "Before marriage keep two eyes open; after marriage, keep one eye closed." Do your digging *before* you make the big decisions; engage in acceptance once you do.

How to Master Problem-Solving
by Mastering Your Own Mind

A patient, Sejal, told me she wasn't valued at work. "My boss hates me," she declared.

I asked her to tell me what evidence she had to suggest that. "They don't invite me to higher-level planning meetings, even though I've asked several times," she replied.

Sejal could be right. But she wasn't equally considering that she could be wrong. Maybe her boss was simply focusing on the tasks and personnel relevant to certain projects, and not considering Sejal's professional growth.[9]

Sejal wouldn't know the answer unless she asked about the meetings issue and for feedback in general. I suggested she request some one-on-one time with her supervisor. She planned a midyear review, instead of waiting for the end of the year.

As she prepped for the meeting, I asked Sejal to consider if there was evidence that might support a scenario where her boss liked her. She told me her regular holiday bonus had been a bit higher than usual and there was some discussion that she might be offered an off-cycle promotion at some point in the future.

Interestingly, Sejal considered not being included in certain meetings post-bonus as further proof of her initial assumption that her boss's dislike was personal. Without explicit feedback otherwise, it seemed, all evidence would support it.

When Sejal met with her supervisor, her boss clarified that the meetings were of a confidential nature relating to company downsizing. Sejal's boss assured her that she was a valuable team member

---

[9] When patients share with me feelings of being treated unfairly at work, I always seek to be sensitive to the intricacies of workplace culture, dynamics, and politics. I follow their lead in exploring the sources of their discomfort, particularly as they may relate to potential bias. In Sejal's case, she did not consider this to be an issue.

and suggested more regular meetings for the two of them. Had Sejal not asked for clarification, her assumption might have completely colored her perceptions, expectations, and happiness in her job.

What sets Practical Optimists apart as problem solvers is that they have expectations of a positive outcome due to their role as agents of change in their life. They engage with reality in real time, asking for feedback and clarification. They've restructured how they think to be hopeful and effective simultaneously. Cognitive restructuring, a highly effective and popular set of techniques that are a cornerstone of cognitive behavioral therapy (CBT), can help you take better charge of your life by taking charge of your thought processes.

Cognitive restructuring is fundamental to problem-solving because it helps us use our mind more incisively to notice our emotions, thought patterns, and behaviors. The full array of techniques goes by the acronym ABCDE.[10] Here's how ABCDE could be applied to Sejal's problem to help her take stock of her situation and move toward a resolution:

Antecedent: We identify the trigger that starts the emotional upset. For Sejal, it was not being invited to meetings.

Belief: Then we look at the belief(s) it conjures up for us. Often these are negative beliefs about our abilities, character, or deservingness, or about how we're perceived. Sejal believed she wasn't invited to meetings because her boss hated her.

Consequences: There are emotional and physical consequences of the belief(s). These may include feeling sad, angry, helpless, or

---

[10] Traditionally, in the original conceptualization of ABCDE, D would mean "Dispute thoughts and challenge your beliefs," and if there is an E, it stands for "Effective new thoughts and beliefs." In my description/conceptualization, D stands for "Distortions" and E for "Embrace." Aaron T. Beck, MD, was instrumental in first describing common distortions and their prominent role in anxiety and depression symptoms. Since then, other experts have expanded on this model, including Dr. David D. Burns.

tense or having knots in our stomach, headaches, etc. Sejal was feeling angry and helpless.

Distortions: Our beliefs give rise to distorted thoughts and skewed perceptions. Identifying these begins the work of reframing them. Sejal was so convinced her boss disliked her that she equated being excluded from the meetings with her boss's perceived disdain for her. Furthermore, she minimized the meaning behind the holiday bonus as something her "boss had to do, not because he wanted to—it doesn't show he really likes or values me," and dismissed the potential promotion as "speculative." She discounted and minimized the positives and magnified the negatives—what we call *negative filtering*—focusing only on the negative aspects of the situation.

Embrace: Finally, we consider what we *can* change (our distorted thoughts and beliefs, possible actions to address problems) and accept what we can't. Sejal took steps to challenge her beliefs by asking for a mid-cycle review. Learning that the meetings were about confidential matters helped calm her concerns so she could examine and embrace her tendency to personalize things that aren't personal—something that happens to all of us at times—and could learn not to read/project negative assumptions into ambiguity: the promotion hadn't been finalized yet, and she interpreted that, plus the exclusion from meetings, as proof that her boss hated her and her job wasn't stable. Result: anxiety.

We'll explore these techniques further in later chapters. Let's look at how to use cognitive restructuring for better problem-solving.

Examine Distorted Thoughts

Are there patterns in your life you'd like to change? Do you notice yourself saying or doing things that are unproductive? If so, some cognitive distortions may be in your mental driver's seat.

Cognitive distortions are unsupported negative thoughts, or biases, that make us more likely to engage in automatic (read: knee-jerk) responses emotionally or behaviorally that ultimately seek to confirm a core distorted belief about ourselves or others. They influence us to act counterproductively. They also increase vulnerability to depression.

Cognitive distortions, although they occur automatically, often reflect and are rooted in negative core beliefs about our self-worth and our future. Negative experiences are part of life, and negative thoughts are to be expected. But only when they're absolute in nature—i.e., when we add something like *always, never, forever, must, should, what if* to them—do they create exponential distress. Examples include all-or-nothing thinking, emotional reasoning, should statements, and what-ifs. They're the inner voice saying, *I'll never find a partner, I should be more successful,* or *I always mess up,* and are linked to deep-core beliefs such as *I'm going to be alone forever,* or *There's something wrong with me,* or *I'm no good at anything/I'm stupid.* Nicole, for example, had a cognitive distortion that said, in essence, *Good mothers shouldn't hire help.*

With practice, you can catch and challenge these rogue thoughts before they grab the wheel and steer you into unproductive actions.

Remember that pause I mentioned that happens during emotional regulation in the headlong rush of a situation? It's in this crucial moment, when nothing seems to be happening, that so much happens as we check in with ourselves: *Oops, there's that distortion that says: "You never finish anything . . . You're not worthy . . . Other people can have love/fun/success/money, but not you" . . . etc.*

In that pause, you can swap in a different thought process. For example: *What's the evidence for my assumptions? I need more information before deciding.*

What You Can't Control, Embrace

Happiness and freedom begin with a clear understanding of one principle: some things are within our control; some aren't. Only by accepting this fundamental truth do inner tranquility and outer effectiveness become possible. Practical Optimist problem solvers try to change what we can, but when we can't, we accept. As my parents often said, "If it's not a problem to be solved, perhaps it's a truth to be accepted."

Embracing or accepting isn't giving up or giving in. It's asking, *What can I change?* There's almost always something (including how you think!). Then it's recognizing what you can't control and letting that be.

Suppose you made a big mistake at work. You assess what you can change: damage control options; future prevention. You report to your boss all that's happened and what you intend to do. She's not happy; neither are you. But as one friend's boss said, with a crooked smile, in such a situation: "And what have we learned?" So you do. Then you let go of what you can't control: the lost client (though you're scouting for new ones), the profits dip (though you've partially offset this by accelerating another project to market), and your boss's displeasure, which you hope will fade with time and your good performance going forward.

The 5 Rs of Emotional Regulation and Real-World Problem-Solving

Emotional regulation, as mentioned, is the interplay between external events and your internal emotional responses, and your attuning to this interplay to make decisions and act in the moment.

In emotional regulation, your goal is to determine what will best serve the situation, others involved, and you. The 5 Rs can help. As you read, consider how these tools could be applied to an emotionally charged situation in your life.

Reassess
Creativity and flexibility are hallmarks of PO problem-solving. These traits are invaluable in reassessing situations. When we reassess, we

choose carefully how, what, where, when, and why we engage in a situation (situation selection) and look for creative ways to modify it (situation modification) rather than defaulting to avoidance—unless, of course, the situation is toxic or abusive. Thus we take back agency and control, two key traits of Practical Optimists, so we don't miss out on life, growth opportunities, or just the possibility of a good time.

This R is especially helpful in stressful situations where avoidance isn't an option, there's an important opportunity, or it's a requirement of our role. Ask yourself:

- Do I need to engage/participate in this?
- How am I likely to feel if I engage/participate, at the event and afterward?
- Do the potential benefits of participating outweigh the risks?
- Is this an overall positive experience—an opportunity for growth, development, or the maintenance of a relationship?
- Does it further an important goal or value in my life?

If your responses were predominantly yes, then consider how you could participate in such a way that the costs don't detract from the potential benefits:

- Which aspects tend to make this situation better or worse?
- Of these, which are deal breakers/non-negotiables for me?
- Can I change any of the variables to make this a better experience, or at least a tolerable and worthwhile one?
- How can I advocate for myself to maximize the benefits and minimize the unpleasant aspects?

Reassessing can help you find just the right amount of stress (see chapter 3, "Processing Emotions") for better performance. Suppose there's a party you know your ex will be attending. Should you go or shouldn't you? If the breakup was brutal and it'll be a ho-hum party, maybe don't. But if it might be a great party with good networking or friends you want to see and you've made peace with your past on the ex front, reassess: is it worth the price of a little (assuming it's a little, and you're able to manage the stress of seeing your ex) anxiety?

To dial down your anxiety, rearrange things to set yourself up for a good time. Contribute your talents—a playlist; overseeing the grill. Since you know your ex would be late to their own funeral, arrive on time and leave before they show up. Dress sharp. Back in the day, I'd say, "Bring your business cards." (These days I might say have your digital business card ready.) See? You've turned a thumbs-down experience into a thumbs-up for yourself.

Or suppose you're invited to travel to an industry meeting. It's an honor to be asked, but you're dreading it because your former boss, who believed a backstabbing coworker whose lies nearly got you fired, will be there, and the coworker, too. You were lucky enough to change departments, but there's still tension there. What to do?

Remember you can set inner boundaries around how invested you get in situations. There's no need to strike up a conversation if you run into each other. You could rearrange: just say hello and move on. You might try that if you decide the meeting is worthwhile for your professional growth. You could also modify things to limit your exposure or add a pleasurable component: attend only the required events, stay with a friend instead of on-site, bring your partner on the trip if permissible.

Reassessing helped Nicole. She'd felt compelled to always show up for her family of origin. Her situation selection started with realizing that she had a choice where, when, and how she wanted to show up.

To prevent her interactions with her mother from escalating, she decided to limit them to a few hours at a time, and only when her mother was sober. She chose to limit most of her family gatherings to Sunday church services, when others would be around as a buffer and the events were positive and on neutral turf. Also, when Nicole didn't feel like talking to her mom on the phone, she'd set up a screen-time call so her mom could interact with Nicole's kids—a positive relationship Nicole was committed to supporting.

Nicole had to firmly stop herself from responding when her mother's negative texts popped up during the day. She had to say, "We can't make it, but have a great time!" to avoid impromptu family gatherings where she anticipated her mother would drink heavily and spiral into judgmental parenting comments. It got easier with practice, and Nicole and her mother both benefited from the results.

Refuel

Our cup must be filled before we can pour from it. When was the last time you refilled yours? Take stock of your physical and emotional reserves. Are you getting good, consistent sleep? Nutrition? Affection? Relaxation? Have you been engaging in activities or using substances that deplete you?

Refueling puts us in a better position to handle what's coming our way. Pediatric psychologists refer to emotional refueling when they are describing how children often return to their mothers or other caregivers for comfort, soothing touch, rest, and reassurance.

As adults, we still need refueling practices. What activities restore your energy and vitality or throttle you down to a purring power-saving mode?

Maintaining important family traditions—lighting the fireplace on holidays; re-creating family recipes—can evoke early feelings and memories of safety. The Danish tradition of hygge and the Swedish mysig focus on creating an environment of comfort, safety, and joy. It can be as simple as lighting scented candles, having cozy blankets at hand, or filling your home with photos of good memories. Some people unwind with music, art, or dance; others go for gardening, exercise, reading, writing, tai chi, or yoga.

Relaxing sounds easy, but for many, putting on the brakes is hard. Just make a start. A soothing bath, a short meditation practice, snapping photos of something beautiful—whatever restores you, make it a priority to set aside time for it. Remember from chapter 2, "Purpose": carving out time for joy helps invigorate us to fulfill our purpose.

Solving Problems in Your Sleep?!

Well, not exactly. But sleep plays a crucial role in emotion regulation and problem-solving. REM sleep helps us process emotions through downregulating reactivity of the amygdala, a brain structure involved in the processing of emotions, including fear. Sleep deprivation is associated with greater emotional reactivity or overreaction to negative and stressful stimuli, creating an overactive brain—not great for problem-solving. Our ability to perceive our emotional state and, in general, to use feedback for real-time decision-making is compromised when we're tired. In fact, research studies point to the performance impairment from sleep deprivation as being akin to performance impairment from elevated blood alcohol levels.

Sleep deprivation decreases all the faculties needed for accurate appraisal and resolution of problems. Effects include delayed/slowed reaction time, impaired judgment, decreased cognitive flexibility and creativity, and increased impulsivity in decision-making. Motor skills, the ability to carry out instructions, and sometimes speech are impaired.

Sleep is especially important because our busy lives make us susceptible to decision fatigue: compromised decision-making from having to make too many decisions over the course of the day, along with other energy-sapping factors like low glucose levels. It's smart not to make things worse by not getting our z's. **(Tip: If possible, try not to make decisions late in the day, or when your stomach is empty.)**

With three young kids, Nicole hadn't slept more than a few hours at a stretch in several years. Her husband decided to take weekend night duty with the baby. After speaking to her pediatrician, she also decided to work with a sleep consultant for her baby—not something everyone can afford, but someone Nicole was fortunate to have access to and chose to engage. Eventually, she was able to get six hours of sleep at a stretch—double what she'd been getting—though she'd continue working on getting more.

Request Input

We can't solve problems effectively without accurate information. Yet we rarely re-engage to request input. Sejal's faulty perception that her boss hated her was corrected only when she sought accurate information about how she was viewed.

Nicole was close to quitting her job to stay home with her youngest daughter. She'd decided that by talking with her boss and her husband she'd come across as a burden, pushy, needy, and demanding. Nicole had been taught to be grateful for any support that came her way. To her, asking for or accepting help would seem as if she wasn't grateful. Nicole's own high expectations of herself added to her burden: "I should be staying up late, I'm the mom." It was only when John, Nicole's husband, insisted that doing night duty with Emma would allow him to spend more time with her, since he worked during most of Emma's waking hours, that Nicole felt comfortable accepting his help. In this case, her husband intuited that this was the only way Nicole could let go of the guilt that was keeping her feeling stuck.

Gradually Nicole started feeling more comfortable challenging assumptions she'd long taken for granted. It was important for Nicole to test her perceptions by requesting real-time input from those in a position to work with her to resolve this problem. That meant checking in with her boss, the day-care center, and her husband. Could she get what she needed from them?

I worked together with Nicole to help her assert herself and explore her options. Six months later, Nicole remained at her job, her childcare situation was worked out, and there was harmony at home. She'd spoken with the childcare center and had been able to get several months' hiatus for Emma to be at home. Nicole also was able to negotiate a four-day workweek so she could be with Emma some of the time, and she found someone she trusted to take care of Emma, based on a friend's recommendation. Her husband picked up more home chores—and this time Nicole let him, guilt-free. "He's actually a pretty good cook; who knew!" Nicole said, turning to John during one of our problem-solving sessions, which John had requested to join in support of Nicole's work in therapy.

I served as a sounding board while Nicole assessed her options and examined the emotions that had kept her stuck. Seeking support promotes problem-solving because emotional regulation is harder when we feel alone with painful emotions. When I feel alone with a problem, I consider:

1. **Would venting to someone make me feel better?** Sometimes we seek input before we're quite ready. I know from my experience with patients in the grip of powerful emotions that we're more able to access our rational problem-solving powers if we first feel comforted, understood, and not alone. Recognition and validation of our emotions (whether provided by ourselves or by others) help in regulating them. If I'm really charged up emotionally, if possible, I hit pause and find someone who can listen and support nonjudgmentally—for me, that helps. My intention often isn't to seek advice. In fact, not every situation requires action, and you can't always change things. Venting is particularly useful in these instances. Remember, dealing with emotions *is* part of problem-solving.

2. **Is there anyone I could talk to for help and advice?** Seeking input from a trusted confidant works best once you're emotionally receptive to suggestions and ready to take proactive steps to change a situation. Beforehand, write down the positive aspects or potentially good outcomes of your issue. This can anchor you if emotions start getting the upper hand.

In either case, find out if the time is right for the other person to talk and whether they have the bandwidth to do so. ("Is now a good time for me to share what's on my mind/bounce some ideas off you/ask your advice?") Don't forget to thank them for their time and attention. And remember, sometimes a therapist can provide that objective ear.

Remind

It helps to remind yourself of your skills, abilities, and past challenges you've met:

- Does this situation have anything in common with anything else that I've done and mastered?
- What skills and abilities have I applied elsewhere that I could apply here? [Example: *Presenting at the division meeting is a big deal. But I've presented to my department several times. Setting up a prep schedule helped me feel less nervous, and I left work on time the day before for my usual workout, so I got a good night's sleep. I went in early the next day for a run-through to check the technology and scope out the room. I'll create a prep schedule and call the IT person about doing a run-through the day before.*]
- What qualities have enabled me to navigate other life challenges? How do I see them applying here? [Example: *I'm persistent, analytical, and organized.*]

Reappraise

When a situation can't be changed, then we need to change our relationship to it. Reappraisal focuses on framing a situation in terms of its positive potentials, its opportunity in obstacles. While reappraisal is not always easy, it's worth practicing as one of the more effective methods of emotional regulation. One way to imbue a seemingly negative situation with positive attributes is with humor. (*It'll make a heck of a story. Nothing bruised but my ego.*) Others take a resourceful approach, like Nelson Mandela: "I never lose. I either win or learn." And Winston Churchill: "A pessimist sees the difficulty in every opportunity; an optimist sees the opportunity in every difficulty."

Let's reappraise the work trip where you'll likely encounter your ex-boss and the toxic former coworker:

It's a great high-level networking opportunity.

I'll meet industry leaders I've only read about.

I could use a getaway.

And those folks you'd rather not see? They become minor inconveniences in an otherwise positive opportunity.

With reappraisal, rejection can be reframed as redirection: *My novel has been rejected by multiple publishers. They say the plot needs work. I'll make a reading list of books by great storytellers and study plot development. I'll redirect for now to plotting in short stories.*

A *no* can be reframed as "not now": *I didn't get the promotion. But I can look for other opportunities in-house, or seek a similar position elsewhere. Meanwhile, I'll work on the necessary skills and on networking.*

It works with everyday aggravation, too. Imagine you've been waiting for a long time to be seen at an office. Just as your turn comes, the service window closes. You're furious. You took the morning off from work (a rare feat) and need to get this done. You rushed to get here, patiently waited, and now will be playing catch-up at work all week.

How you choose to cope depends on your appraisal of the situation. In masterful emotional regulation, we accurately appraise what's at stake—minus subjective negative spins.

Does not seeing the clerk on this particular day have devastating consequences, or can you come back another time, despite the hassle? Are you trying to get a visa to visit a sick relative overseas before they die, or are you there to change your legal name? You might rightfully persist more in the first case.

Instead of taking it personally—which could cause you to leave prematurely in defeat or start yelling—you decide to ask politely to speak to the manager. You request help, describing how difficult it was to arrange being here and how you arrived in good time, waited your turn, and are being held up through no fault of your own.

The manager explains that the clerk goes on lunch break at this time, and the office will reopen in an hour. She says you can wait or return after lunch. You realize you might've missed their office hours on the website, and you decide to acknowledge that, taking responsibility. You calm down, but you decide to ask again if anything could be done to help you so you'll miss less work. The manager, taking pity on you (you do look a little tired), decides to help you herself. Fifteen minutes later, you're en route to work. You got the job done because you didn't cave/leave or yell and decrease your chances of success. You reappraised: looking for alternatives (speaking with the manager), areas of agreement (acknowledging the rules), and opportunities (asking for understanding and help).

Emotional regulation and reappraisal help us reconsider how we can interact with situations and people to meet our needs, with respect and within reason. Our emotions become information (using your work/time pressure to stand up for yourself in an amicable way). We gain the perspective to understand the needs of the other players (time constraints, interests) when we take into consideration what they would need from us in order for our request to make sense to them. This is problem-solving at its best.

P.S.: If there's no way to reappraise a temporary no-fun situation, try the secret sixth R: redeploy. Shift your attention to something neutral. Distraction has been shown to reduce the intensity of painful experiences by decreasing the amygdala activation associated with emotion. So when your ex arrives at the party, head outside to the tetherball game. When you spot your backstabbing colleague and former boss at the business meeting, look around and think, *Wow, look at all the people I want to meet. Who should I talk to first?* Redeploying can help in small doses, but it doesn't solve underlying problems, so use it sparingly.

> **PO Pearls**
> Get the full story. Solve what can be solved. Reappraise, accept, and let go of the rest.

How to Problem-Solve with Others Effectively

With three kids, two dogs, two careers, and one home, Nancy and Sharon felt like they had it all as a married couple. But juggling the good stuff also came with some disagreements. They came to me when everyday stressors like who was going to handle school runs, meal prep, and other logistics got to the point where they couldn't discuss them without yelling or stonewalling.

In any long-term relationship, there will be conflicts. For Practical Optimists, being able to navigate and resolve conflict without creating scar tissue is one of their relationship success secrets.

Often, impasses with couples happen because they know only two possible solutions to their issue: my way *or* yours. I'm stuck with dish duty *or* you are. The real-time emotional regulation strategies in this section help you move from *you* or *me* to *we*. Here are the principles of problem-solving I worked on with Sharon and Nancy:

Step outside the box. If a method hasn't worked, it's not a solution. I asked Sharon and Nancy to brainstorm outside-the-box solutions.

Make it collaborative. Sharon and Nancy were tasked with finding solutions inclusive to each other and receiving them without negative comments. This kept them engaged in problem-solving together. I asked them to accept each other's suggestions as reasonable and worth exploring. John M. Gottman, PhD, the coauthor of *The Seven Principles for Making Marriage Work*, describes this as "being open to your partner's influence."

Resist criticism. Avoid language that blames, name-calls, or character-assassinates your partner. If you must, call out the negative behavior you want to change and focus on the positive behavior you want to gain. (For more on this, see the XYZ technique in chapter 8, "People.")

These strategies helped Nancy and Sharon focus upstream from the "problem" (who does what) and find something they agreed on: while their life was filled with fulfilling endeavors, they felt like they were drowning under the weight of their responsibilities.

They both wanted time for rest, relaxation, hobbies, and interests; time alone, with the kids, and together; time with friends and other family; and time for exercise and entertainment.

Many of us are burdened by elevated expectations and reduced support and need to hone our problem-solving skills now more than ever. Now they could focus on how they were going to get there, instead of on arguing, and devise workable solutions:

- Set up a tighter housework schedule—no more ad hoc arguing.
- Involve the older children in household responsibilities.
- Ask their parents for help with childcare.
- Invest in some household gadgets to make cleaning easier.

- Have groceries delivered.
- Extend grace to themselves on days when the house was a mess and dinner was leftover pizza.

Problem-Solve in a Therapist's Hour: A Guide for Getting to the Heart of the Matter

Maria was clear about her problem: she felt generally unfulfilled, stagnant, and bored by her work. While Maria knew what was bothering her, I wanted to help her figure out *why* it was bothering her. Determining why something matters to us is where the internal part of problem-solving starts.

I posed these questions to help Maria drill down to the root of her problem. I've adapted them in Dr. Sue's Cut-to-the-Chase Question List (see the box on page 119)—with more added, if you'd like to try them out!

DR. SUE: In simple language, can you define the problem?

MARIA: I'm not happy in my day job. I'm not fulfilled.

DR. SUE: What would solve it?

MARIA: Switching to a professional opportunity that I enjoy.

DR. SUE: Does this alternative exist?

MARIA: Not right now.

DR. SUE: What will you have to do to get it?

MARIA: Create it.

DR. SUE: What would that entail?

MARIA: Starting my own business as a side hustle until I can generate enough income.

DR. SUE: How important is this to you, and why?

MARIA: Very. I need to be creative, and I feel stifled. Plus, I want to make my own hours—I really need flexibility. And I like being my own boss.

DR. SUE: What are some possible job options?

MARIA: I'm interested in photography, event planning, teaching, and fitness.

DR. SUE: What's getting in the way, in addition to financial constraints?

MARIA: I'm scared to leave my day job: the comfort, convenience, familiarity, regularity of income, structure, routine, friends. Plus fear of failure. And I don't know which option to pursue first.

DR. SUE: What would you tell a friend who made the same points? [I love this question—we're often more Practically Optimistic with our friends than ourselves!]

MARIA: You won't know until you try. You're good at a lot of things, but maybe you could start with photography, since you have some freelance experience with it. You'll lose the structure and security of a nine-to-five job, and you'll have to be disciplined as your own boss. You might not make money or barely break even, but if you can afford it, it might be worth it. Change is scary. I believe in you; you can do it. You are talented. Start small. Don't quit your day job; do this on evenings and weekends.

DR. SUE: On a scale of 1 to 10, how likely are you to regret not pursuing this ten years from now, with 1 being "not a problem at all" and 10 meaning "lifelong regret"?

MARIA: I'd say 8 to 10.

DR. SUE: How would you solve the problem if time and money weren't issues?

MARIA: I'd take the plunge now.

DR. SUE: Do you have any help or scaffolding to support you if you take the plunge?

MARIA: I have a bit of savings. It's enough to cover some equipment and float me for two or three months.

I'm not suggesting that Maria solved everything immediately, or that any of us can (or even that a typical therapy session is this cut-and-dried). But questions like these can get us out of mental ruts, jump-start creative thinking, and make big hurdles begin to look more like projects we can manage, problem-solving as we go.

Dr. Sue's Cut-to-the-Chase Question List

Below are some questions to ask yourself when you feel stuck in problem-solving or goal-setting. Not all may be applicable to your situation. Don't feel pressured to answer every one—the idea is to get unstuck in how you may be thinking about or approaching the problem. Answer with simple facts—try not to embellish or add emotional interpretations.

1. In simple language, can you define the problem?

2. What is your goal?

3. What would solve it?

4. Does this alternative exist?

5. What will you have to do to get this done?

6. What would that entail?

7. How important is this to you, and why?

8. What are some alternatives if the first solution doesn't work?

9. What's getting in the way?[11]

---

[11] Often we stall on pursuing goals because we have competing, often unacknowledged, goals, and pursuing one comes at the risk of losing the other. For example: "I want to move out of

10. How could you handle these obstacles?

11. What would you tell a friend who made the same points?

12. On a scale of 1 to 10, how likely are you to regret not pursuing this ten years from now, with 1 being "not a problem at all" and 10 meaning "lifelong regret"?

13. How would you proceed if time and money weren't issues?

14. What would be the best possible outcome, and how likely is this to occur?

15. What would be the worst possible outcome, and how likely is this to occur?

16. What would you do about that?

17. If the worst happened and there was nothing you could do about it, could you live with that outcome?

18. What do you think would be the most likely scenario, and can you live with that?

19. Do you have any help or scaffolding to assist or support you if you proceed?

20. Do you need advice, information, or assistance?

21. Who could you ask to help you?

22. Is there a trusted person in your life you could talk with about this?

state, but I don't want to let my aging parents down/upset them." There are no easy answers, but the first step is getting all the goals laid out where you can examine your thoughts and feelings: How accurate is your perception about letting your parents down? What is the evidence that they would be upset? What kind of communication and/or concrete solutions might offset the downsides?

23. What self-care would help you achieve this?

24. How would you feel if it all worked out?

25. Now that you have answered these questions, what might your next steps be?

"We Miss 100 Percent of the Shots We Don't Take"

A common adage attributed to hockey legend Wayne Gretzky and his mentors/coaches relays an important message in the sports world that also applies in everyday life: you can't score if you don't shoot. Effective problem-solving isn't just about handling external obstacles. It's about recognizing the inner dynamics that help or hinder us.

Emotions direct our behavior. They can be lifesaving or life-limiting. What will you choose?

When life challenges you, reflect on what your emotions are trying to tell you. Then look at all the tools you have to address them productively as part of your problem-solving. As an agile Practical Optimist, be ready to shift your perspective to make a positive difference in your world. It will set you on the path to maximizing your life.

To view the scientific references cited in this chapter, please visit doctorsuevarma.com/book.

CHAPTER 5

Pride

A Deep Knowing of Your Self-Worth

No one can make you feel inferior without your consent.

—ELEANOR ROOSEVELT

It was one of those days when the East River sparkles and the Manhattan skyline is etched against a cloudless sky. I'd relished my thirty-block walk to the therapist's office with a guilty pleasure that should have clued me in to some of what we'd be discussing.

I'd had time while walking to mull over some of what had brought me to this point of being a therapist finally ready for therapy. My legs still felt weak, but I had been reassured, following my medical consult, that nothing was wrong with them. It was my mind that needed rejiggering. Still, did I really need therapy? Was I being self-indulgent?

Caring for others' mental health was my mission, but therapy for myself felt at odds with my upbringing. In Indian culture, the focus is on the family. In India, aunts, uncles, and cousins stand ready to pitch in at a moment's notice. During a medical school rotation in India, I had marveled at Indian families' solidarity. The poorest were rich in loving support, with at least three family members literally camped at the sick one's bedside. But for our immigrant family in America, the weight of family support that would've been dispersed over eight or ten relatives in India fell on just the four of us. I don't think my parents realized the toll on me. In my family, you did whatever was needed to maintain harmony, health, and safety for your family and community—even at the expense of the self. And although I was born and raised in the United States, we were expected to live by the examples set by family members in India.

Medicine and psychiatry felt like natural extensions of our values of service and science. But medicine is high-stress and demanding, with a strong emphasis on perfection.

But I loved medicine and my family. So I accepted all the responsibilities with a stout blend of willingness and duty—until the added stress of navigating my mother's cancer diagnosis and treatment overwhelmed me. I couldn't manage all the conflicting priorities. Thus I became the patient.

The elevator opened to an attractive waiting area. I leafed through a fashion magazine, concealing my anxiety.

"Sue?" I looked up to see a tall, slender, stylish therapist. I noticed her welcoming smile first. She was holding a chart—presumably mine. On her wrist was a gold bracelet delicately placed between a few red threads on one side and prayer beads on the other. Stylish and spiritual. I followed her into her office and sat on the couch.

The graciously furnished room with its prizewinning East River penthouse view felt like a sanctuary compared to some of the clinic rooms of my residency. I noticed the box of tissues nearby. Therapists need therapists, too, I reminded myself.

"Welcome," Dr. L said. "What brings you in?"

And there I was, unpacking my emotional baggage in front of a well-dressed stranger.

What emerged during my sessions had to do with a fundamental problem of pride. Not the I'm-better-than-you kind, or the kind tied to accolades and achievement. This was a different pride—one, surprisingly, I needed to build. A healthy pride rooted in self-assurance that helps us act in the face of uncertainty and difficulty, where we may not know exactly what a situation calls for, but we know who we are and what we're worth. A pride that helps us stay level-headed, neither berating nor inflating ourselves, or getting sucked into other people's opinions of us. A pride that cultivates a compassionate mindset in which we look for and encourage the best in ourselves and in others. That's the kind of pride—as well as a five-step blueprint for building it—that we'll explore.

Healthy Pride Defined

Healthy pride, as I define it, means having a stable, kind, realistic picture of who we are. This special sense of self-worth balances confidence with humility, protects us from intrusive thoughts that make us feel ashamed or guilt-ridden, and promotes appreciation for how much we can learn from life and from others.

Healthy pride has four major components:

1. **It's intrinsic.** Healthy pride is rooted in an enduring sense of our inherent worth. Unconditional yet uninflated, it may dip sometimes but doesn't depend on our latest success, failure, compliment, or criticism.
2. **It's accurate.** Some people think they're great, but they're no more wonderful than anyone else. Others don't see just how wonderful they are. Healthy pride means knowing your strengths and imperfections, exaggerating neither.

3. **It's kind.** Kindness toward oneself and others is healthy pride's hallmark. Its first rule is self-compassion, not self-evaluation. We acknowledge our fallibility without self-flagellation and offer this understanding to others.

4. **It encourages growth and positive action.** With self-acceptance comes the capacity for resilience and constructive change: "Things didn't work out today. But I can try again." Healthy pride buffers us against immobilizing guilt and shame, supporting us to adapt, grow, and flourish.

It's Different from Self-Esteem

I'm not a fan of the concept of self-esteem. Research has begun uncovering its potential price. Highly contingent on external achievements, self-esteem can evaporate when it's needed most. Periods of low self-esteem are associated with numerous mental and physiological health problems, including depression, body dysmorphia, eating disorders, and anxiety disorders. In extreme cases, in the context of depression, low self-esteem can increase the risk of suicide. The need to protect self-esteem can lead to a distorted sense of self, prejudice, and even narcissistic behavior and harm toward those perceived as threats. Because healthy pride isn't dependent on external events or on how we rate ourselves compared to others; it's a more stable source of self-worth than self-esteem is.

Allows for Guilt; Protects Against Shame

A little guilt can be a good thing. Shame? Not so much.

Guilt is a feeling of regret or remorse when we feel we've violated our own social norms around a particular circumscribed situation. As long as we aren't plagued by it, guilt can move us to reparation and prosocial behavior. Guilt may even confer evolutionary benefits: follow the tribe's rules, and the tribe looks out for us. Healthy levels of guilt reflect empathy. In fact, guilt-proneness (as opposed to shame) is associated with a more accurate read of others' emotional expressions:

we're aware of how our behavior affects others and take an appropriate amount of responsibility for what we can do about the bad behavior. Studies show that guilt is more likely than shame to generate altruistic behavior and a desire to improve—because a road to redemption seems identifiable and clear.

Shame, in contrast, focuses not on a specific negative behavior, but on the person. Whereas guilt says, "I did something terrible," shame says, "I am terrible."

Shame can feel threatening to the point that we may fear our belonging to or status in the group might be jeopardized. It can lead to severe self-criticism—a type of self-inflicted character assassination. With the negative focus on the self, we have no clear way to make amends. Thus, shame can lead to helplessness, rumination, pessimism, depression, physiological stress (as if we were in physical danger), social isolation/withdrawal, and alienation, as we may avoid the person or situations that generated the bad feelings.

Shame-proneness tends to lower our self-esteem, and vice versa. Its health hazards include a greater risk of psychological problems, especially depression, according to a meta-analysis of 108 studies of a total of more than twenty-two thousand individuals. While some appear to be more vulnerable than others—adolescents, followed by the elderly (perhaps because of their physical changes and sense of frailty)—no one's immune to shame's toxicity. It can lead to negative coping mechanisms like drinking, self-harm, or a failure to pursue what would put a better life within reach, (e.g., losing weight; seeking a better job; cultivating nurturing relationships). Left unchecked, shame can lead us to feel like a burden or even question whether our life is worth living. Cultivating healthy pride strengthens our resistance to shame, allowing room for mistakes while affirming our capacity to remedy them.

Promotes Relationships

Low pride can lead to relentless comparisons with others to maintain self-esteem. If we're "better than," all's well. Fall short, and self-flagellation and jealousy or envy may ensue. Low pride may lead to social anxiety and self-isolation, resulting from the belief we're not lovable, likable (often a by-product of shame or free-floating guilt), or interesting. The ensuing loneliness further reduces our quality of life and longevity.

Healthy pride fosters healthier relationships free of corrosive comparison. We're less likely to fall prey to toxic or abusive relationships (and less willing to accept "emotional bread crumbs") because we know we deserve better, instead seeking out relationships based on mutual support, regard, and love. Love doesn't induce shame, but rather fosters self-acceptance and growth.

It's Good for You!

The wounding self-criticism of unhealthy pride, perceived as a threat to our being, activates our fight-or-flight hormones. Shame releases a stream of stress hormones and the havoc they wreak. In contrast, self-compassionate pride triggers and taps into our mammalian caregiving system, including the secretion of oxytocin (the cuddling/bonding/kindness/caregiving hormone), allowing you to be a nurturing caregiver to yourself. It shuts down powerful stress hormones like cortisol and helps ward off harmful inflammation that may make us more susceptible to depression, medical illness, and immune dysfunction, including autoimmune disorders.

It also encourages healthy habits. Optimists, who have high self-compassion, have better habits, including eating, exercising, meditating, sleeping, resting, and spending time with friends and family. They also have a better work-life balance, in part because they believe themselves worth the investment. They're able to set high standards and goals while being resistant to what's known as maladaptive perfectionism: rigid, harsh, unrealistic standards, with self-flagellation for not meeting them. Research shows that the very high, unrelenting, irrational standards associated with maladaptive perfectionism can lead to someone achieving success at the expense of health and well-being or relationships.

Healthy Pride Influences

Many factors contribute to healthy or unhealthy pride. Let's examine a few key influences.

Positive or Negative Strokes

Psychiatrist Eric Berne, who developed transactional analysis (TA) in the 1950s, used the term *transactions* or *strokes* to describe basic units of social intercourse. A stroke can be verbal or nonverbal (a smile, a hug), positive or negative, and conditional (specific to an event or situation) or unconditional (a broader, more blanket assessment). Examples: "You made a great meal!" (verbal, positive, conditional). "You're a great person!" (verbal, positive, unconditional).

Naturally, our interactions with early caregivers, upon whom we depended for survival, can be formative. A healthy amount of unconditional positive strokes can be affirming—but too many can pump us up artificially and make us unable to cope without them. A few appropriately timed, judicious, constructive negative strokes can usefully correct our behaviors—but too much criticism, and certainly unconditional negative strokes, can be quite damaging and contribute to shame, as they feel like a judgment about our personhood. Indeed, there's increasing awareness that this damage can happen to groups as a result of long periods of negative experiences such as discrimination or any treatment causing feelings of inferiority.

Parents who reliably provide nurturing, kind strokes foster healthy pride, the capacity for self-compassion, and secure attachment—a stable sense of self-worth and an overall ease in interpersonal relationships—and may help counter some people's innate tendencies toward shame and guilt. It's a state of feeling "I'm okay, you're okay," a key phrase and goal in TA and the title of Eric Berne's popular book—a recognition that both you and I are worthy and have intrinsic value. Secure attachments help us develop a sense of belonging and a feeling that we matter.

What if we didn't receive this early conditioning? We can learn to modify our shame-proneness through practicing self-compassion, as you'll see.

Cultural Messages

Cultural conditioning plays a role in the messages we internalize. My parents were indoctrinated by their elders, many of whom had grown up imbued with the idealistic freedom-fighting mindset that Mahatma Gandhi personified. God, country, and family all came before the individual's needs. The mythology and scriptures I was raised with emphasized this. In my family we learned to value selfless service, integral to my parents' commitment to righteous living, or dharma. Do thy duty, don't be attached to the fruits of your labor, respect your elders, obey authority. I told Dr. L how my mother had even postponed marriage until age twenty-nine—shockingly late by Indian standards then—to advocate for women's rights, to work against the customs of child brides and the dowry, and to promote equal education and pay for women.

I honor this cultural legacy. Cultural messages can be richly positive influences. But I also came to see that, as with many principles we're taught, the challenge lies in how we apply and practice them. In some ways, these teachings were akin to those many of us received to inoculate us against egocentric, unhealthy pride. But they can sometimes reduce healthy pride, too (and maybe, by creating shame, they were a way to keep people in check).

Being a doctor, to me, was more than a career; it was a calling. But where did I, Sue Varma—dharma disciple by heritage, American individualist by nationality—fit in? And how could I keep guilt from turning into shame as I grappled with feeling overwhelmed, unable on shaky legs to rise to the occasion and fulfill my many missions?

Comparing Ourselves to Others

At least 10 percent of our daily thoughts consist of comparisons. While they can be a way to assess our abilities, traits, and attitudes or can serve as inspiration (as with role models or mentors), we may also internalize inaccurate, unrealistic upward social comparisons as unreachable expectations, traits of an idealized version of ourselves that we berate ourselves for not living up to. Or we might compare ourselves with folks we might perceive as being less than us (known as downward social comparison), perhaps to boost our mood or ego. Either way, we're tearing ourselves (or others) down or propping ourselves up. Never free to just live and let live.

Tying Our Worth to Productivity

Our society puts paramount emphasis on what we do. In a 2019 report in the *Harvard Business Review*, Ashley Whillans—actress turned social researcher and assistant professor at the Harvard Business School—discusses time famine and time affluence. Simply put, 80 percent of those her team surveyed noted they didn't have enough time to finish everything they wanted to do each day (and always feeling behind can undermine our sense of personal control and agency, further elevating our stress levels). They—we—are in a collective state of time famine.

This concept as described in 2019 wouldn't be on my radar until well after my visits with Dr. L. But as a resident working eighty-plus-hour weeks, sometimes working at four or five hospitals citywide daily, traveling for medical missions (more than one potential suitor asked why I couldn't "just sit still"), and being there in support of my family, I was in its grip.

In my family growing up, duty and service were expressed through productivity. "My parents believed work is worship," I told Dr. L. I shared a vivid memory of the summer they started leaving lists of daily chores: *Paint garage. Paint deck.* All written in my dad's illegible handwriting. No instructions. Execution? A mere detail.

The deck ended up a bilious shade of green. That didn't matter to my well-intentioned parents, who felt that assigning these chores fostered productivity—a word that would haunt me into adulthood. I realized my parents' setting up those tasks was received by me as conditional strokes—as if my success in my mission-driven family was contingent on completing my assigned missions. In adulthood, this translated into super-high—some might say unyielding—standards for myself that made it difficult to cut myself slack.

This is what I internalized from my family's emphasis on selfless contribution: if I'm not doing something impactful, I'm wasting time—meaning (cue nonverbal unconditional negative stroke) I'm nothing.

For many of us, separating who we are from what we do isn't easy. But it's crucial, lest our self-worth be forever tied to the turbulence of the outside world rather than anchored within ourselves.

Exercise: Your Self-Worth Conditioning

Take a breath, open your journal, and reflect on your growing-up years.

1. What positive or negative strokes did you receive? Do you remember verbal or nonverbal examples? Conditional and/or unconditional?
2. What were your takeaway messages?
3. How do you think these messages manifest in your life or your view of yourself today?
4. What cultural messages did you absorb while you were growing up?
5. In what ways do you compare yourself with others or seek others' approval?
6. Do you feel an inner push to be "productive"? Does it feel okay or overwhelming? Where did you get your ideas about productivity?

7. Does self-care, treating yourself, or downtime feel self-indulgent? Do you feel guilty when you do something just for yourself, for fun? If this is so, what was the source of these messages?

PO Pearls

Our self-worth exists simply because we do.

Finding GRACE: A Blueprint for Healthy Pride

What does a healthy sense of pride look like? I wondered. Could I achieve it without seeming cocky? Could I learn to treat myself with the same compassion I extend to friends, family, and patients? Could I come to accept that sometimes, despite my best efforts and intentions, I might disappoint someone?

Cultivating the kindness aspect of healthy pride seemed like a good starting point. After all, it's what I'd prescribe to my patients.

The idea that a caring mindset can improve your life isn't just feel-good verbiage. When excessive guilt or shame plunges us into negative thinking as codified by Dr. Martin Seligman (see chapter 1, "Why Practical Optimism?"), we *personalize* the problem ("I'm bad"), see it as *pervasive,* and deem it *permanent.* Overwhelmed, we become *passive* and disengage.

Research on self-compassion reveals exciting potential in countering these tendencies.

According to researcher Wendy J. Phillips in the *Journal of Positive Psychology and Wellbeing,* "Self-compassion may minimize such disengagement by fostering acceptance of past suffering and skills to overcome future obstacles." People with self-compassion show more motivation to correct their wrongs, glean lessons from their mistakes, make amends for them, and avoid repeating them in the future. One study shows self-compassion can foster a brighter future outlook: a three-week self-compassion intervention helped college students develop optimism. In short, self-compassion not only turns wounds into opportunities for growth but may be a catalyst toward an imagined hopeful future.

It's been suggested that self-compassion throttles down our brain's defensive system and stimulates the brain system involved with a sense of calm and safety—a basis from which we're more likely to experience appreciation and explore. Researcher, professor, and author Barbara Fredrickson's broaden-and-build theory posits that positive emotions (like those resulting from self-compassion) further build positive emotions and psychological resources, allowing us to explore, engage, appreciate, and savor new experiences. Frederickson writes: "Joy sparks the urge to play, interest sparks the urge to explore, contentment sparks the urge to savour and integrate, and love sparks a recurring cycle of each of these urges within safe, close relationships."

The word *grace* comes to mind. To me, grace is a physical, emotional, and spiritual attitude of caring toward all of life, including ourselves. I've developed it into a guiding acronym for engaging our inner caregiver and nurturing healthy pride:

Gratitude for the Good
Recognition of Reality
Acceptance of Imperfection
Compassion for Yourself
Empathy for Others

Gratitude for the Good— in Ourselves and in Life

Gratitude, derived from the Latin root *gratia*, meaning grace, graciousness, or gratefulness, is the recognition or awareness that something good has happened to you for which someone (or something) is responsible—which induces a positive emotional state of appreciation. It's about choosing to positively interpret the good in the world. It is studied as a psychological tool, coping skill, and source of renewable psychological energy. Gratitude promotes flexible and creative thinking, positive emotions, and prosocial behavior.

With gratitude, we see imperfections and challenges clearly, but we equally see potential. Gratitude also helps us find and treasure moments of beauty, calm, inspiration, humor, and kindness in everyday life. Gratitude achieves this not by denying the negative, but through turning toward the good—in other people's actions, in the world unfolding—and in doing so, enhancing the mind. You might think of it as seeing the positive strokes in the world.

Gratitude is mood-boosting and stress-buffering. In one study, participants were randomly assigned to three groups and tasked with one of the following, depending on the group: write about things that had occurred during the week that they were grateful for; write about the week's hassles; or write about the week's events (without being told whether to write about positive, neutral, or negative events). After ten weeks, those who wrote about gratitude had a more optimistic and positive outlook on their lives, enjoyed longer and improved sleep, exercised more, and had fewer physical symptoms (i.e., aches and pains) than those who focused on sources of aggravation or burden. They felt more connected to others and had a greater tendency to offer help and emotional support. In another study with a group of veterans, gratitude was even shown to reduce mental health symptoms in the aftermath of trauma.

Gratitude uses reframing to identify the blessing inherent even in complicated circumstances. It can shift our focus from *What's wrong with me?/Why is this happening to me?* to *What can this situation teach me?/What can I learn about myself?* When I was a resident drowning in work, my heart breaking for my mother's situation, I think my gratitude statement would've been: "I'm stressed, but thank God that I have a family that loves me and a job that's meaningful, and that I'm finally willing and able to seek help. Maybe my symptoms were necessary for me to finally fix what was going to eventually break anyway—and maybe, by seeking help for myself, I can better help others, perhaps even sharing what I learned from my struggles."

Gratitude requires intention and may require cultivating a targeted mindset. We'll revisit it in later chapters. For starters, you might try following the prompt given in the study I mentioned above:

There are many things in our lives, both large and small, that we might be grateful for. Think back over the past day and write down five things in your life that you are grateful for.

PO Pearls

Giving grace to others asks us to choose the most generous interpretation of a situation.

Giving ourselves grace during transition and hardship can be key. A friend who recently moved to New York City shared that she was shocked to learn how high her real estate broker's fee was, and while she was already feeling financially strapped after moving to her new apartment, she then had to deal with the theft of her cell phone. Not wanting these incidents to contaminate her new life that she was otherwise excited about and had worked hard to bring to fruition, she made a conscious decision to seek the positive in daily urban existence. On her morning bus commute, she'd watch for positives: "That nice parent just took her child on her lap so an older person could sit down." "It's kind of incredible that we all manage to deal with rush hour every morning. New Yorkers are amazing." "Wow, look at all the autumn colors on the trees in Central Park!"

We can give ourselves and others grace and acceptance not only in difficult situations (giving someone the benefit of the doubt when something bad has happened or you feel let down by them), but also in neutral or ambiguous situations. So if a coworker picks up the tab for your favorite beverage, you don't think, *Oh, they're just using a buy-one-get-one-free card today,* but rather, *They went out of their way and thought of me.* In this way we can train our brains to actively pursue the positive threads and undertones. (Gratitude, just like Practical Optimism, may not always come easily to us, especially when we're going through a rough time. And that is okay, too.)

Giving Yourself Grace to Just Be

Cultivating a Leisure Practice

Leisure is how we thank our minds and bodies for all they do for us. A leisure practice means intentionally taking time away from obligations, providing yourself with love, kindness, and self-soothing. Especially after a setback, you deserve a period of rest, love, fun, and distraction. Offer yourself the warmth you'd offer others.

Rest and relaxation are necessities, not rewards permissible only when you "deserve them." I'd internalized my parents' assigned chores to mean that I needed to always be productive and in service to others. That had served me well in an American culture that values hustle and productivity above all and the Indian one where deference to authority goes a long way—until I was literally collapsing from the time and self-compassion deficits I'd created.

It's in our downtime that we invest in and reflect on *who* we are, beyond *what* we are. Leisure time, when balanced with productivity, promotes connections with others as well as decreased blood pressure, less depression, and increased relaxation, and is a valuable contributor to our overall happiness. (For more on reclaiming your time, see chapter 7, "Present.")

I realized my dharma could expand to include replenishing my reserves so I could continue serving others.

PO Pearls
You don't need permission to rest.

Recognition of Reality

When we're able to see ourselves as we truly are—fabulousness and flaws alike—we're no longer at the mercy of circumstances or others' perceptions. By modifying outdated scripts, challenging our thought distortions, and recognizing our capabilities, we construct a sense of self-worth rooted in reality.

Suppose you get a surprise promotion. Do you automatically think things like *I got lucky. I was in the right place at the right time.* Or: *What's the catch? They probably couldn't find anyone else.* Or: *I'm the only woman in the department—they want to show they're not biased.* (You might recognize the third response as similar to the example above of the coworker's getting your coffee—the tendency to assume that anything good another does has a self-serving motive. My dad would say to this, "So what? Regardless of their motive, didn't the outcome still work out in your favor?")

Now suppose you're passed over for a promotion. Are the default perceptions along the lines of *I don't have what it takes. They've never liked me.*

Truth is, not everything bad that happens is our fault. And not everything good that happens is to our credit. Getting real about what we're really responsible for protects us from excessive self-blame or grandiosity, helping us discern what's within our control and what isn't. Remember, overidentifying with and personalizing negative events is a hallmark of pessimism.

In healthy, realistic attribution, we take responsibility for our share (good and bad) and nothing more. Appropriate guilt promotes prosocial behavior: taking responsibility for what we did wrong and making amends. If we accomplish something good, we take an appropriate amount of credit, are able to feel healthy pride, and can accept compliments. Shame-prone folks have difficulty accepting compliments but readily absorb criticism and self-blame, perhaps because of strokes from early caregivers.

Truly understanding reality also means being able to see through narratives we've embraced, either consciously or unconsciously, that simply don't serve us any longer. One reality I learned over time is that I have more agency than when my parents, bless their well-meaning hearts, tried to burnish my soul through chores. We can change the old stories, known as maladaptive scripts, we've told ourselves all our lives. Maybe these were the only ways we could cope growing up, but they don't serve us anymore.

Here are some ways I affirmed my agency:

- *Things were a certain way when I was growing up, but they're different now. I can change my outdated scripts.*
- *My parents did the best they could, given their circumstances. With limited support, they had to raise a family in a new, unfamiliar culture. I'm grateful for all they did do for me. The choice of how I live now is up to me.*
- *I don't have to be constantly busy in order to prove my worth.*

Observation, Not Evaluation

There's no better way to see reality than by learning to observe our thoughts and perceptions instead of being consumed by them. In chapter 4, we explored how cognitive restructuring, a core component of cognitive behavioral therapy (CBT) using the acronym ABCDE, can help us see situations objectively so that we don't let negative thoughts or assessments creep in and direct how we evaluate what's really going on. This important reframing tool helps us become effective problem solvers, but it's also a powerful way we can build healthy pride, too. Cognitive restructuring helps us understand that we may be seeing situations through a skewed lens and identify thought distortions that can increase our vulnerability to anxiety and mood disorders. The more we can examine and challenge these irrational thoughts, the more doing so becomes second nature, helping us avoid the spiral of negative thinking and shame that eventually wounds our sense of self-worth. Whether we are dealing with a low-stakes scenario or a situation that hits more deeply, cognitive restructuring can help smooth our path and brighten up our lives.

We looked at an example of how ABCDE can boost our problem-solving skills in chapter 4, but here's an example of how ABCDE could help shift our perspective on an everyday situation that may negatively impact our pride:

Imagine Andie is rushing back from lunch to the office for a co-worker's surprise birthday party. She's carrying her lunch from a food truck, her gym bag, and a bag containing a birthday T-shirt for her coworker. In the lobby, her phone rings. She juggles the things she's holding to pull it from her pants pocket. Next thing she knows, she bumps into coworkers exiting the elevator—and her veggie stir-fry and iced latte spill all over her, them, and the gift. The incident weighs on Andie the rest of the day.

Here's how I'd walk Andie through ABCDE to help her see this situation differently.

Antecedent: In this case, the triggering or inciting events are that Andie's lunch spilled everywhere, she experienced public embarrassment, and the gift is ruined.

Beliefs: Here are some automatic thoughts that may have gone through Andie's mind: *What a disaster. I'm so clumsy. People must be laughing at me, looking like a loser, dripping food. If I hadn't gained so much weight, my phone would've been easier to pull out. If I was fit like some of my other coworkers, I could change into my workout clothes, but I'd look like a huge, inappropriately dressed slob. This wouldn't have happened if I'd planned ahead and packed lunch. When will I ever learn?*

Consequences: Physically, Andie might have felt panic—a racing heart, sweaty palms, and a feeling that her throat was closing. Her face turned red and her breathing was shallow. She cleaned herself up as best she could and offered to pay her coworkers' dry-cleaning bills (they laughingly declined). She was too upset to enjoy the party, and after five minutes, she awkwardly and abruptly left.

Distortions: As we've discussed, distortions are negatively biased errors in thinking and irrational thoughts. They are often an absolute, extreme type of thinking that is harsh and unforgiving. Here are some common distortions, along with examples of how they might apply to this particular situation:

- *Mind reading:* We make assumptions about what others are thinking without supporting facts. *People **must be** laughing at me.*

- *Catastrophizing:* We assume the worst will happen, that bad things are personal, pervasive, and permanent. *When will I ever learn?*

- *Mental filtering/negative filtering/discounting the positives:* We laser-focus on the negatives, which eclipses the positives. *Andie is **too upset** to enjoy the party.*

- *All-or-nothing, aka absolutist thinking:* We think: *Either I show up 100 percent or I don't show up **at all**.* After five minutes, Andie awkwardly and abruptly left.

- *Judgment focus:* We view ourselves as being superior or inferior to others rather than objectively framing people or events. Andie sees herself as *clumsy . . . a loser . . . a slob.*

- *Blaming/labeling/personalizing:* She thinks, *This wouldn't have happened if I'd planned ahead.* Personalizing and blaming ourselves often leads to shame when we start seeing situational failures as character flaws.

- *Emotional reasoning:* We assume our negative self-talk accurately represents external events. *What a disaster.*

- *"Should" statements:* We set high, rigid, arbitrary expectations as a way to motivate ourselves, then feel guilt for not meeting them. [See Stop "Shoulding" on Yourself, page 150.]
- *What if:* We go down a rabbit hole seeking certainty: "What if this/that happens?" The answers we come up with only trigger more anxious what-ifs.
- *Regret orientation:* Andie thinks: *If I hadn't gained so much weight, my phone would've been easier to pull out.*
- *Unfair comparisons (comparing apples and oranges, false equivalents):* Andie thinks: *If I were fit like some of my other coworkers, I could change into my workout clothes, but I'd look like a huge, inappropriately dressed slob.*

Embrace: How do we accept, get past, or incorporate uncomfortable events into the fold of our lives, dealing with them rationally, not letting them weigh us down?

I'd encourage Andie to do the following:

- *See an alternative perspective.* Find a more compassionate way to describe the situation: *I was coming back from the gym with lunch and a birthday gift, and my coworkers and I collided! I'm a thoughtful person who took time to get my co-worker a gift. I'm fortunate I can afford another outfit, and another T-shirt for my coworker.*
- *Look to the five-year view.* Will this really matter five years from now? Will I look back and laugh—or even remember it? *It won't matter. I'll remember it, but no one else will. My coworkers were great sports about it. Looking back, I see I overreacted. No one died (except the T-shirt). Now it's a funny story.*
- *More ways to reframe:*
  - *What's the cost of my thinking this way, i.e., berating myself? I let it ruin my day. I deprived myself of pleasure (the party). I feel alone, defeated about losing weight. I feel upset by how I'm berating myself, because I deserve better.*

- *What's the worst possible scenario? Someone at the party comments on my disheveled appearance.*
- *What's the best possible scenario? We all laugh about it. I enjoy the party and get my coworker another T-shirt the next day.*
- *What's the most likely scenario? People will ask what happened. I'll tell them I was in a rush. Some might think I'm a mess, but most will understand it was an accident and go right back to focusing on the party.*
- *What positives can I acknowledge? I was invited to the party, and I'm generally well-liked and respected at my job. I have great, understanding coworkers. I'm kind and thoughtful—that's what got me into this messy situation!*
- *Try acceptance. My clothes were stained. This can happen to anyone, even the most organized person. I could have stayed and had fun, stained clothes and all.*
- *Separate emotion from fact. Just because I feel like a total disaster right now doesn't mean I am one. People are a lot less focused on us than we think.*

Exercise: Are Cognitive Distortions Holding You Back?

Choose a medium-stakes situation or event that's been on your mind. Walk yourself through ABCDE. Ask yourself:

- What is the antecedent?
- What is the belief about it?
- How am I feeling about it?
- What are some of my distorted thoughts or perceptions? [Do you notice black-and-white thinking—extremes, all-or-nothing thoughts? Are you falling prey to emotional reasoning—"I have strong feelings, so it must be true"—or maybe catastrophizing,

which is assuming the worst possible outcome, especially in an ambiguous/unclear situation? These are some common thought distortions we all engage in at times.]

- How are these distortions holding me back?
- What could I do to feel less this way in this situation?
- What is the problem to be solved? [Try to distill it down into a sentence or two.]
- What can I change about the situation?
- What do I need to embrace or accept about the situation?
- How will I act once these distortions aren't holding me back?

Gradually try this with more complex situations. Jotting your answers in your journal or thought log can help you spot patterns.

Acceptance of Imperfection

Accepting imperfection—in ourselves, others, life—can help prevent our self-worth from seesawing from the inevitable challenges of being human.

Most of us accept our negative thoughts as reality—*I'm a loser; I'm clumsy; what a disaster.* But they're subjective responses.

It's important to stop negative thoughts in their tracks partly because they can lead to rumination, pessimism, loneliness, and depression. They can be so compelling that they shut down the proactive problem-solving parts of our brain. We sink into a low sense of our ability to change things, resulting in learned helplessness (chapter 3, "Processing Emotions") and procrastination. To escape despair, we may cling to unhealthy behaviors, such as excessive eating, substance abuse, or unhealthy relationships. These actions only make our situation worse.

When we accept our imperfections, we realize how exhausting relentless self-criticism is. In fact, one reason programs designed to boost self-esteem frequently fail is that it's hard to reconcile their positive messages with the overpowering inner critic. As we'll see, a more accepting, self-compassionate approach can have a more positive, longer-lasting effect. It doesn't demand that we eradicate our critical voice, but rather accept its presence while persevering in the face of obstacles.

With acceptance, past disappointments and failures lose their power over us. Instead of "Why did they hurt me?" we ask, "Why does this hurt so much?"—becoming curious about our own healing journey, envisioning and pursuing new experiences instead of ruminating on what's done and past.

Implicit in accepting imperfection is acknowledging that change is a constant. That amazing new job will have tough days. Motherhood brings untold joy and also confusion, worry, and sometimes sorrow. And in general, terrible situations can also change, sometimes just in the way we think about them.

The first step in accepting imperfection is validating things as they are right now, while holding firmly to the idea that things change.

Try practicing acceptance with statements like these:

> *I embrace the duality of life—it's not all good or all bad, not simply black or white.*
>
> *I can sit with shades of gray, not having all the answers, not knowing how things will turn out.*
>
> *Growth requires change, and change can sometimes bring struggle, discomfort, and pain.*
>
> *My emotions don't always have to be rational or logical. I'm entitled to how I feel at this moment. This is how I feel right now. Feelings are temporary.*
>
> *I understand things won't always go my way or be all good, and that's okay.*
>
> *What is good will pass; what is not good will also pass; where I am right now will not be a forever state.*

Accepting your imperfections also means taking responsibility for your actions—even if you are not proud of them. If your actions caused someone else pain, take a moment to take an honest inventory of what you've done and how you've impacted someone, without self-flagellation: *I can accept my role in creating this situation, and I need to do better next time.* Also, keep in mind how powerful a simple, sincere apology can be. (More on relationships in chapter 8, "People.")

Exercise: Flip the Script: Turn Self-Criticism into Self-Acceptance

Below are some common self-critical statements and ways to flip the script to practice self-acceptance. In your journal, experiment with flipping your own self-critical scripts.

Self-Criticism	Self-Acceptance
I'm such a disaster, always making mistakes.	I'm human. Humans make mistakes. Why do I expect perfection from myself?
I can't/won't be able to do this.	This is a challenge. Challenges are great learning opportunities. I'm going to learn what I can so next time I'll be even more prepared.
I just wasted all this time, worked so hard, and still didn't succeed.	I'm proud of the work I put into this. I gained knowledge and experience and made new connections with people that will help me in the future. It's not for nothing—I just can't see the benefits right now.
I knew it—I wasn't cut out for this.	Today was rough. I deserve a break to rest and regroup.
What's wrong with me? I should have _____ [insert a goal] by now.	I'm not on the same timeline as some others. Is this really something I want to accomplish? If so, what's a realistic time frame for me? What resources will I need? If not, what's a more authentic goal for me?

Self-Criticism	Self-Acceptance
What will I be if I don't get this job or promotion? What will I be if I lose my job?	I have intrinsic value as a human being that has nothing to do with my external accomplishments. My success doesn't define me.
Why are they so much more successful/happy/wealthy than I am? What do they have that I don't have?	I shouldn't compare my life with the highlight reel that other people project. I don't know the truth behind what they're presenting or what their life is really like. What do I really want?
I don't want to do what they're asking of me, but I'm afraid of the consequences of saying no.	Setting healthy boundaries will allow me to preserve my relationships and my own sense of well-being.
I had a rough day. I deserve to finish this whole [cake, bottle of wine] by myself.	I'm going to give myself a moment to sit with this. I don't need to immediately reach for something that will make me feel more guilty in the long run. I can do something healthy for myself instead, like call a friend, take a walk or a shower, or go to bed early.
This is their fault. or *It's always my fault.*	Sometimes things are beyond our control. Regardless of blame, is there anything I can do to help remedy this situation?
I don't like my body.	My body does so much for me.
I wish I could be more productive.	I deserve rest and will be better able to tackle this when I'm rested.

Compassion for Yourself

If there's one true weapon against that voice inside that says we're not good enough, it's self-compassion. Self-compassion allows us to see ourselves and all people as having intrinsic, enduring worth. Compassion is quite possibly your most important tool in becoming a Practical Optimist. In self-compassion, the basic accepted thought we bring to our life is: *I'm human. This is part of being human.*

According to researcher Kristin Neff, PhD,[12] self-compassion has three key elements:

1. **Kindness:** Throughout this chapter, we've explored kindness in the form of challenging negative thought distortions and rewriting self-critical scripts.
2. **Common humanity:** Understanding that we aren't alone in experiencing hardship, pain, and disappointment decreases the sense that we are isolated in our struggles. Realizing we're connected through common human experience makes us more likely to engage in healthy habits, have better relationships, and enjoy greater well-being.
3. **Mindful awareness:** The practice of observing ourselves and situations without judgment.

Self-compassion helps us make space to process intense emotions, not avoid them. Depression, anxiety, and unexplained physical symptoms (like my leg weakness) are often a result of unprocessed negative emotions—excessive guilt or shame—we feel powerless against. Self-compassion can help alleviate depression that's developed in response to negative life stressors and events, and serves as a buffer against negative emotions, cynicism, anxiety, and ruminations. It's a powerful antidote to shame—often a culprit in depression.

Self-compassion helps us evade the comparison trap. We understand there'll always be people achieving more than we are at any given moment. Instead, we ask ourselves what we can learn from their

---

[12] For more on self-compassion, visit the website of Kristin Neff, PhD: https://self-compassion .org.

example, appreciate their achievements, and share what we know with those who could benefit.

And occasionally when we feel such deep gratitude for the good things in our life that we think we'll never be able to reciprocate for all we've received, self-compassion reminds us that we are okay and are giving what we can.

Exercise: How Self-Compassionate Are You?

Wondering where you fall on the self-criticism/self-compassion scale? Of the five statements below, if you don't say yes to three or more (most people don't, believe it or not!), you may need to practice creating a more compassionate relationship with yourself.

1. When I make a mistake, I'm able to take appropriate responsibility and focus on attempting to correct it, resisting feeling ashamed or retreating into self-blame.
2. I'm patient with myself when I'm learning something new or having difficulty with a new task. I will simply notice that I'm having difficulty instead of judging myself.
3. I understand that when it comes to making mistakes in life, I'm not alone.
4. During a tough time, I'm able to take breaks, rest, and ask for help.
5. I talk to myself in a kind, gentle way.

Four Steps to Living Mindfully and Compassionately

Earlier, we explored how observing our thoughts and perceptions could dramatically change our view of ourselves and the world. Now we'll expand this skill into a real-time self-compassion practice in everyday situations. We'll try it here with a work example of a solo-preneur single parent stressed by missing a deadline with a new client.

Step 1: Observe. Check in with yourself. Be curious, not critical. Label your experience, feelings, and reactions simply and clearly. Example: *I'm not going to meet this work deadline. I feel embarrassed, panicked, incompetent, ashamed, and angry at myself. My kids and I were sick, but this is a new client. As a single mom trying to build my own business, I feel I need to prove myself and show they were right to pick me. I'm afraid they won't understand. My heart's racing, and I feel a pit in my stomach.*

If judgmental statements about yourself come up, acknowledge them and write them in your journal, to help identify your self-criticism habits. If negative thoughts are hard to let go of, use a five-minute meditation or a breathing exercise to return to mindfulness (try the Befriending Your Breath and Befriending Your Body exercises in chapter 3).

Step 2: Contextualize. Now zoom out to the surrounding context of the situation to help put things in perspective. Example: *My kids and I were sick, and I was up much of the night for several nights. I was making mistakes. Delivering on time isn't the whole picture here. It doesn't help the client if the project's full of errors.*

Step 3: Normalize. Now tap into common humanity. Remind yourself: *I'm human, this is normal, we all make mistakes.* Example: *We all get sick sometimes, we can't control everything. Even diligent people miss deadlines sometimes. I'm a work in progress.* Incorporate human values that affirm your worth. Example: *Of course I'm anxious. Anyone would feel this way in this situation. I'm someone who works hard and is committed to doing a good job. I needed to do things thoroughly, and in these circumstances, I couldn't complete my work by the deadline. This was beyond my control.*

Step 4: Act. With gentle accountability, acknowledge your feelings, but simultaneously push yourself to formulate a plan of action. Incorporate self-soothing into your plan. Example: *In addition to being a careful worker, I'm also honest. I need to let them know*

and ask for an extension, and/or get support—engage someone to
help with the project or the kids until I catch up; ask a fellow solo-
preneur for advice. After the call, I'll call a friend and decompress
with a short walk.

Stop "Shoulding" on Yourself

After several sessions with Dr. L, I'd come to appreciate them as opportunities to decompress. So when she asked, "What would you like
to start with today?" I went for it:

"Work-life balance. Something easy," I joked.

Dr. L listened as I enumerated the stressors of my overpacked
weeks, my attempts at balancing work demands with my life and my
family's needs. "Sue, that sounds exhausting," she finally said. "I'm
hearing you speak about many meaningful obligations, but I notice
they seem to be mostly for others. Where exactly do *you* fit into this
equation?"

"I guess I'm not in it?" I said, but kind of asked.

"Do you think that's a problem?" she asked. "By that I mean, do
you think that is *the* problem?"

"I'm just feeling really torn," I said.

I told her I was afraid maybe my problem wasn't just work-life balance, but the collision between the two drastically different world-
views I'd grown up with. In the past, I'd made it work. But now there
was too much—I didn't know what to prioritize when everything was
a priority.

"Something or someone has got to give," I said, "but I don't know
who or what."

"That makes sense," Dr. L said. "You're facing pressures from all
directions, including internal ones, and that would explain the physical manifestation of your anxiety. What exactly is at odds for you?"

And just like that, I could finally come out with the monologue I'd
been preparing for years. "To get ahead in this profession, in this

society, I need to be independent and self-reliant, stand out, speak up, and assert myself. Being shy isn't an option. If I want to be respected, I need to talk about my accomplishments. The values that are imperative to my success in Western medicine and society would make a typical Indian mother shudder. Although my mom was less than typical, traditional Indian values were impressed upon me. Humility, deference, conformity, interdependence, tolerance, acceptance, and obedience are expected as soon as I take off my white coat. Bottom line: Whatever I do, I'm disappointing someone."

I looked up at Dr. L for her words of wisdom.

"We call that shoulding on yourself," she said.

Shoulding, a term coined by famous psychologist Albert Ellis, describes the harsh personal rules we have for ourselves. Indeed, I'd just learned about German psychoanalyst Karen Horney and the phrase she made famous: "The Tyranny of the Shoulds."

We internalize or buy into these idealized, perhaps unrealistic expectations from the environment we grew up in. In times of stress, particularly with large gaps in expectations (i.e., our situation calls for something far above and beyond or different from what we can actually deliver), we tend to respond in certain habitual ways to alleviate our anxiety. The bigger the gap, the greater our anxiety. Some people may become overly compliant (like me), some may turn aggressive, and others withdraw.

What we really need to be able to do is toggle flexibly and appropriately between responses: know when to collaborate, set a firm boundary, or step back. This requires an awareness of how we're feeling (emotional regulation, as discussed in chapter 4, "Problem-Solving"), catching our cognitive distortions (ABCDE), and weighing situations objectively yet self-compassionately (Observe/Contextualize/Normalize/Act).

But people who are aware of nothing but their shoulds see no options. There are no exit ramps on the Maladaptive Perfectionism

Superhighway. They may try to ease their anxiety with unhealthy coping mechanisms such as self-flagellation, disordered eating, self-harm, or substance abuse. They may internalize their anger at themselves or others, which may manifest physically with headaches, digestive issues, insomnia, palpitations, or, in my case, shaky legs.

In the ensuing weeks, I became acutely aware of the shoulds I'd built my life around. They'd had their benefits—helping me collaborate well, pushing me to achieve at levels I might not have dared aim for. But there'd been significant costs.

Our shoulds are basically the face we're told to present to the world, the one we're promised we'll be rewarded for. This ideal self doesn't make mistakes or have inconvenient feelings. It's made of infinite patience, good choices, great outcomes, and a flawless life trajectory. It's the self we feel we should be. But it's not the self we can be, because we're all imperfect humans living in an imperfect world.

My ideal self was uncomplainingly productive and useful. My real self simply couldn't keep up, and my body was giving out under the pressure. If I continued on this path, I'd be of no use to anyone.

Exercise: Rewrite Your Shoulds

Perhaps while reading this, you've thought of some of your shoulds.

- Reflect on the shoulds that have passed through your mind just since you woke up.
- Are the shoulds you've internalized true? Yes, you should brush your teeth. No, you should not be solely responsible for the health and happiness of everyone in your life.
- If something isn't true or is only partially true, can you rewrite it to make it truer?
- Where did this should come from? From you? From what others expect of you? Is it what you want, or are you taking on a re-

sponsibility you don't need or want out of feelings of obligation or fear of rejection?

Next, try rewriting your shoulds to be more specific. Choose words that turn shoulds into actionable decisions and personal choices (not external demands, impositions, or obligations). Example: "I should exercise more" might become "I want to exercise and feel more connected to my body."

Not all shoulds are bad, but not all good or rewritten shoulds are necessary. Would removing this should from your life open you up to more happiness?

Empathy for Others

Do we see the world in first-person singular ("I") or first-person plural ("we")? It turns out that greater use of plural pronouns is linked with feeling less lonely and less depressed.

The natural outgrowth of self-compassion is that we see that others, too—even those who annoy us—may have struggles and pain that we (and sometimes they) cannot see. Attuning to and accepting ourselves just as we are enables us to attune to others, feeling joy for their success, empathy for their pain. We reach an understanding that all humans are flawed and share many common experiences.

Just as through kindness we can build a relationship with ourselves, so we can do the same with others. This benefits us, too: research on people who experienced increased self-compassion indicates that they experienced greater social connectedness and reduced self-criticism, depression, and anxiety.

If shame, with its power to isolate us from our fellow humans, lies on one end of the emotional spectrum, the unifying power of love, powered by compassion, lies on the other. This is the ultimate goal of Practical Optimism.

When we feel interconnected with people, nature, the earth, and a higher being or the infinitely mysterious forces in the universe, we're no longer bound up in our ego and goals. Our world extends to the entire human family. Why wouldn't we try to help our family? Self-compassion, coupled with gratitude, allows us to lick our wounds, let them heal—and then turn back outward in service, connection, kindness, and love toward others, just as we similarly care for ourselves.

It's so easy to give positive strokes. Praise people to their face. Let them know what their presence means to you. Tell them the qualities you like about them ("You're such a good listener"), specific actions you're grateful for ("When you came through for me at my mother's funeral/my child's first birthday party/when I was moving—that really meant a lot"). Praise them to another person, in their presence.

Self-compassion is a powerful way to improve relationships with others. It facilitates empathy, compassion, trust, support, acceptance, and forgiveness. It is a key way to improve interpersonal effectiveness. In later chapters, I'll share more ways to express grace and gratitude and to connect meaningfully with others.

We all have times of need—I'm sure you vividly remember some of yours. We never know how someone else might be struggling and how our kind words or deeds may do them untold good. Can you remember how another's kindness lifted your spirits?

Self-compassion allows us to fill our own cup. Gratitude, as I've mentioned, is the appreciation that someone or something else (a person, nature, an impersonal being, God) has taken the time to fill our cup. Together, when we show ourselves grace and give grace to others for their help, kindness, and love, we begin to feel a part of something greater than ourselves. It can be a scary world, but acts of kindness—toward self and others—unite us as we journey together. They promote mental health and Practical Optimism. To me, they are the essence of my dharma.

The Art of Healing in Kintsugi

One of my biggest hurdles in therapy wasn't just the realization that I needed help, but that I *deserved* it. It created a fundamental shift in my perspective about culture, women, and mental health, but most important, about self-care as an act of self-compassion.

I'd internalized certain ideas growing up that maybe were unrealistic—at least, the way I applied them were—leaving me with an overwhelming feeling of unworthiness. I'd lost my sense of healthy pride in a sea of unreasonable expectations. The antidote to my feelings of inadequacy and relentless self-criticism was self-compassion.

Self-compassion would teach me I have intrinsic worth and value not because of what I do, but simply because of who I am: a human being. And this meant taking rest, breaks, and time for joy and fun; setting better boundaries with myself and others; and prioritizing my health even (maybe especially) when the pace of my life seemed to conspire against it.

Through self-compassion and the self-awareness that goes with it, I was able to go on to become an advocate for applying these dynamics in my profession, both in training and in service to patients. It also opened the path for me to become an advocate to the public. I speak on many mental health matters, but the heart of my message is always this: to remind those feeling afraid to take up space in the world that no one's asking that you say *Me first,* but you must never forget to say *Me too.*

Very few of the ideas I've shared here were in my sight line during my early sessions with Dr. L. In fact, everything she intimated sounded ridiculously out of reach.

"Do you feel like the expectations placed on you by your family and profession mean that you don't matter?"

"I matter—but in a hierarchy of needs that's so much bigger than just me."

"How do you handle conflict between your needs and those of the greater good?"

"I roll with it."

I knew we'd arrived somewhere important by the way Dr. L shifted in her seat and smiled. "That's what resilient people do, Sue. They find the best in their situation or make the best of it."

This didn't sound like a bad thing.

"This kind of thinking can be protective, especially when you don't have much choice, like when you were younger," she said. "And I see many of these dynamics are replicated in the work environment."

Okay, maybe some of it sounded bad.

"You've incorporated many valuable aspects of resilience into your life," she continued. "But another key feature of resilience is adaptability to new stressors and having flexible thinking and coping mechanisms—and in general, being kinder to yourself."

"I'm struggling with that," I said. Understatement of the century.

"That's okay. You've operated one way your entire life. It won't change overnight. It may be time, in your journal, to look at which of these values still serve you and which don't. Then we can focus on ways to redirect or retire them. How does that sound?"

It sounded impossible. No amount of journaling could eradicate millennia of culture. I'd even tried telling her the story of Arjuna, the ultimate warrior in the epic poem about the battle of Mahabharata. When Arjuna must choose between his immediate family and his extended family—all raised in one household like brothers—he's so torn between competing agendas that his body begins shaking uncontrollably; he gets weak and basically breaks down. But I was still too stuck in my deferential ways to tell her she was kidding herself.

I nodded dutifully.

"Same time next week?"

"Yup." Getting up to leave, I took one last look at the East River.

"Sue?"

I turned, hand in pocket, digging for a protein bar to eat en route to the hospital.

"Sometimes even warriors need to vent."

I smiled at her. I felt seen and heard, for the first time in a long time.

As I turned back toward the door, I noticed an object on her elegantly decorated bookshelf nearby. *What a lovely ceramic vase*, I thought. Blue, with gold veining seemingly cementing it together.

Kintsugi. The Japanese art of beautiful repair.

A different piece, of course, than the one in my father's living room. But the same essence: a beautiful object, formed of the earth, made even more beautiful by the loving mending of the broken places. The coaxing of cracks and flaws into a harmonious, unique whole. This was the art of healing. An art I was learning to practice—for others and for myself. I smiled again.

Leaving the warmth and safety of the penthouse suite, I pushed the elevator button.

To view the scientific references cited in this chapter,
please visit doctorsuevarma.com/book.

CHAPTER 6

Proficiency

Believing You Can Achieve

They are able who think they are able.

—VIRGIL

"I feel broken."

That was Shelly's response when I asked her to share a little more about what brought her to the clinic and how she had recently been feeling.

Shelly barely escaped the World Trade Center North Tower's collapse on 9/11. Looking back as she ran, she saw people jumping from office windows. She walked miles in heels, covered in blood and debris. She described a scene of mayhem: almost getting trampled, not knowing where her husband was or being able to contact her children as she boarded a boat to New Jersey, though she lived in Queens.

Her office relocated afterward. She continued doing "what was expected" and trying to "go back to who she was." But she wasn't sure she'd ever be the carefree, outgoing person she'd been. She had nightmares and flashbacks of nearly getting trampled, avoided streets near the towers' footprint, and shunned public transportation, elevators, and crowded public spaces.

I told her I was incredibly sorry for the trauma and losses she'd experienced. Wiping away tears, she thanked me. And then we began, step by careful step, our work together.

After almost a year of therapy, Dr. L and I felt I was doing much better. My leg weakness had resolved itself, and I was better able to manage the demands of my career, myself, and my family. I practiced challenging outdated ways of thinking, kept a worry journal, and regularly did mindfulness exercises. I thanked Dr. L for her help, and we parted knowing that if I needed help again, or a "booster," Dr. L would be there for me. The rest of my residency went well.

Then, a few months post-residency, I was recruited to be the first medical director of a new program dedicated to the monitoring, evaluation, and treatment of survivors of 9/11. Patients got a full battery of mental health questionnaires alongside a medical workup for a host of issues, including asthma and lung problems. Shelly, a thirty-nine-year-old mother of two, was one of my first patients for further evaluation of anxiety, depression, and possible post-traumatic stress disorder.

That night I wondered: *Am I ready for this?* I had years of experience with patients whose medical needs were complex, nuanced, and varied. But assisting in survivors' recovery from mass trauma was uncharted territory. I'd immersed myself in trauma therapy training but was still building knowledge. It was enough to shake even the most confident practitioner's feelings of proficiency. I needed to address my own feelings of inadequacy so I could assist those like Shelly who trusted me to help them.

Trauma comes from the Greek word for wound. Working with Shelly and others in the program, I came to see that in addition to any physical wounds, my patients suffered from a feeling of inner "broken-ness." Trauma had ruptured their faith in other people, in the world, and in their confidence in being able to navigate it.

Our sense of self and our capabilities—our sense of proficiency or self-efficacy[13]—is integral to our identity. According to social cognitive theory, self-efficacy is our perceived ability to navigate a task or situation (known as task-specific confidence), or how effective we feel overall in our ability to get things done (general self-efficacy), cope with stressors and challenges, regulate our emotions, and self-soothe (emotional self-efficacy). All the Pillars of PO are meant to help us not only *feel* more efficacious, but to actually *be* more efficacious. And our belief in our ability to do both helps us get better at both.

No one feels equally proficient at everything. You might feel generally capable, but your confidence may waver in certain domains, such as public speaking. The key is having an accurate understanding of your abilities—feeling confident in them (even a tad overconfident)—and believing you can increase your abilities, should you choose.

Proficiency can mean the difference between a stressor causing a minor shakeup or a major breakdown. But what happens when massive trauma estranges us from confidence built over a lifetime? If Shelly's worldview wasn't the same, how could she ever be the same? Could I help Shelly discover who she was *now*—and help restore her confidence in her ability to live a happy, fulfilling life, with all its ups and downs, not letting the past trauma dictate her future? As I'll explain, that's the heart of proficiency. It isn't knowledge or skills. It's knowing that we *have the ability* to know, learn, adapt, and flourish despite challenges, capable of handling what comes our way.

Strong self-efficacy is related to better health, higher work and academic achievement, and better social and romantic relationships.

---

[13] For the purposes of this chapter, I'm using self-efficacy interchangeably with proficiency (or to be more precise, our perceived proficiency).

It leads to greater effort and can increase your motivation—your desire to achieve—further driving and sustaining effort. Research shows that when people have been primed to think they're capable in a set of circumstances—for example, they're told they have higher chances of winning a game in an experimental situation—they work harder, longer, and stronger. Proficiency pushes us to keep trying, especially in the face of adversity and failure.

Self-efficacy comes easy to toddlers—they believe they can do anything! But we soon discover not everything is instantly or easily attainable or possible. We build self-efficacy through years of trying, failing, succeeding, and trying some more. When I graduated from medical school, I was handed a diploma, a white coat, and a big bucket of self-confidence. Oh, wait. I just got the diploma and coat. My proficiency was built over years of practice with patients. Proficiency is a journey. Expect some hiccups along the way—it will ebb and flow—that's totally normal. And, as we'll explore, there are ways to speed the process along.

I'll teach you a variety of ways to approach an event that might be seen as a big T (as in *trauma*) in order to blunt its capacity to damage morale and self-efficacy, as well as turn lowercase t's, more mundane stressors, into opportunities to build proficiency as never before.

A Word to the Wise

When the Going Is Hard

Proficiency can make all the difference between opportunities we do pursue or don't because we think we're not capable. At the same time, I recognize there are opportunities we don't pursue because of factors or barriers outside of our control. Our environment, the people around us, our early life experiences, the chances we were (or weren't) given—all influence self-efficacy. When limitations are imposed on us, it can be hard to experience proficiency. In fact, repeated attempts without a sense of progress can feel limiting and demoralizing and can even (as I'll discuss) lead to learned helplessness—a feeling that nothing we do will make a difference.

Sometimes you may decide to stop pursuing a particular goal in service of your mental health. But before you stop, try to pause. Give yourself grace: time, rest, and opportunity to assess the situation. Are there some aspects that are within your control? Are there ways to pivot? I hope that turning to the tools in this chapter will help you. Also, check out chapter 9, "Practicing Healthy Habits"—because proficiency is a habit that strengthens with practice.

If things don't work out, or if you decide it's best to stop, know this: though it may feel like a loss, you haven't lost. The effort of trying actually builds new pathways in the brain. You build skills. You build agency. You build proficiency.

You may not see or feel that right away. But trust that your trying has put you in a better position to address your goals, when you are ready, in the way you know best.

No Believing, No Achieving: Proficiency Demystified

Ever bought a gym membership and stopped going within months? Downloaded productivity apps and never used them? Talked yourself out of seeking a well-deserved raise?

If so, then you know that proficiency, self-efficacy, is a mindset first and foremost.

Your *perception* of your ability supports agency—your actual ability to execute tasks. Our perception of our abilities is just as important, if not more so, as actual ability. Indeed, researchers have found that confidence in our ability to succeed may predict desired outcomes better than actual health behaviors.

The pathway to proficiency goes something like this: Confidence leads to your attempting something, putting in effort. Consistent effort (persistence) leads to steadily increasing ability or agency, leading eventually (hopefully!) to success and wins. These make us feel good—I call this positive emotional response (PER). Each win boosts our confidence, making us more likely to attempt, persist, and complete the next step or task, leading to more self-efficacy, more effort, and better odds of winning. A virtuous cycle!

Each component must be present for proficiency to grow. Sometimes, though, despite our efforts, we don't see positive results, or we have trouble mustering effort. Various barriers may be in the way. Maybe you catch yourself thinking or saying, *I can't/won't be able to do this, I don't know how, and I don't know where to start.* We don't realize that these statements, if we let them fester without putting them to the test, can lead to avoiding, stressing out over, or prematurely quitting at things that are important to us. Procrastination, avoidance, pessimism, and excessive worry are both preceded by and result in low proficiency. These repeated hits to self-efficacy can lead to learned helplessness, spill into other areas of life, and become a slippery slope to depression.

Self-efficacy isn't overconfidence or narcissism, nor does it lead to unscrupulous tactics like cheating, stealing, or shortcuts. (In reality, it's low self-efficacy coupled with high aspirations—expecting a top outcome but lacking confidence in one's capability to achieve it—that might lead to taking shortcuts and the complications that can ensue.) Self-efficacy leads to the healthy, venturesome behavior often necessary to catapult us to the next level in our goals.

Research shows that self-efficacy can improve work performance and happiness. A 1998 meta-analysis of over a hundred studies pertaining to self-efficacy and job performance found that workers who felt a sense of proficiency in their work were happier and higher performing. Strong self-efficacy has been shown to boost positive surgical outcomes, prevent relapse in addiction, and increase well-being and quality of life in patients with coronary heart disease, cancer, spinal cord injuries, and osteoarthritis. Students with high self-efficacy do better academically partly because they recognize their own efforts have impact and can result in a better score. They also exhibit better health, better coping mechanisms, and higher personal satisfaction, resulting in higher retention rates.

Self-efficacy is made up of two active states:

1. **Self-efficacy expectations.** Confidence in your ability to carry out a specific behavior. Suppose losing weight is your goal. Self-efficacy expectations are your confidence in your capability to execute a weight-loss plan. People may know or understand the value of cutting out fast food, but if they don't feel competent at healthy meal prep, they may continue eating fast food.
2. **Outcome expectations.** Confidence in your ability to succeed in a particular goal once you initiate and follow through. In our weight-loss example, your outcome expectations are your confidence in achieving your desired results by engaging in your plan. Some people give up because they think that despite their efforts—healthy meal prep, etc.—they won't succeed.

Ideally, we want to be high in both expectations. Many of us have a distorted idea of being less capable than we actually are, tending to believe that *good things are outside my control or happen to me because of luck or chance* (known as an external locus of control for the positive) or that *bad things are always my fault; there must be something wrong with me* (an internal locus of control for all things negative). It's best to have a healthy, realistic view of what our responsibility is in a particular situation, and which factors are outside of our control—so that we give ourselves chances to try and see that our efforts can produce results, while also knowing when to cut our losses. This is especially important for survivors of trauma, such as Shelly, and anyone suffering powerful loss, so they feel empowered to embark on and continue their healing journey, despite challenges along the way.

Self-efficacy has a bearing on every obstacle or goal (which ultimately can impact everything from personal finances to success in relationships and work). And feeling in control of our future is essential for good mental health.

When a patient named Lina first came to see me, she'd all but given up at work. Lina said she could identify with the term *quiet quitting*—where you continue working but feel far less engaged. Soon, she feared, she'd be doing the bare minimum—and that wasn't who she was.

Lina enjoyed her work but was concerned that some of her peers, who hadn't worked there as long as she, were getting new projects and more face time and were on the cusp of promotion, while she, equally qualified, literally didn't have a seat at the table and was being overlooked for new responsibilities and promotion, despite trying.

Lina's self-efficacy was wavering, leading to learned helplessness—a conviction that nothing she did mattered: *They'll never let me into their circle [low outcome expectations]. I'd be too scared to ask [low self-efficacy expectations].* Her resulting reduced output could lead to her feared outcome—no promotion; maybe no job—and further demoralization. This is the dangerous downward spiral of low self-efficacy (more on how Lina pulled out of it later).

A healthy sense of proficiency can mean being undeterred (or minimally impacted) by setbacks instead of demoralized or stressed out, approaching a task with gusto rather than dread.

The good news: Proficiency isn't magic. It's built step by step. Confidence begets confidence through practice.

Pathways to Proficiency

According to noted psychologist Albert Bandura, PhD, self-efficacy develops in four main ways:

1. *Personal experience.* Your own direct experience—overcoming obstacles and experiencing success via your actions or contributions—is, whenever possible, one of the most important ways to build self-efficacy.
2. *Vicarious experience.* You can enhance self-efficacy by seeing how others overcome obstacles and attain goals—something I found invaluable as a new doctor.
3. *Verbal persuasion.* Seeking feedback and reinforcement, encouragement, and reassurance from the right people (who know you and the task at hand) can promote self-efficacy. This shapes much of our early learning. As adults, we get fewer such opportunities and need to seek them out. But feedback needs to be given carefully, as we'll discuss.
4. *Physiological feedback.* We gain self-efficacy through how situations make us feel while navigating them. If a task makes us feel bad about ourselves or thoroughly bored, we're more likely to avoid or abandon it and feel low efficacy, even if it was easy to master. (More on the connection between positive emotional feedback and developing healthy habits in chapter 9.)

These four aspects are embedded in how we build proficiency and the steps we can take when we are struggling.

Barriers to Believing in Ourselves—
and Overcoming Them

Sometimes barriers arise in our minds or lives as we seek to build proficiency. They can impact how we view ourselves, the world, and even our future. Below we'll look at the three barriers I find people tend to experience most often—and the barrier-busting strategies to help address them:

Barrier 1: Helplessness. *I feel broken/powerless/alone.*
   Barrier Buster: Validation

Barrier 2: Stuckness. *This is overwhelming/I can't do this/I'll never get it right.*
   Barrier Buster: Flexibility

Barrier 3: Fatigue. *This is too hard/I feel like giving up.*
   Barrier Buster: Self-Support

———

Barrier 1: Helplessness. *I feel broken/powerless/alone.* → Barrier Buster: Validation

In chapter 3, we looked at how emotions serve as powerful forces that can propel us in positive or negative directions. When we feel emotionally and physically safe and understood, including receiving acknowledgment of difficulties, changes, pain, or losses we've suffered, we're more able to risk change. Validation and safety are especially important if we're dealing with trauma. I began my work with Shelly by validating the profound change that had occurred. The world as she knew it (as we all knew it) wasn't the same. I gave her time and space to grieve the old happy-go-lucky Shelly who came to work in six-inch heels and accept the new Shelly who wore sneakers for fear she'd need to escape another attack. Would she wear heels again? Yes, but they'd be different. Eventually she'd feel comfortable donning a pair of kitten heels, keeping a pair of sneakers and sweatpants with her in a backpack.

Validating her physical and emotional needs included promoting calmness. We gradually dialed down Shelly's immobilizing sense of hypervigilance so she'd feel able to engage in problem-solving to feel safe and effective again. She also needed rest, time, and space for treatment. She'd taken no time off after 9/11. As part of our work together, she asked her manager for vacation leave, but when her manager found out it was related to Shelly's post-9/11 distress, she suggested Shelly use her accrued sick leave—and let her know that should she need more time off or any special accommodations, including medical and therapy appointments, it was available and wouldn't impede her advancement.

"You don't know how affirming that was," Shelly told me. Afraid of being viewed as "not a team player," Shelly had kept it all in. Ashamed to take sick leave, she didn't feel entitled to take time to tend her emotional wounds, because they weren't "visible" like some of her coworkers' 9/11 injuries.

Barrier 2: Stuckness. *This is overwhelming/I can't do this/I'll never get it right.* → Barrier Buster: Flexibility

Feeling that we aren't prepared for change or challenge or that the challenge is too great or hard can paralyze us. The ancients knew resisting change causes suffering. "There is nothing permanent except change," said the Greek philosopher Heraclitus in 500 BCE. Impermanence of life is also central in Buddhism, with the important distinction that often it's not the change itself but rather our resistance to it that leads to the suffering. Just as we update our computer software to better meet our needs, so we must update our mindset to meet the demands of current circumstances. Here are some ways to get unstuck by promoting flexibility in thought and action, loosening ourselves up for better performance.

View Challenges as Opportunities for Growth

There were some tangible reasons for my trepidation about my new role. This program was breaking new ground. There was no blueprint. I'd never been a medical director before, much less treated such extreme trauma.

It really helped to grab a growth mindset—a term coined and researched by pioneering psychologist Carol Dweck, PhD. A growth mindset, unlike a fixed mindset, doesn't set a cap or limit on ability. When we internalize or believe statements like "Some people just aren't/I'll just never be good at math or engineering," or "No matter what I do, I won't be able to lose this weight," or (as Lina said) "They'll never let me into their circle," we're assigning a ceiling to our self-efficacy and are more likely to become discouraged and frustrated and to give up. Pessimistic thinking gives us permission not to study as hard . . . to skip workouts, to sneak snacks . . . to lose enthusiasm for work. In a self-fulfilling prophecy, our worst predictions come true simply because we let them; in fact, we even create them.

> **PO Pearls**
> The first and most important glass ceiling you want to shatter is the self-imposed one.

To encourage yourself to view obstacles as growth opportunities, try seeing your situation not as a threat to your comfort zone, but as a way to practice and gain skills. *This won't be easy, but I'm going to learn so much* nudges the needle on positive expectations, increasing our perceived ability to withstand stress, which increases our actual ability to withstand stress!

Challenge Distorted Thoughts and Reframe Skewed Perceptions

People who constantly criticize or question themselves are likely to be distracted by their negative self-talk in challenging situations. Confident people are more likely to perform better under pressure because their self-talk is under control so they can stay in flow, focused on the situation. The more you can lower your task anxiety through positive self-talk, the better you'll perform. The cognitive restructuring skills in previous chapters (ABCDE, the 5 Rs, worry journaling, thought logs, and more) can help you challenge negative self-talk and perceive situations in more empowering ways.

As Lina acknowledged her pessimistic thoughts—*I can't get on the boss's radar, and even if I perform well, no one will notice*—and began to challenge them, she was more able to hold a growth mindset. Taking responsibility for her attitude, her efforts, and the things she could control helped her stop avoiding taking action to begin addressing her concerns.

While having high standards and pursuing excellence for learning and growth—known as perfectionistic striving—can be healthy, rigid standards, unchecked inflexibility, and unrelenting self-flagellation from what's called maladaptive perfectionism can seriously impede progress toward a goal. When we need or exclusively rely on something to turn out a certain way in order to feel okay, we're adopting an all-or-nothing view that limits access to our coping skills. The relentless need to succeed raises the stakes and fear of failure sky-high, causing a flood of stress hormones that can cripple performance. Research shows that maladaptive perfectionism can compromise successful goal attainment, lead to someone's achieving success "by all means necessary"—including less-than-ethical ones—or may result in other goals falling by the wayside. Flexibility coupled with self-compassion (*It's okay, everyone makes mistakes/has setbacks*), as we'll explore on page 174, can help combat some of this self-imposed criticism.

Practicing flexibility by reframing perceptions can be powerful for any situation that seems to push your buttons—from work to relationships to parenting. As one example, parents with low self-efficacy in parenting resort to more punitive parenting styles. Gaining skills and feeling more capable leads to better social, emotional, and academic outcomes in kids. If you think you're skillful as a parent, you're less likely to perceive your kids' natural push for autonomy as pushing your buttons, making you less likely to take things personally, feel threatened or helpless, and resort to unhealthy means of coping.

After the 9/11 attacks, Shelly's perception was that she'd never feel safe again. We worked on modifying this view by identifying and using her thought log to document all-or-nothing thinking (*I can't relax unless I know for sure there'll never be a threat again*), catastrophizing (*I'm destroyed/broken*), overgeneralization (*You can't trust anyone or anything—why leave the house*), and negative filtering (*I've made some progress, but I really have so far to go*). We challenged these distortions with techniques like cost-benefit analysis (What's the cost of thinking this way? What would be the benefit of thinking differently?), future perspective (reviewing a situation from, say, a five- or ten-year perspective), and analyzing the situation as a caring friend would (compassion and validation versus judgment).

After we had worked together approximately eight months, Shelly would say, "I mostly feel safe." This view empowered her to take steps to reclaim agency over her life.

Connect to Meaning, Purpose, and Identity

If you're feeling stymied by or undecided about a challenge or goal, try asking yourself why this would be meaningful for you, reflect what you stand for, or fit with the kind of person you feel yourself to be—i.e., your identity. A patient, Katie, wanted very much to become a psychologist when she was a kid. Her parents told her she wasn't cut out for a PhD in psychology. She applied anyway but didn't get into the handful of (mostly research-oriented) PhD programs she applied to. Her sense of proficiency took a big hit. But Katie had a built-in silver lining. She was flexible.

When I asked what her underlying reasons were for pursuing this work, her answer was instantaneous: helping others and advocacy. She realized that a plethora of other health professional careers met this goal that held meaning for her. Awareness of her larger purpose toppled the barrier of all-or-nothing thinking that only psychology could be fulfilling, revealing other options. Katie eventually became a successful nurse practitioner and was promoted to an administrative position at her hospital. Several years after we ended her treatment, she emailed me to say she'd become chief wellness officer at a major corporation. She later sent a press release about receiving a leadership award for women in business. With it was a plaque for my office: "Write your purpose in pen, your path in pencil." Katie attributes her career success to being able to pivot to Plan B when Plan A didn't work.

There were some courses in med school I wasn't excited about, but I got through them by connecting with my core sense of medicine as my calling. Understanding our health as an intricate web of mental and physical relationships is one of the most valuable vantage points I can bring to my patients—it's one of the reasons I chose to pursue a medical career and psychiatry. Coursework in everything from anatomy and physiology to pathophysiology, neuroscience, pharmacology, and microbiology and training in clinical rotations ranging from surgery, obstetrics, and gynecology to pediatrics afford psychiatrists a global picture of health and allow them to be meaningfully involved in integrated treatment plans for their patients. From medication interactions to common medical manifestations of psychiatric illness and psychiatric symptoms of other medical disorders, we are attuned to just how intertwined the mind and the body are. Being a psychiatrist has taught me one thing for sure: There is no health without mental health.

Connecting goals to your purpose or core values can also help you determine whether your push (or hesitation) might be more about pleasing or proving yourself to someone else than about your interest in the task itself. Being driven by the need for others' approval, by a desire for accolades or other external indications of success, or by fear of criticism can lead to harsh self-criticism that erodes proficiency and causes procrastination, giving up, and self-sabotage. It's okay to know when you aren't interested in something and take a pause or step back to reassess.

Remind Yourself of Past Masteries

Most of us have far more proficiency than we give ourselves credit for. You may need to be reminded of what a capable, smart, strong human being you are.

Come up with fact-based observations about your strengths and accomplishments. Look back into your childhood, and think about your schooling, sports, social skills, work life, hobbies, and relationships. You're borrowing competency from another area to bolster a domain where your self-efficacy is faltering.

For example, growing up as the eldest of five kids, Lina often took on a caregiving role with her siblings. Frequently her needs weren't first on the list. I asked Lina to describe, despite her childhood disappointments, the positive lessons learned. "Well, my parents relied on me. I was dependable, or at least I became that way. I was able to take charge, I guess." Had that served her life in any way? "Definitely," she said. "But it's interesting—I don't think I wanted to see it that way."

Sometimes others see our potential more clearly than we do—which is helpful in moments of self-doubt. A distinguished colleague who'd known me through my training and international work suggested I pursue the opportunity for the trauma program's medical directorship after they reached out to recruit me. I respected her enormously, and if she thought I could do the job, then perhaps I could.

If counseling the younger me, I'd say, "So you're not the number one trauma specialist in the country—that's an unfair comparison. But you have all the foundational elements. You're a good listener and empathetic. You've worked with people from diverse socioeconomic and ethnic backgrounds. You know how to draw out the key points with patients. If you don't know the answers, you know how to research and seek information and support. You were selected from a competitive applicant pool. They wouldn't have chosen you if they didn't think you could do the job. Plus you have a great team, and the program founder is a dedicated female clinician whom you admire."

Remind yourself that while you may not have done this particular task before, you've handled other difficult situations.

Barrier 3: Fatigue. *This is too hard/I feel like giving up.* → Barrier Buster: Self-Support

Self-support through self-compassion is your proficiency superpower. At work, in school, and in relationships, with self-compassion we recover better from setbacks and feel more hopeful about future attempts. One study showed that students with self-compassion approached a midterm exam failure with better, more flexible positive emotional coping strategies. In another, students with self-compassion were able to re-engage and try harder and longer on tests. Holding a self-compassionate mindset relating to work, research shows, increased job engagement and resilience, leading to more headway on work objectives and an increased sense of life meaning.

By allowing you to accept yourself without harsh judgment, self-compassion frees you to learn, ask for help, and try again. Thus self-compassion is always moving you toward your best self. For a deeper dive into this topic, I invite you to spend some time in the GRACE section of chapter 5, "Pride," if you haven't already. Your proficiency will thank you!

Self-support includes physical care. Especially when pursuing goals or surmounting challenges, you need rest, relaxation, sufficient exercise, healthy food, and restorative sleep. I'm especially alert to patients who say, "No matter what I do, I can't seem to . . ." We often explore whether some medical or mental health problems might be posing barriers to (for example) losing weight, feeling energized and positive, or staying on task. Sometimes we need self-support helpers, such as a registered dietitian or a health or fitness coach.

In addition to rest, Shelly and I focused on progressive muscle relaxation and mindfulness during sessions and at home. She joined art therapy and yoga therapy and a CBT trauma group in our program, and continued being monitored for lung and sinus issues resulting from exposure to the dust and debris on 9/11.

Experience = Empowerment

Rumi said, "Don't be satisfied with stories, how things have gone with others. Unfold your own myth." As mentioned, the best way to develop self-efficacy is through firsthand experience. But try not to throw yourself in at the deep end! Success builds self-efficacy: we need some return on our investment; otherwise proficiency can be hard to sustain. Tasks should ideally be just challenging enough to stimulate you and encourage you to persevere, since perseverance can be that extra little something that decides whether a person succeeds.

Take small chances before fully committing to big changes: Want to become a better, more persuasive presenter? Read up on it, for starters. Watch videos of masterful speakers. Take a webinar on public speaking. Try some low-stakes situations, such as heading a committee at your house of worship or coaching or tutoring kids. Study tutorials on preparing compelling slide decks. Incorporate your new skills into work pitches and presentations. (More on turning aspirations into action in chapter 9, "Practicing Healthy Habits.")

Encourage yourself with reminders that this is how you build proficiency: *inch by inch; baby steps; walk before you run; base hits, not home runs; one foot in front of the other; easy does it.*

If anxiety's keeping you stuck, try behavioral activation (chapter 2, "Purpose"): don't wait to feel like doing something. Just start— inch by inch. Simply doing it builds self-efficacy—a powerful weapon against anxiety.

Don't downplay your wins: Many people chalk up their positive outcomes to luck, or otherwise minimize their success. These are distortions of negative thinking.

As Shelly started feeling better, her mood, sleep, energy, and concentration improved. Feeling more focused at work, she started volunteering for projects. She even began feeling more comfortable in large groups and with public speaking again. Her boss noticed and gave her a promotion—a big self-efficacy win. "I can get better," she said. "Things can get better." Self-efficacy builds hope.

Shelly's evolution, and what I saw in my other patients, was a turning point for me, too. Their pain and loss had happened outside my office—and so, I realized, would their gains. Empowering someone means restoring their faith in themselves, their world, and their future through their experiences of success. Helping my patients gain agency through real-world wins would become the foundation of my Practical Optimism program: empowering individuals to be agents of change in their own lives.

Vicarious Experience

Ever witnessed your boss adroitly negotiate a deal? Admired a parent's ability to soothe a child? Watched videos of a baseball player's swing? Been inspired by how someone handles adversity or infirmity? Any time you've learned by observing, you're practicing vicarious experience. After direct personal experience, watching a skilled practitioner is the best way to learn. It's why shadowing is a big part of medical training.

Social comparison theory, according to psychologist Leon Festinger, PhD, suggests that people have an innate drive to evaluate themselves, often in comparison to others. Seeing the accomplishments of peers (lateral social comparison) or of role models (upward social comparison) helps us size up our own abilities, traits, and attitudes. As long as the comparisons aren't so out of reach as to make us feel hopeless about our prospects, they may instruct and motivate us: if this person I identify with can do it, so can I.

Keep Learning

We talked earlier in this chapter about adopting a growth mindset, or a lens in which you view yourself as capable of improving at a task or reaching a goal. Having this mindset keeps you open to learning key information needed to move ahead, gaining specific skills, and developing emotional insight as your mastery grows. Staying curious augments flexibility and adaptability (*What else can I try/do I need to find out?*) and helps you feel a sense of progress (*Look how much I know now, compared to when I started*). And it helps you move through the inevitable challenges that arise (*I need to keep working and putting in effort* vs. *I'm just no good at this*).

> **PO Pearls**
> External approval can help you attain success, but it won't help you sustain it. Authentic success and the happiness it brings come from building mastery over small obstacles over time.

Setbacks, even failure, offer opportunities to regroup and try again with self-compassion, and research shows this supports persistence: "This is challenging and new to me. It's going to take me some time to get the hang of this. It's natural to feel intimidated, or to stumble."

I vividly recall failing my first Organic Chemistry exam. It was more than just a bad test score. Organic Chemistry is infamous for being a course that stands between premed students and their dream to become a doctor. It was essentially one of the biggest barriers that could keep me from doing the work that meant everything to me. If I couldn't pass the first exam, how could I pass the rest? Then I learned I wasn't the only one. That helped me tap into the common humanity

aspect of self-compassion: this can happen to anyone. I was still intimidated, but I persisted—doubled down on study and determina-
tion, got extra help—and eventually did (very) well, despite also
juggling three jobs. Later, I took great satisfaction in becoming a tutor
for the department (and continued teaching it to individuals and small
groups of premedical and health science students well into my medical school years), helping demystify this subject that derails so many.
Since then, when I've had to surmount obstacles, I've encouraged myself by reminding myself of not only the breadth of knowledge I gained
from that experience, but also the lessons in mastery and self-efficacy:
I've done it before, so I'll be able to do it again.

In this newly created directorship, I had a lot to learn. I decided it
was a matter of acquiring specific abilities. What do you do if you lack
ability? You go out and develop it, right?

In the months before starting the job, I intensively researched
how mental health programs are organized and administered. I attended conferences and met heads of clinics, finding out about their
programs, and learned from the director of the larger comprehensive
program.

On the job, I tapped into my colleagues' collective knowledge. We
relied on one another, meeting to discuss complicated cases as we sought
to treat this diverse population—executives, servicepeople, first responders, neighborhood residents—each uniquely affected by their
collective trauma. We had a journal club to read and discuss relevant
articles. In retrospect, I believe my need and willingness to learn resulted in a less hierarchical team culture that benefited me, my coworkers, and our patients.

A growth mindset, as I mentioned, includes emotional insight.
While I don't think everyone should be in therapy, it can be an important step in learning productive new coping skills—it certainly was for
me. Lina told me she felt invisible sometimes in her large family. They
literally didn't have space at the kitchen table for everyone to fit. "I was
expected to help with dinner, which meant my mom and I ate last,"

she said. How did she feel about that? "Like I wasn't important enough to be part of the family meal."

We talked about how this caretaker role might be replicated at work, where she got her work done and helped others, but found it "hard to ask for what I want—and that it was selfish to do so."

"I honestly don't mind helping other people," she said. "I just want to sit alongside everyone else at the table." This reminded me of a famous saying by New York congressperson (and the first African American woman in Congress) Shirley Chisholm: "If they don't give you a seat at the table, bring a folding chair." Creativity, flexibility, and persistence were helping Lina boost her proficiency and eliminate some of the "invisible" obstacles that she had control over.

Getting the Right Feedback

As Lina and I discussed the closed circuit she might have created in her singular focus on visibility and promotion, which she equated with how much her company valued her, I asked what else might indicate her worth to her team and supervisors. "I could ask for feedback," she said—tapping into one of the four self-efficacy builders identified by Bandura. We decided she'd seek feedback from her boss. With that, she could decide what her next move would be: ask for a seat at the table or look at other options.

Seeking feedback is part of a growth mindset. In Lina's case, her boss's feedback would help her focus less on her perceptions of how things were going and more on concrete things she could do to be a visible and valuable contributor. But feedback might also come from someone who knows you well, has your best interests at heart, has relevant experience with what you're dealing with, and maybe has more life experience.

Asking for information and input or inviting constructive feedback, as Lina did, can help prevent the self-efficacy drain of wondering how we're doing. Input or feedback can be knowledge-based, skill-based, or mindset-based. What makes it constructive? Ideally, it is:

1. *Authoritative:* It comes from someone in a position to know what they're talking about. Maybe they've known your work over time, worked with you closely, or know areas where you could improve. *Authoritative* doesn't mean they must be an authority figure. Sometimes we learn best from someone we respect who isn't a direct authority figure. While Lina decided to seek feedback from her boss, we also discussed her seeking out a mentor through a program at work, where she built a strong rapport with a senior partner at the firm. Lina much preferred receiving input from someone without direct authority over her, compared to being vulnerable with her boss, whose constructive criticism she admitted to sometimes taking personally.

   If you're approaching someone you don't know, that's where advance preparation and networking come in. I couldn't just call medical directors and take hours of their time asking about running a treatment program. I'd attend conferences and meetings I knew they'd be attending or speaking at. I put in the time to search people out, introduce myself, ask for a few minutes to share their experiences as program directors, and go from there. Sometimes I made the initial contact beforehand based on papers of theirs I'd read in advance and asked to follow up on at the conference, or I approached them after their talk or even asked questions as part of the general Q and A session.

2. *Specific:* Focus on specific areas where you need a boost in agency. I did background reading so that I arrived informed, with specific questions targeted to fill knowledge gaps. I sought knowledge-based input on trauma—for example, we invited leading experts to speak to our team about trauma-informed psychotherapy and to serve as consultants on cases. For skill-based input on administering a program, I connected with medical directors. Mindset-based input was Dr. L's department.

3. *Candid but kind:* Tactful truthfulness is ideal, but sometimes feedback is harsh. Take a self-compassion chaser: *Wow, that*

didn't feel good. But that person is an expert in the field. I'm grateful I got to talk with them. I'm glad I had the courage to ask.

Sometimes people fear they'll look stupid, insecure, or unqualified by seeking feedback or help. You must actively work to keep self-eroding beliefs like these at bay. Use self-compassion: *No one knows everything. It's a sign of strength to admit what you don't know.*

A Word to the Wise

All Praise Is Not Alike

If you're getting or giving feedback, know that there are ways to praise that enhance proficiency (or not).

Studies suggest praise can be a disservice when it provides blanket reassurance. In fact, one study showed that kids who were getting Cs were less motivated when reassured that they were great. Telling someone—particularly a young person—who succeeds at a task that they "are a wonderful person" doesn't necessarily help them build the connection between their efforts at the task and the resulting success, but rather leads to a perception of a ceiling on capability. In contrast, giving conditional effort- or task-focused praise—"You worked hard on this—and you did an excellent job as a result. Way to go!"—spotlights effort, something we have control over. It connects us with our power to become proficient—a growth mindset.

There's a sweet spot. There's no harm in a balance between unconditional praise that validates a person's worth as being important and deserving (and a worthy human being) alongside conditional, task-focused praise spotlighting what they're doing to effect change. For example, in a work setting: "You're a valuable asset to this company and we're so glad you're on this team (unconditional). When you work hard on the client proposals, we get good results from your team—something magical happens (conditional). I look forward to more great work on the next project." Or, in a school setting: "You brighten this classroom (unconditional). And the time and effort you've been putting in—taking notes, reviewing your tests to see how to correct errors—have paid off (conditional). You're really working hard; keep going!"

The Importance of Visualization

We've discussed the two components of self-efficacy: confidence in our ability to carry out a specific behavior (self-efficacy expectations) and confidence in those actions leading to the desired outcome (outcome expectations). Here are two ways to boost self-efficacy by "seeing" both more positively.

Role Play

I often use role play to help my patients envision themselves meeting goals and to enable them to prepare for stressful situations. With Lina, I played the boss as she practiced asking for what she needed in her feedback session. As her boss, I gave Lina some pushback, saying things like "I'm not sure we need additional people at the meeting." To which Lina, with some practice, would say (first to me during role playing; later to her boss), "I understand [acknowledging his point]. At the same time, attending the meetings helps me understand the company's broader vision and priorities, which I can apply to my work and articulate to our clients to build their confidence in our company [making a strong case for why her attendance could benefit her boss and the company]." We also role-played asking for a promotion in the future once she'd ramped up her performance (she admitted that her low self-efficacy had kept her from putting in the necessary effort over the past quarter and it wasn't realistic to expect advancement at this time) and fielding a response to the statement that there was no room in the head count for a promotion.

Guided Imagery

You can also spend a few minutes daily using guided imagery to imagine the best-case scenario. If you're trying to lose weight, see yourself doing your workout and (this is key) visualizing the rewards associated with exercise: feeling more energetic, focused, and happier.

Creating the "Good Feeling" Proficiency Loop

Experiencing positive emotions as we navigate new experiences is a key way we develop self-efficacy. Pay attention to how you feel when doing the task or challenge. Don't just move on to the next task or challenge. It's an important learning cue to remember just how good this process of hard work—learning, trying, and succeeding (even if it's not a complete success)—feels.

When you meet with success, embrace the good feelings, the sense of accomplishment, and the satisfaction. If things don't go well, revisit the strategies I discussed in the earlier section on overcoming barriers to validate your emotions, make sure you're not falling into negative thinking and distorted perceptions, and offer yourself support to ease back into the process.

Although her feedback session with her boss went well, Lina continued to be met with resistance in her efforts to be more included in new projects and meetings, but she didn't give up or take it personally. One Friday, the day before her boss left on vacation, Lina volunteered to cover meetings in his absence. While it made her a bit anxious to ask, she'd had practice at managing her anxiety in other conversations with her boss (inch by inch!).

He agreed! That boosted her self-confidence—just what she needed to revive her flagging engagement. "I'm learning to ask for what I need. It's important, because otherwise I'll end up checking out mentally!" she told me. "My boss is slowly learning to loosen the reins a little more. He let me join a few more meetings after he returned from vacation." How did this impact how she felt at work? "I feel a lot better. As if I've finally gotten some recognition. I feel more interested and willing to go above and beyond—something I always did until recently."

Lina used her increased self-efficacy from those wins to be seen and heard at the table. This didn't happen overnight, but it happened because of Lina's commitment to fostering her sense of proficiency, driving the virtuous cycle of enhanced proficiency, productivity, and performance. Lina finally felt a sense of proficiency in her work, giving her the added boost to eventually ask for and receive a well-deserved raise, breaking the low proficiency/high avoidance/low engagement cycle she'd been caught in.

Shelly's commitment to emerging from the paralyzing effects of her trauma allowed her, step by step, to move toward healing. When our work together came to an end, her husband asked to join us for one last session. "Dr. Varma, it makes me so happy to see her smile again. I fell in love with her because of that smile, her laughter, her carefree nature. I wasn't sure I'd see that side again. She's a hopeful person again. Thanks to all of you at this program for giving me Shelly 2.0."

Shelly 2.0?

Shelly told me that her husband noticed there was something calm about her. "He says I've become more serene. When he complains about seemingly small things—like a driver on the road honking at him or waiting on line too long, I just laugh. I tell him, 'Don't sweat the small stuff. We have each other, we're healthy, we're alive. That's all that matters, right?'"

Your Personal Proficiency Power Questions

Here are a series of proficiency-building questions you might find useful if you're facing a challenge, task, situation, or goal. Don't feel pressured to answer them all—they're just here to help you consider ways to reframe or reconsider things from a pro-proficiency point of view. Consider the role your thoughts, emotions, and behaviors play in proficiency—how they help you; where they cause confusion, delays, and inefficiencies; and how you can gain actionable clarity.

Understanding my emotional needs:

1. What feelings am I having that need to be accepted and validated (and by whom)? Validation by others may not always be possible. In this case, write your feelings in your journal.

2. Do I need some time to grieve a loss? If so, what can I do to promote emotional and physical calm and extend grace to myself? **(Tip: Visit Finding GRACE in chapter 5.)**

3. What physical sensations did I notice in working toward or doing my goal activity? Was my heart racing? Were my palms sweating? Was I a little shaky? Was my heart pounding with excitement or fear?

4. What did I do as a result of these emotions? Did I want to call someone and share how amazing I felt? Or that I wish I'd done better? Was it a mix?

Understanding my thoughts and perceptions:
If the task or goal seems too hard, ask yourself:

5. What is my why—i.e., what is my underlying purpose in wanting to achieve this? Am I doing this for someone else's approval or to gain recognition? If so, what do I hope will change in my life as a result? *Who am I trying to please; what am I trying to prove?*

6. Am I avoiding new challenges and opportunities because I'm projecting past struggles (or distortions) onto future possibilities? If so, what cognitive distortions come to mind? Examples: catastrophizing ("I'm hopeless at this"); all-or-nothing thinking ("It's too late"); unfair comparisons ("They're so much better than me"). **(Tip: Try applying ABCDE, described in chapters 4 and 5.)**

7. How could I reframe it—the situation or the way I'm perceiving the situation—to help decrease the negative mental associations? **(Tip: Try the 5 Rs of Emotional Regulation and Real-World Problem-Solving in chapter 4.)** Could I see this challenge as an opportunity instead? Can I speak to and treat myself more kindly as I approach this?

8. If I can't change the situation, my relationship to the situation (my participation), or the outcome of the situation, what can it teach me that is of value, even if things didn't turn out as I hoped?

Translating thoughts and emotions into behavior:

Putting a plan into action involves several components (in no particular order), all of which have immense benefits for proficiency building.

9. *Building confidence:* What qualities do I already possess that are transferable?

10. *Building resources:* What do I need tangibly? Are there tangible needs I could express to others (e.g., time off) or provide to myself (e.g., rest)?

11. *Building knowledge and skills:* What do I need to know or learn—in terms of information, skills, or mindset—and from whom or which source? What courses, videos, or lectures might help? Can I request a brief informational interview with someone? What abilities have served me well in other situations?

12. *Building support and accountability:* What kind of feedback would be helpful—knowledge-based, skill-based, mindset-based—and from whom? Who might be willing to share their experiences with me and let me periodically check in with them as I proceed (perhaps someone who has already achieved what I'm setting out to do)?

13. *Building vision:* Can I commit to three minutes a day of visualizing myself engaging in actions leading to the best-case scenario? In my journal or with a trusted friend, can I role-play some options?

14. *Building commitment and alternatives:* How can I get started so I can learn from my own experience? Can I break it into small steps, tackling one at a time on a regular basis? What's my Plan B if Plan A doesn't work?

15. *Building proficiency and value by giving back:* What can I offer as a result of what I've learned? How can I reciprocate to those who've helped me along the way? (*Personal note:* Building proficiency is about building confidence, skills, and knowledge so you can eventually put them into practice. For me, looking for ways to offer value to others in my daily life is how I give back the benefits I've received from my proficiency. In the beginning, you may not feel like you have much to offer, and that's okay, too. Expressing gratitude to those who've offered their time, skills, encouragement, and feedback is a great start and is always appreciated.)

Strength and Healing Through Love

Working with Shelly was one of my most powerful professional lessons in self-efficacy. I couldn't give Shelly back the life she'd had. I couldn't remake the tapestry of her life or anyone else's—including my own. We can't change the past. But with self-efficacy, we can make the most of our present and seek to forge our future. Thinking of the beautiful kintsugi vase in Dr. L's office—the art of making a thing more beautiful and valued because it has been broken and repaired—I realized I could help my patients apply the golden glue of love and compassion to their broken places, not hiding them away but embracing them, crafting a stronger self and a better, healthier, happier tomorrow.

This is the very essence of what I do. It is the very essence of our life's work. Practical Optimism empowers us to take responsibility for our own healing. It is the golden glue we all need from time to time to reclaim the beauty of our lives. May it do for you the great good it has done for me.

To view the scientific references cited in this chapter,
please doctorsuevarma.com/book.

CHAPTER 7

Present

Being Here Now

Attention is the rarest and purest form of generosity.

—SIMONE WEIL

"*Uma mesa para dois, por favor,*" I said to the elderly gentleman behind the counter of what was perhaps the only café in town. During a whirlwind trip to Portugal, my husband and I had taken a wrong turn and ended up in a small café in a fishing village in southern Portugal.

As we sat and took the proffered menus, I asked, "*E por favor a senha do Wi-Fi, senhor?*" I knew some Portuguese, but I'd need Google Translate for the menu. Our phone batteries were dying; the cell signal was spotty. Wi-Fi would make things much smoother.

He smiled, pointing to the sign behind him. In English, it read:

WHERE THE WI-FI IS LOW, THE CONNECTION IS HIGH.

I was hungry, tired, and desperate for the Oracle of Google. It told us how to get where we needed to go, how much we should tip, and what the weather would be.

When did I become so reliant on Google, nervous when I couldn't access it? Yet we'd relished our impromptu conversations and adventures in Portugal—where, ironically, we'd used the tools of the internet to be "off the grid." So perhaps this sign was a timely reminder to stop plotting our course and simply sit and enjoy a coffee.

João—who, as we learned, was the owner of the café—was eighty-five years young. When my husband explained that we planned to drive to Lagos for dinner, João's chuckle spoke volumes. "In our restaurants, you are our guest. We want you to eat and drink," he said. "You won't be leaving before two and a half to three hours minimum—it's why our restaurants have only one or two seatings. No, you will not be eating tonight in Lagos without reservation, sorry." He waved his hand, muttered something in Portuguese, and walked away.

So much for a quick espresso with a side of Wi-Fi!

We ordered the traditional dishes João recommended. He and his wife cooked. His son and daughter-in-law managed out front. They all checked on us. João joined us for Porto and pastéis de nata—Portuguese custards. Two and a half hours later, we left, supplied with good food but even better stories.

I wondered how our dining experience might've been different if there'd been Wi-Fi. Would we have talked less, interrupting our meal to scroll through our phones, checking maps, work emails, and social media? Would we have talked with João and his family?

These habits have become routine. I understood the attraction of the parallel world online—technology has afforded me many opportunities, professionally and socially. I understood its convenience for keeping in touch with loved ones. And how insidiously it could co-opt attention—like when I found myself checking work email in the wee hours after delivering a baby . . . my own.

I wanted the virtual world to occupy a right-sized place in my life. I longed to be cognizant and present enough to fully appreciate all the beauty unfolding around me in the real world.

And I knew that finding that balance was—is—up to me.

According to the MobileDNA app, which shows smartphone usage, as of this writing, on average, we unlock our smartphones eighty times a day and send or receive ninety-four text messages daily. The BBC reports that according to app monitoring firm data.ai (formerly App Annie), we spend around five hours per day (a third of our time awake!) on our phones. A study by Common Sense Media shows that teens spend on average nine hours per day on their phones. A 2018 Pew Research study shows that approximately half of teens are online "almost constantly."

Those numbers may shock you. But what is even more troubling is that studies are connecting technology use with reduced empathy. A 2011 research paper looking at seventy-two studies done over a thirty-year span found a 40 percent decline in self-reported empathy in college students—with the most significant drop after 2000—in part thought due to technology. What else has decreased? Our moral/ethical attention and good Samaritan behavior; cognitive performance (it's as if IQ dropped); reading, writing, and social/emotional skills in kids. How does this impact our depth in interpersonal exchanges? Just the sight of the possibly interrupting phone, studies reveal, alters conversations: their quality and depth suffer, and both parties in an exchange feel less invested in it, potentially reducing their connectedness and even the empathic connection they feel toward each other. The uber-availability of tech matters. In a study carried out at a device-free camp for children, it was found that after only five days without phones, the children showed improved recognition and interpretation of facial expressions and a greater ability to pay attention to and interpret social cues compared to a control group whose screen time hadn't changed.

The increasing lack of depth in our encounters is known as the shallowing hypothesis. Experts theorize we're starting to expect the same convenience from our relationships and the world that we derive from technology, leading us to be impatient or dissatisfied with others and the world (our tolerance for frustration has declined), and, in extreme cases, to lose empathy for others. Inevitably the world and people will never be nearly as predictable or as able to provide instant gratification as our technology (and mind you, even our devices are imperfect!), setting us up to be disappointed with the real world and relationships.

The shallowing hypothesis also extends to how we consume information. Our reading comprehension is declining, yet we're overconfident we've understood what we've read. Online reading gets us in the habit of quickly scanning and scrolling, which might be at odds with the careful consideration and rereading often necessary for deep comprehension.

But . . .

I've come to realize it's not the digital world alone driving these and other shifts. Society has changed a lot in the last thirty years. While the prevalence and usage of technology are associated with a decline in empathy, research led by Sara H. Konrath of the University of Michigan at Ann Arbor and published in the *Personality and Social Psychology Review* considered potential factors for the changes in self-reported empathy (the impact of which may be influenced by technology):

- Changes in who our role models are and what they value will impact us. There's been a huge rise in reality TV, which exalts self-centered behavior and narcissism and rewards aggression.
- We increasingly value external achievement at the expense of friendships, investing less emotionally in friends and more in outward measures of success. As a result, we may begin seeing friends as competitors and potential threats. Furthermore, roughly four in ten teens cite "too many obligations" as a reason they don't spend time in person with their friends outside of school, according to a 2018 Teens, Social Media, and Technology survey conducted by the Pew Research Center. Could lei-

sure time spent alone on tech be better spent in person? The same survey shows teens are contending with the negative aspects of social media use—pressure to present themselves in a positive light, bullying, and unnecessary drama in their friendships. And another study found that time spent in person for people ages fifteen to twenty-four has declined significantly, from roughly 150 minutes a day in 2003 to just 40 minutes a day in 2020, an approximately 70 percent decrease.

- We're bombarded by news and media sources with violence, war, terrorism, and other disasters and risk becoming desensitized, with less emotional bandwidth available to experience and express empathy.
- We're reading less—and reading (fiction in particular) is correlated with better perspective-taking, or perceiving a situation from another's point of view.
- As parents, we may not always have the time or patience to validate our children's experiences, giving them the space to express themselves emotionally and to build their perspective-taking abilities.
- We spend less time seeking to understand the thoughts and feelings of others close to us because our attention is divided and because we experience temporary satiety with more superficial relationships, not developing the give-and-take and emotional attunement necessary for deeper relationships.

While this list could seem discouraging, there's an upside: it highlights the idea that empathy isn't a fixed trait, but a fluid one. If it can be decreased, it can be increased—but this needs to be made a practice. The importance of intentionality can't be overstated, because empathy is not only an essential component of interpersonal success but also a marker of a humane society.

This leads to my main point. I believe tech has magnified a fundamental problem: too often, our time and our mind aren't our own.

In small *intentional* doses, social media can give people a sense of connection, meaning, and purpose—as long as their basic needs for connection are being met in the real world. In fact, social media has created learning opportunities and given a platform for underrepresented people and communities to share ideas, experiences, and causes.

The harm really comes when the virtual world:

- Takes us away from face-to-face interaction—or more commonly, if we continue using our devices in each other's presence and our conversations center around what's on them.
- Exposes us to content (comparisons to others or to an unrealistic ideal) or experiences (cyberbullying) that make us feel bad about ourselves. (Interestingly, these comparisons are found to decrease with age, a finding that, not surprisingly, correlates with an increase in happiness as we grow older.)
- Prevents us from doing what's needed to care for ourselves physically and emotionally (specifically sleep, exercise). According to an observational study of almost ten thousand adolescents carried out over three years (2013–15) and reported in *The Lancet Child & Adolescent Health*, very frequent social media use by teen girls (defined as three to five hours of daily use) was linked to depression, with key behavioral habits being implicated in this connection: reduced sleep, less exercise, an increased exposure to harmful content, and cyberbullying.

These needn't be the default destinations on the information superhighway. All of us can ask ourselves these questions:

As a result of my digital habits, am I:

- Sleeping less or has my sleep quality decreased?
- Not seeing my friends in person as much anymore?

- Frequently seeing disturbing, negative content or engaging in negative interactions in person or online?
- Forgoing physical exercise or activity or finding myself more sedentary in general?
- Wasting time on social media instead of accomplishing other tasks I intend to do?

We can't change our genes, but we know lifestyle changes can influence their effects, sometimes dramatically. It's no different with tech. We don't need to begrudge ourselves our tech, but we can be very intentional about its role in our life and can modify or adjust our behavior accordingly. Remember, you have control over your digital intake.

Practical Optimists don't let events (or poor habits) control where and how they direct their attention. We can reclaim the agency of our attention. In this chapter, we'll examine what divides and limits our attention, and I'll share strategies for reclaiming it through the practice of being present.

> **PO Pearls**
> Our time and attention are among our most precious resources. They're not limitless. They must be protected.

Our Monkey Mind

Imagine toddlers in a toy store. They'll point, shout excitedly, and pick up every toy, insisting on taking it home.

This is what your mind does when you are thinking. Our monkey mind, as Buddhists put it, swings between thoughts like a monkey between branches. It grabs notions, spins narratives, assigns judgment: *Wow, cool! Ooh, scary! Ugh, hideous!*

It's natural. We can thank our prefrontal cortex for this novelty bias, which incites us to pay attention to new stimuli. Staying alert to the sudden rustling of leaves kept our prehistoric ancestors alive to kick back by the fire.

Now, in the digital world, where we're exposed 24/7 to the monkey minds of millions, novelty bias drives our impulse to check our email when it pings or the social media we follow for new posts. We seek to close the "curiosity gap" between what's happening out there and our knowledge of it.

We're also hardwired to seek pleasure in the form of dopamine, a brain chemical associated with feelings of pleasure. Evolutionarily speaking, dopamine encourages us to seek positive, rewarding behaviors through a chemical reward akin to the feeling some people experience from drugs.

Throughout history, we've learned to get a little high from numerous fairly innocuous aids like music and books that add great value to our life along with a dab of dopamine. Before cell phones became the villain du jour, there were similar concerns over the destruction of the human mind by radios, television, video games—even books. But the rapid dopamine hits we experience from being constantly connected makes our phones more addictive. The more hits we get, the more it takes to get that high or even to return to baseline happiness.

Choices and decisions also may become more arduous in what's called the paradox of choice. Choices are great—except when we have too many. Many people, when presented with more options, feel overwhelmed and walk away. According to a study reported in the *Harvard Business Review,* a jam stand at a farmers' market equipped with more options to choose from made fewer sales than one that just presented a few (even though the larger selection attracted more passersby). Fatigue and choice overload further erode our decision-making ability.[14]

---

[14] In a form of sensory overload called cyber-based overload, we're flooded with information and communication, leading to an erosion of social responsibility, estrangement from our social and physical surroundings, and less empathy for others. Cyber-based overload can be

So while the modern world offers countless options to fit a variety of lifestyles, it leaves many of us with decision fatigue.

Then there's distraction conflict, which is the difficulty of being present when two things you value vie for attention: the person in front of you versus the notifications and other people's calls/texts on your phone. We simply don't have the mental bandwidth for incoming high-speed internet information and the deeper, slower processing needed to enter into the intimate conversations that allow us to really see one another and forge lasting emotional connections.

Swept into this stimulus tsunami, our monkey mind goes into overdrive to figure everything out. But it can't differentiate between what it needs to act on—an actual problem to be solved—and stuff for the "no big deal" pile. What should be a transient thought or mood can ruin a day, week, or month because our mind doesn't separate what's rational and real and needs our attention from what isn't and doesn't.

Exhausting.

So why does the brain do this? Well, as we've said, our brain's job is to keep us alive, not necessarily to ensure that we're happy. Being happy? That's our job. And that's where being present comes in.

> **PO Pearls**
> To become present is to become aware of the natural tendencies of the mind and use intentionality and awareness to help direct our attention.

---

considered a modern offshoot of the urban overload theory, initially identified by psychologist Stanley Milgram to explain why people in cities are less likely to help a stranger than those in small towns. The theory states that city dwellers are exposed to such a large number of external stimuli on a daily basis that they've adapted to tune out their environment in order to get through the day.

Reclaiming Our Attention:
The Three Cognitive Traps

When our monkey mind prevails, we're rarely living intentionally in the present. We get caught up in neighborhood gossip, next week's meeting, that mistake we made, that thing someone else has or did that we want to have or do, and on and on. There are three main ways we can get stuck in monkey mind. I call them the Three Cognitive Traps:

1. **Trapped in the past:** Rumination and regrets about yesterday.
2. **Trapped in the future:** Worry and what-ifs about tomorrow.
3. **Trapped in comparisons:** Judging our current life in comparison—whether to people we know or to a certain standard we've internalized.

Let's take a look at how these traps commonly manifest.

Trapped in the Past

Symptoms

- Focusing on past events, blaming yourself for what didn't work out, or wishing things could be different than they are right now.
- Holding on to grudges or having difficulty forgiving or letting go.
- Regretting missed opportunities or obsessing about "the one that got away"; believing there was one right person, job, or opportunity that slipped through our fingers.
- Avoiding current and future experiences or being reluctant to try again based on past "failures"; insisting it's too late (despite what others say).

- Believing something needs to change but feeling stuck and un-
sure about how to move forward.

Ruminating about the past can conjure feelings of regret, guilt, and shame that, if left unchecked, can lead to depression. Some say regret sticks with us more than failure, and inaction and indecision also come at a cost. When we cultivate the ability to act mindfully in the present, carefully weighing risks and benefits for each course of action, we're in a better position to do the things now that will head off those regrets down the road.

Trapped in the Future

Symptoms

- Frequent what-if thinking, catastrophizing, jumping to conclusions. Difficulty handling uncertainty, almost preferring a certain, however negative, outcome. Indecision is another form of this trap, as it's essentially fretting over what-ifs.
- Difficulty relaxing, always focusing on what's next, even after a major project/accomplishment. Difficulty celebrating wins—feeling pressure to get back into action immediately.
- Physical symptoms, including a racing heart, a clenched jaw, frequent tension headaches, irritable bowel syndrome, insomnia, restlessness, irritability, and fatigue.

Obsessing about the future keeps your body and mind on high alert, unable to rest in the present or calmly plan for the future.

Trapped in Comparisons

Symptoms

- Frequent self-comparison with others.
- Feelings of not measuring up to what others have, how they look, and/or what they've accomplished, and berating ourselves or feeling extreme pressure to keep up as a result.
- Thinking the good life seems to come easily to others.
- Feelings of being left out, leading to sadness, loneliness, and heightened sensitivity to social consequences (fitting in, being liked, being excluded, etc.).

This is the trap I think the digital world has made us even more vulnerable to. We are social creatures, so our interest in others is normal. Comparing ourselves with others is also normal. As we saw in chapter 5, "Pride," it's one way to realistically assess ourselves or aspire to improve (via role models or mentors). These comparisons can sometimes lead to the healthy pursuit of excellence, but when the standards we hold ourselves to become rigid, arbitrary, and unrelenting, they can be considered maladaptive perfectionism, which puts us under great pressure to measure up and often leads to our feeling bad about ourselves. And when our mood is low, we often reach for things we imagine will make us feel better. For many, that means picking up our cell phone. Most people check their social media within fifteen minutes of awakening, and eight to twelve times an hour throughout the day.

Similar to watching a movie, social media scrolling can offer temporary mental escape. But constant exposure to the carefully curated feeds of others, including images of beautiful bodies, successful careers, and perfect relationships, can lead to feelings of inferiority and can translate to distorted expectations in everything from achievement to romance: *I'm working really hard. How come it's not happening for me?* As mentioned, we may feel disappointed when the people in our lives don't match what we see online. Because trends related to beauty and success are constantly changing online, they can seem unachievable—as does the happiness that's tied to them.

Comparisons may lead to envy. Benign envy can be wanting what someone has. Malicious envy goes a step further: wishing they didn't have it. Thus comparison can rob us of joy in our own life and of our ability to be happy for others in their good fortune or to empathize with them in their misfortune (i.e., schadenfreude).

So while self-comparison may sound relatively benign, it can become all-consuming to the point that our sense of self is under threat. Our attention gets hijacked, lessening the consideration we can give others. The focus becomes how we see ourselves and are seen by others. This can lead to depression and anxiety and problematic technology use. We may post to boost our mood (consciously or not) with positive feedback—but this now triggers envy in someone else, who then posts, and so on. Thus the cycle of envy continues.

A Word to the Wise

FOMO—More Than Fear of Missing Out

It's Friday night and you've decided to stay in after a long workweek. But by nine P.M., you're curious what everyone else is up to. You start scrolling through social media. There's a beachy post from Greece. Rock-climbing adventures. A romantic dinner. A girls' night out. Snuggles with the baby.

Why is my life not nearly as exciting? you wonder.

According to researchers, FOMO, or fear of missing out, is "the uneasy and sometimes all-consuming feeling that you're missing out— that your peers are doing, in the know about, or in possession of more or something better than you." It's thought to be comprised of three key states: irritability, anxiety, and feelings of inadequacy. FOMO is more than just the fear of missing out. It's the fear of being left out. Of not belonging—which, along with competence and autonomy, is one of our three innate needs, according to self-determination theory.

The result can be an unsettled feeling we may try to alleviate by constantly checking and scrolling. Despite knowing it's disruptive, people check social media when they wake in the night or while they are driving, eating, spending time with family, working, or studying. The switching costs—loss of focus interfering with returning to task— are high. FOMO can negatively impact our mood, life satisfaction, sleep, and attention, and erode our sense of self-worth.

I've had patients describe stomachaches, palpitations, dizziness, insomnia, irritability, tension headaches, and more when FOMO overlaps with feelings of rejection and social isolation.

Self-comparison and FOMO have always existed. But FOMO, as we experience it through social media, is self-comparison to the max—a level of comparison that can threaten our sense of self.

Most of us periodically get stuck in these Cognitive Traps. But as we'll learn, they need not be our default destinations. The danger in spending time in them is that they lead to excessive preoccupation with the self, which scientists attribute, at least in part, to the escalating mental health crisis. Some self-referential thinking—how we relate what happens in the outside world to ourselves—can be helpful when it leads to self-reflection. However, excessive self-referential thinking personalizes everything too much and shows up as maladaptive rumination (*What's wrong with me?*), a key feature of pessimism.[15] When we focus

---

[15] Pessimism has real health consequences, and rumination is thought to be associated with the severity and duration of a depressive episode, as well as with risk of relapse. If you are struggling with rumination and want to explore this further, consider speaking with a mental health provider.

on this gap between who we are and who we think we should be, we're no longer experiencing or enjoying the present moment.

Heightened self-focus and rumination can be seen on functional brain imaging as increased brain activity in prefrontal cortex midline structures. All the techniques we'll explore in this chapter quiet these overactive regions of the mind.

Let's start with accepting that we're built to be curious and investigate novelty, and that we are vulnerable to information and decisional overload and often fall into self-comparison sinkholes. Rather than demonize the digital world or chastise ourselves, let's instead use our rational minds to counter the fallacy that we can actually keep up with it all, or even that we *should*.

The rest of this chapter offers a path for getting there along with my Present Prescriptions for working gently with your monkey mind to guide and direct your attention.

Cultivating Present-Moment Awareness

Present-moment awareness (PMA) is a mindful practice that enables us to see and observe reality in the here and now. PMA allows you to pause, creating a space between an outside stimulus and your response. In this neutral, healthy emotional distance lie freedom, choice, power, and attention.

PMA can increase joy, helping you remain in the moment to appreciate the beauty before you, from the infinite hues of a sunset to the hug of a dear friend. Even concentrating on more mundane moments in life—dressing, bathing, sipping coffee, making breakfast—can keep you anchored to the present and clearheaded. Become single-minded in your focus and I promise you'll get more done, with more accuracy and efficiency.

Part of PMA is learning to be kind to your monkey mind. I suggest to patients that they observe their thoughts like baggage on an airport carousel. You notice other people's baggage, but you don't pick it up, examine it, or take it home. You might comment briefly to yourself about it, but you're not invested in it. You let it pass.

Many of my patients notice that after practicing mindfulness, they approach conflict differently, feeling more patient, less stung if things don't work out. PMA gives them the perspective to see that others may be caught in their own distorted thinking or fear.

Books and materials abound on cultivating PMA. Explore, enjoy! I also offer a few tips for using PMA in the prescriptions below.

Savoring the Moments You're In

Picture this: a tall, frosty drink.

Feel this: a cat's plush fur.

Smell this: freshly baked chocolate chip cookies.

We're built with sensory capacities for savoring. We can savor just by *thinking* about things. With comparisons a constant distraction, we may forget to savor the present moment blooming before us. I think of savoring as my joy practice.

You can inject savoring into daily life by deciding to dress up for a weeknight family dinner or taking your office to the beach in the form of a laptop and a small folding table and chair (I've done it!). I used to wear a favorite outfit to my less exciting med school classes and to bring treats for the hospital staff when working overnight shifts over the holidays.

We can also lift our spirits in the here and now by savoring past events and future ones (called savoring reminiscing and savoring anticipating, respectively).

Then there's savoring people: real-life relationships with all their vulnerability, baring of souls, and incomparably good times. There's a time and a place for texting friends: lists, directions, photos. But you can't savor a text the way you savor a loved one's voice. It feels like a balm to your soul because those interactions release a hormonal response that reduces stress and increases positive emotional responses.

A 2010 study published in *Proceedings of the Royal Society B: Biological Sciences* that followed sixty-one preteenage girls seeking contact and reassurance from their mothers in a period of distress found voice-only contact (via phone) reduced their stress levels and facilitated the release of natural bonding and soothing hormones in a way that didn't happen when they received the same sort of feedback from their mothers via text message (when voice-only and text were the only two options provided). There's more on cherishing real-time relationships in chapter 8, "People."

Present Prescriptions

- Deep breathing and body scan exercises are two PMA processes I use with patients. Incredibly relaxing! Try Befriending Your Breath and Befriending Your Body in chapter 3, or experiment with meditation apps to find what works for you. I also like progressive muscle relaxation—tensing and releasing muscle groups one by one—for tension relief. Here again, online resources abound.
- Savor details of your day: The smell of the breeze . . . the softness of your bed at night. Or try slowly savoring a meal. Admire the food on your plate. Take smaller bites and chew slowly, absorbing aromas, textures, flavors. How does this change the experience?

Having a hard time staying present? Try an hour of pure play. Give your attention to something fun and moderately challenging—a board or video game, fun with your kids. Stream or watch a benign distraction (not sensory overload or binge-watching)—a comedy or a relaxing nature documentary, maybe. Or do something healthy requiring no mental energy—a walk, a shower—then something fun and interesting.

Overcoming Mental Fatigue

Remember the example of the jam stand? We can shut down over seemingly simple arrays of choice. With our attention constantly divided across competing demands, we may experience mental fatigue even when our bodies don't feel tired.

Memory, cognition, attention span, learning, creative thinking, altruistic tendencies, and decision-making are compromised when we are sleep-deprived. One study showed sleep deprivation led to decreases in empathy, willingness to understand and listen, generosity, and impulse control. Judges are less likely to grant parole at the end of their day; sleep-deprived doctors are less likely to prescribe pain meds when requested by patients.

When our energy flags, we tend to magnify our losses and feel vulnerable to the self-comparison trap. We can get caught up in worry about the future, feeling daunted by "everything we have to do."

Resources abound on healthy sleep hygiene. Apps with soothing nature sounds, guided meditations, and music can help. And sometimes getting *more* rest isn't what you need, but rather the right kind of rest. It's important to note that going to bed one hour earlier and waking up one hour earlier can reduce depression.

But there's more to rest than sleep. Rest can be divided into three categories, and it's ideal to have a daily dose of each:

1. **Physical rest:** There's *passive rest*—sleep and short power naps as needed—and *active rest* such as stretching or massage.
2. **Mental/sensory rest:** Pause the internal and external noise of life. Try the Present Prescriptions below.
3. **Social-emotional rest:** Find your aloneness-to-togetherness balance (more on this in chapter 8, "People"). Become intentional about friendships: invest in those that energize you; prune out those that drain you. Decide when, how long, and how often you should be with others. This may change as your life and

daily needs change: "Could we meet for a walk when I take the baby out?" "I'm on a crazy deadline, but could we catch up by phone?"

Present Prescriptions

- Designate a home space where you can be there for yourself. It may have a comfortable chair for reading, pillows and a blanket for power naps, candles, a journal, plants, special photos, mementos, or artwork—anything that invites peace and calm for you. For some people, simply a cleared space or an organized area feels therapeutic, inducing productivity, reducing stress, and lifting your mood.
- Have a wind-down ritual, a clear end to your day. Shut down your computer and put away your phone (turn off alerts!); play music or burn some incense.
- Let there be peace in your mornings. Often our days start with serving others or checking social media or messages. If possible, reserve a slice of the newest part of the day for a just-for-you routine. Awaken twenty to thirty minutes before anyone else. Enjoy coffee by a sunny window or outside. Morning sunlight exposure tells the brain to shut off melatonin, making you more awake when you want to be alert. This allows melatonin to then gradually rise in the evening, contributing to nighttime sleep.
- Meditate, read for pleasure, journal, walk.
- Carve out what I call oasis moments—small blocks of time, sometimes as little as five minutes, to recenter in the now, versus what's next. Close your eyes. Take a few deep breaths.
- As mentioned in chapter 5, "Pride," a leisure practice helps ensure that you engage your inner caregiver not just when you can spare the time, but as a worthwhile activity in itself. Leisure time promotes connections with others as well as decreased blood pressure and depression and increased relaxation; it

contributes to your overall happiness. Enjoy a cup of tea, have a healthy lunch solo or with a friend, take time to exercise, re-evaluate your goals and timeline, go to therapy, take a nap, call a friend.

Importantly, the happiness associated with leisure isn't only driven by whether we engage in it, but by whether we find value in it. Folks who don't are more prone to depression, anxiety, and elevated stress levels. Time isn't something that's earned. It's a precious gift as part of being given life.

Releasing Worry and Rumination

As I discussed earlier in this chapter, negative thoughts about the past or future can block us from feeling peace and connection to the present moment. Here are some strategies to release these kinds of nagging thoughts that can consume us:

- Deliberately invite worry at times *you* designate with a worry journal or worry diary. Set a time: get your worries out of your head and onto paper. Thank your worry for sharing. Proceed with your day. (This may help you sleep—many of us are so busy that worry hits when our head hits the pillow.)
- Another worry-buster: Park your obligations in to-do lists, clearing your mind to focus on current tasks.
- Try writing about how you feel about the things in the past that are preoccupying you. What would you do if you could go back and help yourself? How would you have rescued or consoled the younger you? Do this with a therapist if you are struggling with anger or past trauma. If you're writing about the future, what can you do to solve the problem?

- If you are harboring anger at someone for a past circumstance (one that did not create trauma), consider writing a letter to them even if you never send it. Is it worth repairing a relationship if the person is alive? Do you wish to forgive yourself and/or them? (For more on forgiveness, see A Word to the Wise: On Forgiveness in chapter 8.) No one's saying you need to forgive, but experiment with seeing the situation from the other person's point of view. What would make this anger less dominant in your life?
- Every time you think or say "It's too late," list one thing you could do now. (Example: "It's too late for me to _____." Replace with: "I can still _____.")
- Do you have regrets about losses? Try journaling: "This was taken away from me: _____." Then add: "And here is how I'm going to give it to myself now: _____." Many people regret lost time—not spending it with loved ones, cultivating interests, or asking for promotions. Try saying, "That has happened, but now what am I going to do about it?" If nothing can be done, ask: "What's the underlying unmet need I'm trying to meet?"

For some, feeling settled in the present requires accepting the past. Not everything can or should be changed. Sometimes accepting or simply honoring the past—acknowledging what did or didn't happen—helps us gather ourselves, apply balm to our hurt places, and feel more whole again.

The Grounding Effect of Gratitude

In chapters 5 and 6 we discussed how gratitude, coupled with self-compassion, can profoundly boost our sense of self-worth and our confidence. Gratitude also helps us enjoy our life and relationships in the present—we avoid the Cognitive Traps of past and future by loosening the grip of past disappointments, regrets, shame, and failures. It helps us open ourselves to future thinking and possibilities.

Gratitude takes just seconds. Pause. Make a mental note of several things you're grateful for at this moment. Maybe for the few minutes you're finally taking to finish the book on your nightstand, for the many unseen hands that bring food to your table, or for life itself.

Gratitude also provides a major antidote to FOMO: JOMO—the joy of missing out. JOMO is about living your life on your terms, based on your intentional, appreciative choices. It's opting out of the party because you've decided what's best for you is a night recharging at home, investing in your relationship with your significant other or a friend, or just doing nothing. JOMO and gratitude allow us to take back our attention and honor our life choices. When we're busy relishing our own present, we don't have time to compare it with other people's.

Instead of sinking into a funk about a friend who's doing the fun stuff you stopped doing since starting your new job (*I used to be more carefree. Now I'm a drudge*), let gratitude moderate your black-and-white thinking: *I'm in a different life phase right now. Taking this job was my choice. I'm grateful for this amazing opportunity that I worked hard for.* You might even feel grateful for your friend's example: *No one's stopping me from making some changes. I can start by finding an hour a week for fun time.*

Remember, too, you're likely only getting a well-curated piece of that person's story. They've probably faced challenge, even heartbreak. Grace lets you be glad for their good day.

In relationships, saying "I'm grateful for you" extends grace. Or instead of falling into a self-comparison trap over someone's dream vacation, destination wedding, work win, or kid's big milestone, cheer for them with a comment, text, email, call, or (handwritten!) note. Expressing gratitude to an acquaintance is more likely to turn them into a friend.

In communication, you can extend grace through mutual disclosure and deep listening, offering the gift of your complete presence. In compassionate listening, as Thích Nhất Hanh puts it, "You listen with only one purpose: [to] help [a person] to empty [their] heart."

Present Prescriptions

- Create a gratitude mantra: "I'm grateful for what I've been able to accomplish. I'm grateful for opportunities and support provided to me. I'm grateful for the health that I do have."
- Express your gratitude to others in writing or verbally.
- Did someone help you today? Comfort you? Remind yourself of kindnesses.
- Dealing with a challenge? Write a supportive note to yourself. One study showed that parents who did a fifteen-minute self-compassion writing exercise felt less parent guilt and were better able to handle parenting challenges. Allow yourself the same compassion for your journey, obstacles, limitations, and celebrations of your wins and accomplishments as you would a friend.

Finding Your Flow

In chapter 2, we discussed flow—or what many of us think of as being in the zone—a totally immersive mix of challenge, fun, interest, and meaning. Flow experiences plunge us into the present moment so deeply, we lose track of time—a lessened sense of self that may come from brain changes perhaps propelled by norepinephrine, while dopamine and serotonin boost pleasure and tamp down fatigue. (Engaging in flow is a problem only if you're doing it as a way to avoid other important present-moment obligations, but for the most part, flow is an antidote to many of the hijackers of attention.)

Associated with decreased self-focus and worry, flow can help quiet turbulent emotions about past, present, or future (as brain scans confirm). It's a far more productive, healthy coping mechanism than endless scrolling.

Peak flow usually comes from activities of high interest to you, in which you experience some degree of competence and some degree of challenge, but not enough to produce stress. They unite purpose, play, and the present moment in a potent brew. Result: joy.

If you are having difficulty finding the activities that move you into a flow state, consider ways you once enjoyed spending your time that may have fallen by the wayside as you juggled other demands in life. Almost every person I know can find at least one activity where they feel as if they lose track of time because they are so immersed. For me, it was doing the research for and writing this book, or when I'm deeply engaged in teaching medical students, or giving talks on things I'm passionate about. For my husband, it's when he is skiing with our kids. He and they encourage one another to build their skills so they can tackle the more challenging courses—the black diamonds and moguls, which require a unique combination of focus, relaxation, and mastery. For one of my patients, it's dancing salsa to Marc Anthony's music; for another it's cooking Sunday dinner. My mother's surgeon's office was full of sculptures and paintings; that was how he experienced flow when he was outside the OR. For one fifty-five-year-old patient of mine who worked long hours in a stressful investment banking job, I suggested he connect with something that brought him great joy. He decided to dust off his guitar—a remnant of his college rock-and-roll-band days. The bonus: he got to perform onstage with his sixteen-year-old son, a whiz at the drums, in his son's band. Another patient, deciding he didn't want to be consumed by or limited by symptoms of social anxiety, agoraphobia, depression, and OCD, got back into cycling cross-country with a group and tours, eventually winning races and triathlons.

We all have a place where we feel in the zone. Reconnecting with these activities helps us feel fully connected to the present again and can drown out the noise—whatever that means for you.

It could also be time to find a new hobby or challenge. If you are feeling curious about your friends' hobbies or sports fun, the classes they're taking, or their accomplishments, it could be a sign that you've been putting something on the back burner for too long. Lean into those curiosities—you may just find a new source of fulfillment and flow time.

Present Prescriptions

- Try out hobbies or experiences that you've been curious about or return to pursuits that once fulfilled you from the inside out.
- Schedule flow time. Try for a minimum of fifteen minutes. Tell your family you'll be MIA. Phones and computers: out of sight/earshot. Use this time to engage in or explore possible flow activities.

Connecting to Nature and Awe

Scientists are studying nature relatedness—how connected we feel to nature—on three levels: cognitively (whether we see nature as part of our identity and health and see value in taking care of it), emotionally (whether it elicits positive emotions), and experientially (whether we seek it out or have comfort and familiarity with it). But one thing is clear: The more connected we feel to nature, the greater our positive emotions, life satisfaction, and vitality, as well as our autonomy, personal growth, and sense of purpose in life. To me, that makes spending time in nature a "one-stop shopping" proposition. Since the United Nations predicts that 68 percent of the world's population will be living in urban environments by 2050, we need to be intentional about seeking out (and taking care of) nature.

But the word *nature* here is really a catch-all term for anything that induces awe. Awe allows us to transcend the mundane, tolerate the unbearable, and sometimes even confront difficult truths when we're ready. Awe experiences allow us to transcend the limits imposed by our negative self-talk, preconceived notions, and judgments shaped by past experiences. It's almost as if there's a momentary suspension of thought where only the present is unfolding. In that precious moment, there is no monkey mind—a halt to judgment, comparison, regret, future thinking, and sometimes even words—because there are no other experiences our mind can compare it to.

Anything that gets us out of the rumination in our head is an opportunity for present-moment wonder. Maybe you have to get up before dawn to catch your morning train—but how amazing, the sunrises you see; what a feat of genius, the bridge you cross.

Present Prescriptions

- Sit outside for fifteen minutes. Close your eyes. Tune into the sounds around you.
- Try activities like hiking, gardening, mountain biking, walking, swimming, stargazing, or camping.
- Seek out "awe-some" new environments or experiences. They might be just a short drive, commute, or walk away. Check out architecture, a park, an art gallery, a forest, a historic site, a museum. Take in some music or dance.

Taking Back Your Time

Only you can change how your time on earth unfolds.

It may start with letting go of some things. I never want to relinquish anything that's important to me. But while I was writing this book, many social events went by the wayside. I had to give myself permission for the balance of my activities to be flexible so that I could be more effective. It's important to keep a "for now" mindset when you are not able to keep up with obligations as you might like to—e.g., *I don't have time to keep up with friends the way I'd like to right now.* This removes the pessimistic assumption that what's happening is permanent and will continue for the foreseeable future.

If you are feeling overwhelmed, consider the top three things that you need to prioritize and dedicate your time to those tasks. If you can, edit out tasks that drag you down; focus on the tasks that lift you up, adding meaning and purpose. This may require asking for help and support, maybe from your partner, your boss, or coworkers; engaging helpers or bartering tasks with a friend; or saying, "I am letting go of this task for now." If these people support you in any way—by helping you carry out important tasks related to your meaning and purpose, or by being there to cheer you on—let's call them "purpose partners" (see chapter 2, "Purpose").

Present Prescription

- Rushing from task to task? Appreciate the positive effects of each task: *Dishes washed. Now I can enjoy seeing a clean sink tomorrow morning. Got that tough email sent. Good going. It was nice to run errands today with my daughter. We got to talk and got the errands done.* This heightens your present-minded awareness and sense of purpose.

I'd love to tell you that after my dinner in João's café, I never again felt internal tug-of-war between being fully present to the world in front of me and the quick dopamine hits of social media. But that's not true. Technology has allowed me to connect with others in a way that wasn't possible in previous generations. I'm not exempt from occasionally being called out—"Mom, you're on your phone *again*?"—as I respond to messages from patients, friends, followers, and the media.

At least for now, social media and a blurry work-life balance are here to stay, certainly for me; the same is probably true for many of us. It's how we get news, information, keep up with loved ones, work, and sometimes play. So let's navigate it in the healthiest way possible. For me, that means being intentional about my tech time. I'm mindful, too, of the material I gravitate to online, and I find that FOMO is kept at bay when I make time to keep my life, mind, body, and connections enriched, nurtured, and active.

Not all social media use leads to lower well-being. There's less negative impact on social well-being when we're actively engaged versus passively scrolling. For example, use social media to message and keep up with people, writing them directly and engaging with them.

Regarding posting sensitive information about yourself, be aware you're leaving a digital trail; be intentional about what you decide to share. To a patient struggling with that, I'd suggest they consider: *What's my aim or goal? Upside and downside? Can I live with the downside?* Suppose the goal is: "I want to be open so I can get support." If so, are you really getting support? Are there ways to get support other than sharing on social media?

Present Prescriptions

- *Take Back Your Tech: Level 1*
  - Track your screen time. Many devices have preprogrammed time limits. Apps can block websites and app usage or let you set an alarm when scrolling.
  - Bring present-mindedness to scrolling. Note what you use social media for (info/interests? following friends? news? inspiration?) and supplement those areas with offline activities.
  - Establish sacred times and spaces: tech-free times and zones during meals and before/during sleep time.
  - Start and end your day with meditation instead of scrolling.

- *Take Back Your Tech: Level 2*
  - Take a timed social media break once or twice daily. I sometimes don't post on weekends. It removes the urge to check: *Who liked/commented?* And: [crickets] . . . *No one likes me.*
  - Delete apps you don't regularly use.
  - Those newsletters and solicitations you delete daily? Unsubscribe.
- *Take Back Your Tech: Level 3*
  - Become present to how you feel after scrolling social media. Inspired? More anxious? Aimless? Jealous? This can be a catalyst for changing unhealthy behaviors.
  - See with your eyes, not your phone: Resist taking photos. Notice the people, sights, smells, and tactile sensations around you. Compile a mental album of vivid present-moment experiences.
- *Take Back Your Tech: Level 4*
  - When with friends, put your phone away. (If you feel you must check your phone in case someone really needs to reach you, let your friends know you need to do that at selected times, but try to keep the intervals brief.)
  - Read with intention and attention, adding printed material and books to the mix. Our brain often assumes we can skim an online resource quickly and overestimates its comprehension of what it's just read. Thus our understanding is often compromised. Encourage your brain to focus and allocate more mental resources by deliberately slowing down, recognizing a given task as important. Shut off notifications (messages, updates, alerts). Decrease other distractions, pick a quiet space, and take notes—on-screen or on paper—jotting down key words and summaries, as if trying to explain it to someone else in simple language.

- Since our brain associates online materials with scrolling, reading a book cues our brain to slow down, absorb, and reread. Visual cues of where key points appeared on the page help anchor and reinforce them. A meta-analysis of studies involving over 170,000 participants titled "Don't Throw Away Your Printed Books" shows that printed material has advantages over digital texts in reading comprehension. Skimming and scanning happen because we're used to quick rewards—such as the dopamine hits of likes online. Balance that by enjoying the slow simmer of reading printed material.
- On vacation or holidays, take social media time off. Post afterward, if you choose.
- Ask yourself: *Does my technology use align with a life purpose for me (e.g., building my career, helping others, educating myself, actively strengthening my friendships)? How often am I using it purely for distraction? Is it landing me in FOMO or unfair comparisons?*

PO Pearls

May your past be at peace, your present productive and joyful, and your future worry-free.

Star Light, Star Bright

When we see the stars at night, their light feels immediate. Yet we know there's a delay between the moment those wavelengths begin and the moment they hit our retina. According to NASA, the light of our sun—the star closest to us, at about 93 million miles away—takes about 8.3 minutes to reach us. We always see the sun as it was about 8.3 minutes ago. The next closest star to Earth is over four light-years away. That starlight we see is the light it emitted years ago.

So maybe it's impossible to live literally in the moment. But this is one of those things where the reward is in the effort, as many spiritual traditions understood. In ancient Greece, the Stoics wrote about the practice of attention (*prosoché*) as the cornerstone of a good spiritual life. At the beginning of this chapter, there's a quote from French philosopher, mystic, and political activist Simone Weil positing the pure gift we give when we bestow our attention. The practice of being present is precisely that: a practice. How you do it will vary day to day, because the stream of time and life is ever-changing. That's the beautiful possibility of the present. Like starlight, it streams toward us. We meet it somewhere on the way. What happens at the moment of contact . . . is up to us.

To view the scientific references cited in this chapter,
please visit doctorsuevarma.com/book.

CHAPTER 8

People

Creating Nourishing Relationships

*If you want to go fast, go alone. If you want to go far,
go together.*

—AFRICAN PROVERB

*There is a brief discussion of suicide in this section; however, the larger
themes focus on developing and maintaining healthy relationships. You can
skip ahead if the topic feels too triggering or stick around longer if you feel
up to it. And please discuss with a trained mental health therapist any signs
and symptoms of depression or suicidal ideation.*

In her early sixties and an accomplished, recently retired New York
ad exec, marathoner, mother, and grandmother, Liz[16] was the sort of

---

[16] What you are learning about Liz is a condensed version of her story. I am of necessity selecting aspects of her case and treatment relevant to the points in this chapter, which focuses
on the importance of relationships and how our relationships are informed by our early childhood experiences and loneliness. Each individual's journey is unique. It's not my intention to

person you look at and think has it all together. And she'd jumped off a bridge.

She survived, but she had serious physical injuries and a long road ahead for recovery. She'd been transferred to the psychiatric ward after multiple surgeries and nights in the ICU.

"They're trying to put me together again," she quipped from her wheelchair. It was my first glimpse of Liz's New York sense of humor—which I was happy to see she still had.

While Liz had suffered severe depressive episodes for thirty-plus years, this was the first time she'd tried to end her life. "I didn't want to be a burden to anyone anymore," she said.

I could see many of Liz's physical wounds. And from her chart, I learned about her history of chronic depression and recent surgeries. But I was most struck by something no cast, bandage, visible scar, or medical chart would reveal: the wounds of loneliness. I was reminded of the time I spent working in a hospital in India, where family members were always at patients' bedsides. The idea was that we could cure physical illnesses with medicine—but the treatment for despair and loneliness was love, support, concern, and compassion from others. And ideally, people received both.

After Liz's divorce, her kids lived with their father. "I didn't know how to be good at much besides my job. I was also battling my depression—my chart's like a psychopharmacology textbook."

Liz hadn't seen her kids or grandkids in "a while. They're busy. I don't want to burden them." Again, that word *burden*. "No one needs me anymore," she stated. "I don't see a point to living."

When I spoke with Liz's sons and their partners, who were traveling to her bedside from around the country, their love seemed far more palpable than Liz perceived it: "I think they just feel sorry for me." Did

suggest or attempt to present a comprehensive discussion of suicide, its risk factors, or available mental health treatments (nor to suggest that they are widely available to all individuals, given the disparities in healthcare).

Liz have a problem perceiving support? How did that play into every-thing she was contending with now?

––––––

A good friend[17] gives you permission to be yourself. Are your friend-ships what you want them to be? Whether your social life needs a lift or a lifeline, my aim is to help you approach friendships as Practical Optimists do: with resourcefulness and intention.

A thriving "people practice," as I call it, is a virtuous cycle: a posi-tive mindset fosters positive actions, and vice versa. Our relation-ship mindset—our positive or negative expectations—can actually shape how people treat us by shaping how we behave toward others. A study of classmates' perceptions of their classroom social environ-ment (chilly or welcoming?) showed their perception of the social en-vironment depended mostly on their behaviors within it. Those who engaged with others regarded it as friendly. Those who kept to them-selves saw it as unwelcoming. It's what's known as the acceptance prophecy.

If you can't see yourself clearly, you'll likely have a distorted view of how others see you, affecting your relationship behaviors. It's said the best way to have friends is to be one. That includes befriending yourself, too.

This chapter shares ways to forge nourishing relationships with others and with yourself. I'll troubleshoot the thought distortions that commonly undermine friendships. Although friendships require effort—indeed, research shows that people who think their friend-ships don't require work are less likely to have successful ones—they needn't be complicated. I'll help you understand your relationship

––––––

[17] In this chapter, *friends* refers to any or all of your interpersonal connections—be they family, love relationships, work, community, or other social connections.

history and style, the various types of friendships, and steps you can take to strengthen your relationships and create new ones.

Lonely Planet?

Social isolation has been used as a form of torture throughout human history for good reason. Social connection is a basic human need—one we must prioritize, like food, shelter, and rest. So statistics like these are worrisome:

- A survey released in January 2020 by insurance provider Cigna of over ten thousand people ages eighteen and up throughout the United States revealed that 61 percent of Americans are lonely. (This was *before* a global pandemic forced much of the population into prolonged isolation.) Post-pandemic data published by Cigna show that high rates of loneliness remain consistent. A 2022 study revealed that 58 percent of adults reported feeling lonely, with younger adults (twice as many individuals in the eighteen to thirty-four bracket felt "left out"), parents (especially mothers), lower-income people, and underrepresented racial groups experiencing some of the highest rates of loneliness. While social isolation was once associated with older adults, in 2021, young adults were reporting rates of loneliness twice that of adults over the age of sixty-five.
- In 2021, an ongoing social survey by the Survey Center on American Life showed the number of Americans' close friends has declined substantially. Thirty years ago, 33 percent of Americans could identify ten or more close friends, not counting family members. Today, it's just 13 percent. Fewer than half surveyed said they had a best friend.
- The same report shows people are talking to and relying upon their friends less often for personal support—even more so for

men: "Four in 10 (41 percent [of]) women report having received emotional support from a friend within the past week,
compared to 21 percent of men."

Our friendships are getting put on the back burner for myriad
reasons: longer work hours; an emphasis on productivity, status, and
achievement; longer commutes; remote work; parents spending more
time with children than in previous generations; reduced involvement
with places of worship and less civic engagement; social media use—
even the shift to online shopping. Many of us have moved away from
our hometowns and thus may have lost many of the "soft tissue connections" that extended family, classmates, and hometown neighbors
and community members once provided.

Loneliness is more than a few too many nights alone bingeing
Netflix. It's a state of longing for meaningful connection. Loneliness
has nothing to do with our number of social contacts, but with their
quality. We can have few social contacts yet be satisfied with their quality or can be surrounded by acquaintances yet feel no true connection. As the character of Lance Clayton, played by comedian Robin
Williams, says in the film *World's Greatest Dad*: "I used to think the
worst thing in life was to end up all alone. It's not. The worst thing in
life is to end up with people who make you feel all alone."

I believe many people aren't totally satisfied with their relationships but don't consider that loneliness—although it is. Amanda (whom
you will meet on page 251) loved her friends but felt they weren't tuned
into her—something many of us experience.

Loneliness can be insidious. If you'd asked Liz during her one-
hundred-hour workweeks if she was lonely, she'd have rattled off
business luncheons and charity galas to prove she wasn't. Liz was
surrounded by people but was lonely, as she realized when those connections evaporated when she retired—a danger in a culture that re-
veres professional accomplishment and tangible displays of success.

The health consequences of loneliness are striking. Loneliness alters gene expression and causes inflammation—which, when chronic, can impact everything from heart health[18] to cognitive decline, increasing the risk for cancer, stroke, and mental health disorders, and even accelerating aging. Loneliness changes how our brain functions. Acute social isolation creates a unique neural signature in the brain that isn't that far off from depression. The stress response associated with loneliness can make us more likely to perceive danger in social situations, impairing the very skills needed to pull ourselves out of isolation.

Relationships provide a buffer against stress, illness, and depression. And for those like Liz who might be predisposed to loneliness and depression because of biological and environmental factors, I believe an intentional relationship practice can be an important part of a thorough and comprehensive treatment program. For Liz, that included medication and psychotherapy, along with various group therapies offered in the inpatient unit. Importantly, Liz told me she felt committed to getting better.

Social connection lowers the risk of premature death by half. In a study of midlife women, those in highly satisfying marriages and marital-type relationships had a lower risk for cardiovascular disease than those in less satisfying marriages. But you don't have to be married to your support system. Scientists now suspect that hanging out with our friends can help mitigate the physical manifestations of stress. Reaching out to friends in times of stress induces a tend-and-befriend response that increases oxytocin and endorphins and can help reduce our stress.

Social support may help lower cholesterol, boost our immune

---

[18] In a 2016 meta-analysis of twenty-three studies involving 181,000 adults, published in the journal *Heart*, lack of social and emotional support was associated with a 29 percent increase in heart attack risk and a 32 percent increased likelihood for stroke. The study found cardiovascular risk associated with loneliness rivaled that of smoking and obesity. According to a meta-analysis published in *Perspectives on Psychological Science* in 2015, loneliness impacted our mortality—specifically the increased likelihood of death was 26 percent for reported loneliness, 29 percent for social isolation, and 32 percent for living alone.

system, hasten postsurgical wound healing, and decrease cortisol levels. Scientific literature on the benefits of social support abounds across all specialties in medicine. And it's not just close social ties in our personal life that provide benefits. Having close social ties in the workplace positively influences employee engagement, creativity, productivity, and retention rates; maximizes employee health; and minimizes workplace accidents as well as sick days due to stress, illness, and/or workplace injury. Not having peer support in the workplace even impacts mortality rates. The benefits of social support also extend to communities, boosting their ability to prepare for and recover from natural disasters more quickly.

And, well, chronic conflict has the opposite effect. Studies have linked disappointing or negative interactions with family and friends with poorer physical and mental health. One intriguing line of research has found signs of reduced immunity in couples during especially hostile marital spats. Broken heart syndrome is a real thing. People can develop an arrhythmia, or irregular heartbeat, and vasospasm as a result of major or chronic stress in a relationship. Some even experience heart attacks.

Research suggests that four to five close relationships, in a mix of family and friends, may be the loneliness-reduction sweet spot—but others say we should count our blessings to have one or two people we feel get us. I think even one close confidant can go a long way. While the internet provides instant access to all sorts of people, evidence is mixed regarding whether digital-only relationships are as beneficial as real-life connections.

Our best defense against loneliness is to view it as an internal cue steering us toward our need for belonging. Although some people have a genetic predisposition to loneliness,[19] genes don't seal our fate. As

---

[19] One of the first genome-wide association studies of loneliness, involving more than ten thousand people and published in the journal *Neuropsychopharmacology*, showed that while no one gene was responsible, loneliness may be a heritable trait.

you'll see, Liz likely had a genetic predisposition to loneliness coupled with ongoing severe depression, but with time, self-compassion, and continued mental health treatment, she was able to put into practice new thought patterns and habits and to flip her social script—because environment and effort play a much larger role in how those genes are expressed than many of us might think.[20]

If our perceptions and actions mainly shape our relationships, what shapes those? It starts with our first lessons in connection.

Attachment: Our Earliest Relationships

When we're born, the human brain is ready to go—teeming with 100 billion neurons, primed to learn. But even in the womb, we're learning. Our early caregivers are so crucial for our physical and emotional survival that the baby starts learning about its mother in utero—experiencing sound and touch and detecting odors and tastes in the amniotic fluid—and shows a natural preference immediately after birth for the mother's smell and taste, voice and touch. Thus begins the imprinting that will continue, in a process called attachment, throughout our early years.

Our ability to readily bond with others varies depending on our attachment style, which is formed in early childhood. Attachment is considered an instinctual need, born of our biological need for survival and our psychological need for security. British psychiatrist and psychoanalyst John Bowlby described attachment as the lasting psychological connectedness between humans, which sets the tone for everything from our capacity for emotional regulation and self-soothing as adults to how we interact and whether we're secure enough to form

---

[20] If you are experiencing loneliness accompanied by depressive symptoms or feelings of helplessness and hopelessness, please talk to a trained mental health professional.

trusting bonds, seek comfort and help from others, and explore. Secure attachments foster a healthy balance between valuing ourselves and valuing others—Eric Berne's "I'm okay, you're okay" equilibrium discussed in chapter 5, "Pride."

How well (or poorly) caregivers respond to our needs as infants ultimately determines our attachment style. During the 1970s, psychologist Mary Ainsworth, PhD, and others studied the mother-infant relationship, leading to the classification of key attachment styles: secure and insecure. When warm, caring nurturing is absent or inconsistent, the result can be insecure attachment—avoidant or anxious.[21] Both can undermine relationships if we aren't aware.

Avoidant Attachment Style

When children's feelings are invalidated and they aren't shown empathy, they internalize the message that there is no room for their feelings. As adults, they might be less emotionally attuned to others and themselves. They may erect walls, mistrust others, attempt to become overly self-reliant, appear aloof, prematurely end relationships, and have low tolerance for others' emotional displays.

An overreliance on oneself can sometimes have serious consequences. In general, clinicians believe suicide rates have risen due to a societal expectation in the United States that we should be self-reliant, including when we are struggling with mental health, leading people to avoid seeking professional help: *I should be able to figure this out by myself.* (I told you those *shoulds* were dangerous!).

In general, a tendency not to seek help in interpersonal relationships may be especially pronounced in people with avoidant attachment style. They may also be less able to recognize and respond to needs for help from others, unless those individuals explicitly ask for it.

---

[21] Another type added later, known as disorganized, is in some ways a combination of these, but we'll focus on anxious and avoidant.

Those with avoidant attachment style may appear cool and collected, but their heart rate and blood pressure are elevated when these are measured during tough times, revealing stress they aren't consciously aware of. This wears the mind and body down. I've seen patients collapse under the weight of suppressed emotions. I always say if you're suppressing emotions in one place, they're coming out in another, in the form of (take your pick) upset bowels, headache, skin breakouts, and more. Insecure attachment is associated with higher rates of cardiovascular disease, pain, fatigue, anxiety, and depression.

Liz had been subjected to the harsh, controlling, cold, overly strict and critical parenting that can foster an avoidant attachment style. A family history of chronic anxiety and likely untreated mental illness contributed to her painful home life. Liz described her mother as having a lot of anxiety in interpersonal relationships and being fearful of rejection, while her father avoided conflict and to some degree closeness in relationships in general. Given her family history, Liz perhaps already had a genetic vulnerability to depression and loneliness. The science of epigenetics now reveals that the chronic stress of extremely punitive childhood environments can cause changes in how our genes ultimately get expressed and is associated with depression later on (not to mention that chronic stress in childhood can be associated with accelerated brain aging). Indeed, our parents' epigenetic life changes from adverse conditions can get passed on to us.

From her earliest days, Liz was taught that her value was in her usefulness to others and in the achievement of outward measures of success; that having emotions, seeking help, or reaching out signaled weakness. Liz perceived that she was alone in the world, not well-liked, a burden, and weak if she showed vulnerability.

In adulthood, Liz poured her energy into professional achievement and joining charity boards. Her self-protective wall made her seem aloof, but inside, she was perfectionistic, self-critical, distressed, and isolated despite her many activities. If Liz thought she'd received a slight at work, she'd berate herself (she'd internalized her parents' voice) and double down on work, further isolating herself. She recip-rocated when her sons reached out, but rarely initiated contact. Her attempted suicide shocked the family. Liz was accomplished and re-spected, had many interests, and was loved by her children—but her genes, chronic depression, and early life adversity blinded her to these positives.

Anxious Attachment Style

In contrast, someone with an anxious attachment style—thought to be a result of inconsistent nurturing—tends to crave connection, have difficulty tolerating the natural ebbs and flows of relationships, and become extremely anxious and hypervigilant when that connection is perceived to be threatened or in the face of perceived rejection. Similar to Sam, Nicole, Sejal, and Lina, whom you met in previous chapters, they work hard to please others, often at the expense of their own well-being, becoming disheartened or frustrated if they don't get the level of approval, reassurance, or praise they need and living in fear of rejection or of severing of ties. They may be plagued by self-doubt, afraid to seek help at work or preoccupied with interpersonal dynam-ics, and hypervigilant for clues that "prove" their fear that a relation-ship or job will end. Sometimes their fear becomes a self-fulfilling prophecy because their behavior (in extreme cases) alienates others.

Secure Attachment Style

If I had to sum up insecure attachment styles, I'd say it's like hav-ing one arm that's overdeveloped or overactive and one that's under-developed or underactive. In avoidant attachment, self-reliance is overdeveloped (hypertrophied) and help-seeking is underdeveloped/ underactive. It may lead to ending relationships prematurely or abruptly. However, when their partners show appreciation, this can have great benefits to individuals with avoidant attachment style, showing them they're cared for and enhancing their willingness and commitment to reciprocate. In anxious attachment, there's an over-developed threat system (a heightened sensitivity to perceived loss, abandonment, rejection, or distance in a relationship) and an internal self-soothe system that may be underactivated or underdeveloped. It may lead to staying in or holding on to friendships too long (even unhealthy ones). In both styles, low self-compassion translates to withdrawing or being too pushy socially. But with time, intention, and help, whatever our style, we can strengthen and gradually practice tapping into our inner caregiving strategies, while also seeking to bring emotional processing and regulation to our relationships with others.

Ideally, as we see in secure attachment, we feel we can rely on others and can reach out to receive (and offer) help, but we can also self-soothe and rely on ourselves appropriately, allowing the same space to others. Perhaps thanks to more consistent comforting from caregivers, people with more secure attachments demonstrate greater self-compassion, enjoy a healthy pride, and are able to effectively regulate their emotions: *I have realistic, positive regard for myself and work on being attuned to and addressing my feelings.* They're able to trust their instincts when they aren't treated well, ask for what they deserve, and move on when necessary. They expect partners to be supportive and tend to see the best in people: *I believe I matter to you and that you have positive regard for me. I know I can ask for help and rely on you in moments of need, as you can with me.* This positive expectation enhances how they support others—*I have positive regard for you*—and tends to bring out the best in others.

The numerous health benefits associated with secure attachments include less pain, fatigue, anxiety, depression, and irritability; improved energy and ability to make and maintain healthy habits; and an avoidance of the maladies of loneliness. Even some employers are starting to pay attention to their employees' attachment style and how it plays out in the workplace in an effort to maximize trust, collaboration, and communication (and fun!).

Exercise: Learning About Your Attachment Style

The thought prompts below may feel like big questions and can stir strong emotions. Feel free to skip questions that feel overwhelming. But if something resonates with you, take time to ponder. We may not personally experience trouble with something but realize it's an issue because others have brought it up.

Your mix of answers may help indicate which circumstances tend to trigger or elicit certain thoughts, emotions, and behaviors in you. No one answer puts you in one category or the other. You may feel one way at work and another with friends—some variation is normal. What matters is your overall response pattern. This exercise is meant just to help you gain clarity regarding your general tendencies. You may wish to explore this more deeply with a trusted source or a trained mental health professional.

Therapy might be helpful to address the questions, concerns, and emotions that come up.

Each set of questions below is organized according to the overactive/underactive dynamics discussed earlier:

Overactive Self-Reliance

1. Generally, in most relationships, do you prefer space over togetherness?
2. In difficult or stressful times, do you tend to rely almost exclusively on yourself and take pride in that?
3. Do you find you frequently rely on yourself because you perceive that others can't be relied upon or depended upon?
4. Do you notice you don't react strongly to what others might consider a stressful situation? Or do others describe you as "cool as a cucumber" or say that you "underreact" to what they might consider stressful events?

5. Do you sometimes wonder what all the fuss about friendships is all about, since you've got you to turn to?

Underactive Help-Seeking/Help-Giving

1. Do you avoid opening up to others about your feelings?
2. Do you avoid confrontations or situations that would stir up feelings, and/or prefer sticking to facts?
3. Do you keep people at arm's length (or have others observed this trait in you), or do you lose interest when they start moving closer—either as friends or in a romantic relationship?
4. Do you avoid asking for help, thinking others won't help or that you don't want to burden them?
5. Have others expressed disappointment/dissatisfaction in your ability to show appreciation and affection, provide emotional comfort, and/or do you find it difficult to comfort/console others or tell them what they mean to you?

Underactive Self-Soothing

1. Do you crave togetherness, afraid you couldn't manage alone?
2. Do you find yourself constantly seeking attention/praise/reassurance from close others, despite knowing you're loved or positively regarded in the relationship?
3. Do you engage in frequent people-pleasing and approval-seeking behaviors, even to the point of denying your boundaries, or do you turn to many people for help, soothing, and advice when in distress?
4. Do you frequently feel disappointed by others' attempts to soothe you or feel your attempts to soothe yourself are inadequate?
5. Do you have a hard time comforting yourself when slighted or rejected?

Overactive Threat System

1. In general, do you tend to assume the worst in relationships?
   For example, are you often afraid a relationship is ending? Do
   you ruminate about others (including friends) not liking you, or
   fear something's wrong when you don't immediately hear back
   from someone?
2. Are you (secretly) afraid your partner will find someone better?
3. When others don't agree with you, do you think they dislike you?
4. Could your relationships be categorized as tumultuous or un-
   stable?
5. Are you very impacted by/sensitive to others' moods and do you
   try hard to keep everyone happy?

Many of us struggle if our early caregivers' nurturing was hit-or-miss
or downright neglectful or harsh. Maybe despite their best intentions
and efforts, what the caregivers provided simply didn't fit our needs.
Maybe their own limitations prevented them from providing for our
needs.

If you didn't have a secure attachment, please know that your early
life is not a life sentence. While there's a strong neurobiological basis
of attachment style shaped by early environment, it's not irrevocable.
Your marvelous adult brain is sophisticated, and you're in charge of
shaping it. It takes insight and persistence, but you now sit in the
driver's seat and can choose to steer yourself along a different road.
Just as Practical Optimism is within reach of people who might not
have been born with optimism or had it modeled in their relationships, so PO can help us take steps to understand our attachment
tendencies and become aware of potentially counterproductive or maladaptive behavioral patterns.

The Four Types of Friendships

We don't need lots of great friends; just a few good ones we're in touch with regularly. Awareness of the different types of friendships can help us cultivate them more intentionally.

1. *Deep friendships:* All the clichés apply: they're there for you, they have your back, and they get you. You've seen each other through thick and thin. You cheer each other's successes and are lovingly candid about foibles and struggles.

   Positives: You know you're loved for who you are, not for what you have, what you've accomplished, or what you can do for them. You're in each other's lives because you deeply care about each other.

   Connecting Tips: Even the closest friendships may fade without the intimacy-building sharing of life's ups and downs. Sure, text fun stuff and photos—but be conscientious about contact, preferably with regular face-to-face and voice connection.

2. *Meaningful friendships:* These friendships vibrantly combine shared experience and moderate emotional closeness. Maybe you're both navigating life situations (e.g., starting businesses, raising kids, going to school, or newly single/retired).

   Positives: You make each other's life better—tangibly with information and experience; intangibly through listening and emotional responsiveness.

   Connecting Tips: Shared activity and talk time may lead to deep friendship. Other connections are just right as they are or naturally fade when your lives mesh less.

3. *Interest/activity/professional partners:* Examples: your favorite running mate, folks you chat with at board meetings, trusty project partners at work, business sounding boards.

Positives: You don't exchange deep secrets, but you enjoy each other's company. You make each other's immediate experience significantly better.

Connecting Tips: This group can incubate meaningful friendships as trust builds through regular interaction, progressing together toward goals, and the sharing of resources. Deepen if you feel like it: "Hey, want to grab coffee/lunch sometime?" If these friendships unite multiple contexts in your life—your yoga buddy is also a parent at your kid's school; your running partner is also a coworker—it may help deepen the connection, but if not, that's fine, too.

4. *Micro-connections:* I use this term to describe small but emotionally satisfying interactions (*micro-moments,* as researcher, professor, and author Barbara Fredrickson, PhD, terms them), available in our everyday activities—maybe with the barista, the bus driver, the crossing guard, the store clerk, the security guard, other parents at school drop-off/pickup, fellow pet enthusiasts or commuters. Not exactly friends, but friendly acquaintances in your shared world.

Positives: We underestimate the power of these undemanding but frequent contacts with strangers or known people around a shared experience. Micro-connections combat loneliness and provide a small but potent lift. Dr. Fredrickson calls it "positivity resonance . . . a type of interpersonal connection characterized by shared positivity, mutual care and concern, and behavioral and biological synchrony." Eye contact initiates behavioral synchrony, in which our nonverbal gestures match as our emotion sparks around a shared moment—sweet dog, cute kids, busy checkout line, great weather. Nothing heavy. But your mood and your day feel brighter. (FYI: Receiving or even witnessing acts of kindness is thought to buffer/dampen our stress response system.) Maybe the world brightens, too: social experiments

involving people receiving small acts or gestures of kindness demonstrate that, given the opportunity, recipients are
more likely to pay it forward to someone else than somebody not primed with an act of kindness.

Connecting Tips: Start with eye contact, a smile, or a nod.
According to Fredrickson, positive emotional nonverbals
(the positive strokes mentioned in chapter 5, "Pride") invite
our brains to mimic one another, entering synchrony. Signal
availability for conversation by turning toward the person
and pausing. Make small talk: share some humor or mutual
appreciation. Deepen the connection by asking appropriate
questions ("How are things going?" "How's Sparky's paw?"
"Did Anya enjoy her birthday party?"). If they ask how
you're doing, say something pleasant/upbeat or admit it's
hectic if that's the case.

While micro-connections aren't substitutes for deeper
relationships, with nurturing, they can become delightfully
supportive. The store clerk sets aside an item they know we
want. The security guard watches our double-parked car
while we fetch something we forgot. We trade pet-sitting
with a neighbor, pick up each other's mail when out of town,
maybe ferry each other to medical appointments.

Micro-connections or social snacking effortlessly add
variety to our social diet, bringing us in contact with people
of all life stages and backgrounds. Regular microdosing can
feed our soul, providing positivity, safety, belonging, and
connection—increasing mood, health, and overall well-
being.

Exercise: Your Friendship Style

Without thinking too much about it, jot down your answers to these questions:

1. Do you feel energized by the idea of socializing? Or if you feel less fed emotionally by social interaction than others you know, do you avoid making social plans?
2. Do you sometimes overextend yourself socially (i.e., you feel exhausted, can't get your own stuff done, or feel resentful because you're not getting enough alone time)?
3. Do you feel heard and understood by people in your life, sure that a few people really have your back?
4. Are you completely satisfied with the balance of deep friendships, meaningful friendships, interest/activity/professional partners, and micro-connections in your life? (For example, is the scale tipping toward many superficial social interactions, but not much depth? Or a few close friends, but mostly scattered across the country, and no one to call for an impromptu activity or an urgent situation? Which categories, if any, do you feel could be improved?)
5. How proactive are you about prioritizing your social life? Do you tend to wait for the invitations to come to you? In the last month, how often have you called people out of the blue to say hi? Met friends in person, via video, or by phone? If time is an issue, are there moments in your day (e.g., during a walk or your commute) when you could build connections in?

The questions in this exercise are intended to give you an idea of your basic friendship style, what kinds and qualities of friendships you might be missing, and how intentional you are in shaping your social life—not to assign blame or responsibility, but to figure out what feeds you socially, what doesn't, and what you might be able to do about it.

If you used to enjoy certain people's company but don't even want to see your bestie anymore—and this worries you and the people you care about—plus your mood, motivation, energy, and interest in things you once cared about are low, you may want to speak with a therapist.

The Practical Optimist's Guide to Meaningful Engagement

The techniques below will help you bring more intentionality to your connections. Some facilitate conversations; others help manage the mind and emotions in real time.

Supportive Listening: Detect, Reflect, Act

Whether I'm speaking to the public, patients, friends, or my kids, I try to remember a simple formula: Detect, Reflect, Act. It incorporates a technique called active listening, a skill that can transform relationships and safeguard health.[22]

- *Detect:* That means listening—without interruption and interjection—as someone tells you what's going on (*what are they trying to convey?*). Observe, too: maybe they say they're okay, but a downcast face, slumped shoulders, and a monotone voice suggest otherwise.

---

[22] A 2021 study published in *JAMA* found people with a genetic predilection toward cognitive decline but with supportive listeners in their life had less of a chance of developing both stroke and dementia. Another fun fact: Having supportive listeners in your life decreases the age of your brain by as much as four years.

- *Reflect:* Next, verbalize what you've heard, first with *message receiving*: paraphrase what they've said: "What I'm hearing you say is . . . Did I understand you correctly? . . . Did I get that right?" This is also an opportunity to reflect on observed behavior, displays of emotions, or facial expression (something we therapists do): "You seem tearful" or "You seem cheerful." Then let them keep talking. This allows for clarification. Resist the urge to inject your interpretation, experience, or advice, or fill silences with platitudes of positivity or reassurance—these can all sound like discounting someone's feelings and situation. Being able to update your thinking based on what someone's telling you is the hallmark of cognitive flexibility.

  - Then there's *message registering*: express appreciation of the emotional impact of what you've heard: "I'm picking up on how sad/angry/worried you are feeling." "Wow, it's hitting me, the pain you are in."

  - Finally there's *message response*. This is the time to show you get it. Instead of analysis or advice ("maybe you should . . ."), try something like "I get that this is hard for you." "It sounds like it's been a stressful time." "You have a lot on your plate." Giving advice, though well-intentioned, shuts down the opportunity for someone to share. Don't underestimate the benefit of simply listening as someone shares their pain, allowing them space to find their way toward those aha moments that can come when we freely confide in a trusted other.

  - Now may be the time for appropriate self-disclosure. Again, delicately, without offering advice or shifting the focus to yourself, simply extend your compassion in order to decrease the isolation people feel when they're suffering. Reassure them they're not alone and perhaps share an experience that might resonate: "Though I haven't gone through what you've gone through, I once experienced X and it was really hard.

I'm so sorry." Keep it short, without comparing situations. If self-disclosure doesn't feel appropriate in the context of the person describing their pain, refrain.

- *Act:* Here you turn empathy into action—the essence of compassion:
  - "I'm here for you." "What can I do to help?" You might offer tangible solutions if appropriate, warranted, and welcome. Or offer specific assistance if you're able and genuinely wish to. Simply being a sounding board is action, if that's what's wanted and needed.
  - Then consistently show up with reminders of your support, rooting for them with words, deeds, or both. Even a card with a message—"I've been thinking of you/Please take good care of yourself"—can mean so much.
  - If you can make a person who's suffering feel genuinely supported through consistently showing up, you, my friend, are an angel.

This approach can work with any of the four friendship types. Suppose I'm new in town. I sign up for a walking tour series to get to know the city and meet people. I start chatting with one woman, and we end up walking together on the first two tours. After the second tour she asks, "How'd you end up moving here?"

Maybe by then I feel safe sharing that I moved here wanting a fresh start after a breakup, followed by a company restructuring in which I was laid off. She listens and responds with validation and compassion: "Wow. That's so much change in a short time. How have things been going?" Suddenly our conversation is deeper.

Then she puts empathy into action: "I'd love to introduce you to some of my friends. Why don't you come to my yoga class? Some of us usually have coffee afterward." And just like that, both of you are expanding and deepening your social circle.

Part of Liz's treatment involved connecting with others. Much of her sense of self centered around her work, but her fellow patients were interested in *her*, not her professional awards. Gradually she learned to connect by being receptive to and vulnerable with others, not just performing. Her curiosity and attention to detail, which had made her successful at work, also made her successful in her relationships. She became a peer leader for a book club, leading stimulating discussions. Liz told me teaching had been her passion, but her father had devalued it. I could tell she was an educator at heart.

Resolving Conflicts: The XYZ Technique

The XYZ technique[23] is powerful for real-time interactions, especially when emotions are running high. While the program was meant to help couples build key skills to strengthen their relationships, to promote conflict resolution, and to prevent escalation of marital problems and divorce, I find it equally useful with people in long-term relationships and in different types of relationships, from friendships to adult children and parents. It can work not only in conflictual relationships, but to maintain healthy relationships.

The XYZ technique keeps discussions focused on a behavior and a situation, not a *person*. There's no character assassination or "kitchen sinking" (generalizations about a person) or all-or-nothing statements. Here's the formula:

"IN SITUATION X, WHEN YOU DID Y, I FELT Z."

- **"In Situation X"**: Describe the specific situation that has created an issue in your relationship—one moment, not a laundry list of fails.
- **"when you did Y"**: Describe the specific behavior.

---

[23] Adapted from the Prevention and Relationship Enhancement Program (PREP), which teaches couples how to resolve conflicts effectively and enhance emotional closeness, friendship, and connection.

- "I felt Z, and I [fill in action/reaction]": Explain how you felt or were affected, and own your reaction, using "I" statements. This feedback can help target negative behavior.

Remember Nancy and Sharon from chapter 4, who were arguing over household duties? They practiced this technique in our session and at home. For example: Sharon: "Nancy, when you wait until the last minute to pack the kids up before our vacations, I feel incredibly stressed and devalued. I get very anxious (and sometimes feel hurt)."

Focus on how the situation made you *feel*, rather than a blanket statement about who the other person *is*. As discussed in chapter 5, it's the difference between a conditional negative stroke, which gives someone actionable feedback about how their behavior negatively impacted someone else, and an unconditional negative stroke—those wounding messages that induce helplessness and shame about our very identity, which leads to avoidance rather than reparation. I recommend practicing this technique in lower-stakes situations so it's more accessible when tensions rise.

XYZ works for positives, too. Nancy and Sharon used gratitude XYZ statements to reinforce positive behavior: "When you offered to take the kids out on Sunday morning so I could sleep in, I felt grateful, appreciated, and pampered." Conditional positive strokes encourage more of the positive behavior we appreciate. Remember, too, the power of unconditional positives: "Thank you!"; "I love you"; "You're an amazing person"; hugs and smiles; doing someone a good turn. According to leading relationship researcher John Gottman, PhD, the magic ratio in relationships is 5:1—for every negative interaction during conflict, a stable and happy relationship has five (or more) positive interactions.

Challenging Your Perceptions

According to a 2014 study published in the *Journal of Experimental Psychology*, subway commuters in Chicago generally believed interacting with strangers was uncomfortable or unwelcome or reduced their productivity time. But when they actually chatted with their neighboring straphanger, they overwhelmingly found the experience mood-lifting and a positive addition to their short-term well-being. If that can happen when we challenge our assumptions about micro-connections, imagine what could happen with our deeper friendships!

Feeling supported by others signals to our brains that we can relax, that we're taken care of and are safe. As we're pack animals by evolution, being relegated to the outskirts of the tribe can feel threatening. Thus thinking you're protected is protective for your mental health.

This perception of feeling supported can lead to a more robust social network system, fostering a hopeful, upbeat atmosphere and contributing to relationship success. This effect extends beyond our immediate circle. Patients who feel supported or understood by their doctors will have a better rapport with them and are thus more likely to adhere to treatment and follow-up visits, resulting in better health outcomes.

Positive relationship expectations create positive outcomes because we come to the table with a win-win attitude. Remember the classroom study mentioned earlier: if we expect acceptance from others, we're more likely to exude warmth, in turn leading others to accept us.

With positive expectations, we're less likely to personalize neutral behavior as negative. *Maybe they weren't brushing me off, but were busy with their fussy baby, were embarrassed that I saw them with their shirt smeared with ice cream, or were just having a bad day.* We also see clearly when people repeatedly disappoint us, treat us poorly, or trespass our boundaries, and we don't avoid confronting the problem.

Sadly, sometimes because of early attachment experiences, our negative assumptions about ourselves and how others will view us hold us back from meeting new people, deepening acquaintances, or reconnecting with old friends. Or we may feel so anxious about belonging that we lose ourselves in relationships, fearing the worst over even minor turbulence. Either way, we fear rejection: not being liked.

We assume we like others more than they like us, a dissonance known as the liking gap. We don't start out this way. Kids under age five don't show it—it kicks in only around the age when we start concerning ourselves with what others think about us. Also, in what's known as the beautiful mess effect, we may fear even appropriate self-disclosure, thinking being vulnerable will lead to negative or critical judgment.

> **PO Pearls**
> We often underestimate how much people like us.

Cognitive behavior techniques like the ABCDE approach and the 5 Rs of Emotional Regulation and Real-World Problem-Solving (see chapters 4 and 5 for a refresher on these and more!) can help you challenge cognitive distortions and give yourself and others a chance.

Coming to a New Perspective with ABCDE

Liz struggled to see her situation outside the narrative she'd built around her aloneness, to the point of believing her family visited her at the hospital because "they just feel sorry for me." We needed to work on her perception of support. Here's a hypothetical model for how Liz's assumptions can be challenged using the ABCDE approach:

Antecedent: *My family flew in to visit me in the hospital.*
Belief: *They did it only because they feel sorry for me.*
Consequences: Feeling alone, worthless, emotionally numb.
Distortions: *They came only because they pity me [mind reading, discounting the positives]. If I'd been a better mother, maybe they'd really want to see me [regret orientation]. Without my career I'm worthless/uninteresting [all-or-nothing thinking]. No one really cares [catastrophizing], so I'm on my own [emotional reasoning and negative filtering].*

Embrace: *I have a history of depression and a family history where I was told I didn't matter. It's painful, but I don't have to let it run my life. I can believe the best of my children, in ways my father didn't believe in me. If they see positives in me, maybe they're right. I've made friends in the hospital. They like me for who I am and remind me I have inherent value and am more than my accomplishments. My struggles make me more able to empathize with others. Reaching out helps others, and me, feel good. I don't have to be perfect—if anything, the constant need for perfection has been harmful. I can be kinder to myself.*

None of these insights came to Liz overnight. But as we practice, the ABCDE technique helps us catch and challenge negative automatic thoughts and encourages our brains to reframe with more realistic, accurate, positive but true associations.

Perception Hacks
Here are some ways to hack common relationship perceptions:

Situation: There's a group of close friends that always hangs out.
   Perception: *They're cliquey/unfriendly.*
   Hack: What evidence do you have that they're really this way? Ask yourself what you've done to engage with them. If you've tried and they've turned you down, that conclusion may be warranted. But if you've kept to yourself and resent that no one has approached you, it's time to own that perception and decide if you'll approach them and see what happens or let it go.
Situation: You're invited to an event where you won't know most of the people.
   Perception: *I don't want to meet new people, although I know it would be good for me. I can't imagine it being fun. I won't*

know anyone, don't know what to expect, and won't know what to say.

Hack: Often all-or-nothing thinking lurks behind these perceptions: *I'm not good with people/I don't fit in.* Or self-comparison: *I'm not as funny/pretty/smart/cool/interesting/popular.* Or body image self-consciousness: *I don't feel good about my body right now/don't look good in my clothes right now/don't have anything to wear for social outings.* Or feeling vulnerable: *I just lost my job/broke up with my partner and don't want people to ask about it.* Remind yourself of your abilities, of past challenges you've met, of skills you have that you could apply, as Liz applied her curiosity and insight about people to making friends.

Do you know anyone who's attended this event in the past? Ask what to expect and what made it a good experience. If you know anyone who's going, could you go together? If you're allowed to bring a guest, invite someone along. Are there event particulars that would help put you at ease (e.g., the opportunity to learn)? Don't know what to say? Switch your focus—most people have plenty to say about themselves. After smiles and introductions, chat about the event: what brings them there? Listen; ask follow-up questions. Ask open-ended questions. I might ask someone how their summer went or what books, movies, or podcasts they've enjoyed—info nuggets that provide valuable insights and potential mutual connection points based on shared interests. Expressing genuine interest in others is enough to make you a success among them.

Situation: You need some help but hesitate to ask.

Perception: *I don't want to impose. I'm embarrassed. What if they say no?*

Hack: A 2022 survey by the market research firm OnePoll revealed that almost half of respondents don't ask for help until they feel overwhelmed. The reality: people aren't as bur-

dened by our requests as we imagine they'll be. A bond forms
when we show people our authentic selves.

The benefits to both parties of giving and receiving are
severalfold: lowered blood pressure, a drop in stress hormones,
and a boost in immunity.

Start with small asks: extra napkins at a restaurant, or
whether someone at the gym could spot you for heavy weights.
In time, it'll feel less uncomfortable. For bigger asks, be specific (no dropping of hints, hoping someone will read your
mind): "I'm going to a party and will likely run into my ex—
it'd be a big help and lots more fun if you came along." "I'm
going on a first date and I'd like to have something planned for
later so the date's not open-ended." A wonderfully proactive
example: one woman shared her Google Calendar with the
members of her hiking club, saying that she didn't need nursing the week after her surgery, but that she did want company,
and she invited people to sign up to visit her.

Then, of course, express gratitude and reciprocate in their
time of need.

Situation: You've fallen out of touch with someone, or it's been a long
time since meeting someone you'd like to get to know better.

Perception: *I screwed up. It's been too long.*

Hack: Some version of "it's too late" is a major reason why
people don't reach out in friendships old and new. Variants
include: *I'll be bothering them/I don't want to impose/They don't
need more friends/I'm too old to make new friends/We had a
falling-out—they'll still be mad.*

Modern life doesn't lend itself to spontaneous connections.
We have to create opportunities. Weeks, months, even years
later—it's never too late to let someone know you're thinking
of them. Indeed, studies show people appreciate receiving
texts from others, and the more unexpected, the greater the
benefit to the receiver. When I was younger, I wasn't great at

keeping in touch. Then I'd think, *It's been too long; it'll seem weird.* Now I realize maybe the other person might feel the same! So I just reach out.

People love hearing from us when we open up, share, ask for help. We minimize how much we mean to others and how much a text out of the blue means. Expressing and receiving appreciation has mental health benefits, increasing your life satisfaction and well-being. It creates and solidifies bonds and is associated with greater relationship satisfaction and relationship commitment.

As part of reestablishing connections, Liz reached out to her college roommate, a tenured professor of economics at their alma mater in Boston. Liz had started doing calligraphy again—a hobby she'd shelved along with many other comforts in hopes of earning her father's approval. Liz sent one of her hand-calligraphed cards to her old friend. They hadn't spoken in about ten years. She received a letter in reply, addressed to her at the hospital—a sign that she was not only reaching out, but opening up.

So reach out to an old friend from school, work, or childhood. Email them saying you were thinking of them, wondering how they're doing. Remind someone how much you enjoyed their conversation, where you met, and an anecdote or joke you might've shared. Send an article that might interest them. You don't have to open up or suggest a meet-up. Just rekindle the conversation. If you hear back and the connection feels mutual, build from there. Be open to the possibility that sometimes our efforts aren't reciprocated. Sometimes I get a response; other times I don't. Either way, I feel good about reaching out.

If the silence is from a simple misunderstanding with an old friend or you think someone doesn't like you anymore, be open and honest. "I miss you. It's been a while. I'd like to talk about what happened." Be ready to discuss hard things, take responsibility for your part in any misapprehensions that may have taken place, and indicate you are open to moving on or finding closure.

A Word to the Wise

On Forgiveness

Forgiveness is the power to let go of resentment toward someone who caused us harm. If others' actions have disrupted a relationship, you still can give yourself options:

1. *Free someone completely from blame.* It's easy to exonerate someone in the case of a genuine mistake, if the person truly didn't understand the import of their actions (for example, was very young), or if they completely accept responsibility and you want to maintain the relationship. Of course, the best apology is a change in behavior. But in the absence of that, below are some ways of handling continued hurt or bad behavior, or when someone hasn't quite owned up to the bad behavior or corrected course yet.

2. *Trust but verify.* This may apply in the case of an insincere quasi-apology in which somehow you also get partially blamed (the person rationalizes or tries to explain away their behavior, and not for the first time) or an inauthentic relationship. Maybe you're in a position where you don't have a choice—you need to continue the relationship for important reasons and/or you simply need to move on. You forgive but don't forget, and your watchwords are "trust but verify."

3. *Live and let go.* In this option, based on the idea of nonattachment or radical acceptance, we don't condone or approve the hurtful behavior, but choose our sanity and peace of mind

over it through acceptance, nonattachment, and letting go. According to Buddhist ideas, pain is a part of life, and suffering is the spin we put on it through our attachment to ideas, memories, people, and the past. Trust me, I've been there: "If only this hadn't happened." But it did. Accepting a bad situation isn't condoning it; we are releasing ourselves from the hold it has over us because we don't want to be a prisoner of the past.

Sometimes allowing ourselves to feel anger (and not necessarily do anything about it other than acknowledge it) allows us to grieve and forgive. It's possible to be angry at someone who's done a lot for you. Sometimes what we're mourning might be the loss of a relationship or simply our expectations of it. We sometimes equate acceptance with resignation or with tolerance of a bad situation or a bad behavior. Not so. Forgiveness keeps anger from calcifying into resentment, allowing you to heal from the associated negative feelings.

Healthy Boundaries

Often relationship conflicts are really about competing agendas—others' values, goals, needs, and wants may be incongruent with ours. But there's frequently also an inner conflict: we don't like to let people down. Yet consistently putting others' needs and wants before ours is a recipe for resentment.

The solution? Boundaries. Boundaries can protect and honor all involved. They help us replenish our emotional reserves so we have the resources to show up for those we love.

Years after I'd worked with Liz, I met a patient named Amanda. While Liz's high emotional boundaries walled her off from others, Amanda's lack of boundaries had created a recurring problem. Just starting out in her career, she was finding it hard to find her footing because she felt beholden to her social commitments. As is true for many of my younger single patients, friendships were vital for Amanda. She was social by nature, and community was central to her cultural heritage. But now that her friends were getting engaged and married, "attending weddings is my full-time job," she said. That meant showers, gifts, time off, and travel expenses—plus, if she was an attendant, "the dresses, shoes, parties."

In many ways, Amanda had perfected the art of making and maintaining friendships.

But her need to belong was clashing with her other basic needs for autonomy, competence, and financial security. She missed alone time to hang out, bike, and take a yoga training that interested her. She found it hard to say no to the unspoken expectation to drop money and show up. She was prioritizing her friends' needs but felt her needs never entered the equation.

While Liz and Amanda seem like polar opposites, both needed to examine their understanding of relationships and think about how their emotions influenced their relationship decisions, and what they could do for more fulfilling social experiences.

In Amanda's case, what struck me most were her ruminations about how her friends would drop her if she didn't do as they asked. Her sense of self-worth seemed contingent upon their approval. She had spent years and thousands of dollars prioritizing her friends' needs above her own. Her lack of healthy boundaries had created resentment toward people she loved. Her need to be liked and to belong conflicted with her financial goals and her desire to make life decisions that felt more authentic and fulfilling.

Healthy boundaries, when created with people we respect and trust, are aimed at preserving the relationship. When the inevitable next invitation to be a bridesmaid came, Amanda and I strategized ways to erect healthy boundaries while supporting her friends.

To start, she told her friend she was thrilled for her, thanked her for including her in such a special day, and gave herself time to think:

"I really want to attend all the events you've invited me to. I'm so excited for you both. Let me look at my calendar (and budget!) and get back to you in a few days." Subsequently, she got back in touch and said she'd be honored to be a bridesmaid but wouldn't be able to travel to the bachelorette party in New Orleans, giving her friend the option of accepting her very reasonable boundaries regarding her time and finances or finding another friend to fill the role.

Amanda's boundaries were:

1. **Intentional**: Healthy boundaries aren't reactive or based in anger. Amanda considered her options.
2. **Compassionate**: Thoughtful, kind boundaries may include what you *can* do alongside what you can't: "I'm really sorry, I won't be able to make it to the bachelorette party in New Orleans—my schedule and budget don't allow for it, unfortunately. But I'm so excited to attend the wedding!" Gratitude shows you value the relationship and the intention behind the request: "Thank you so much for thinking of me." "I'm so grateful you are trying to include me." "I appreciate your asking."
3. **Collaborative, cooperative, often creative**: Amanda's biggest realization—and the one that most effectively prevented any potential resentment—was that she could still "show up" for her friends by contributing to the party planning and pitching in for decorations and games (activities within her time and financial means). You might adapt this idea: "While I won't be able to host the dinner, I'm more than happy to bring a few dishes and help clean up." Different people bring different strengths, resources, and ways to show their caring. Some offer their time, others their homes, others their wallets. Play to people's strengths.
4. **Explicit**: Amanda was clear about both her excitement for her friend and her enthusiasm for attending her wedding *and* her inability to attend the bachelorette party. No guessing or surprises.

5. **Flexible:** Friendships are rarely all-or-nothing. Amanda realized she didn't need to be all in to be a good friend.

6. **Reinforced:** When her boundaries were tested, Amanda remained compassionate but firm. When her friend said, "I'm so bummed—isn't there any way you can make it to the bachelorette?" Amanda gave it some thought and then clearly reinforced her boundaries (without reiterating her budget constraints, which her friend already knew about): "I can't wait to see you at the shower and the wedding. I can't make it to the bachelorette. But I'm so excited to help with the planning and glad the other girls can make it!"

7. **Open:** Depending on the closeness of the relationship, you may choose to share more of what's behind your decision: "I really need to focus on school/work/family/rest/mental health." Among friends, it's a way of letting them know "it's not you, it's me" looking out for my health right now.

Amanda was pleasantly surprised that although some of her friends naturally expressed mild disappointment, none stopped talking to her. In time, Amanda normalized her new routine of boundary setting.

Setting boundaries can feel daunting, so remember its benefits:

- **Boundaries are meant to facilitate closeness.** Boundaries may sometimes require us to deliver short-term disappointment for the long-term preservation of the relationship. Ultimately, they help manage expectations, making for fewer misunderstandings.
- **Boundaries help us take care of ourselves.** I set boundaries so I can be the best version of myself when I show up for others.
- **Boundaries needn't always be absolute.** In an otherwise supportive relationship, boundaries can be more like hedges than walls, as with respect for each other's needs, we each agree to be flexible with boundaries when needed.

- **Boundaries can act as a bridge to strength**. Sometimes hedges need to become walls. Establishing boundaries may be the first step toward making the decision to end a relationship.

Befriending Yourself

At the beginning of this chapter, I noted that the best way to befriend others is to befriend yourself. Particularly when you are feeling unsettled or in distress, studies show people can sometimes be helped to feel more secure through key words, images, and exercises that invoke memories of caregiving and invoke their inner caregiver—a process called security priming.

The ideas below focus on nurturing our closest friendship—the one we have with ourselves—as an integral component of healthy relating to others. Few of us had idyllic upbringings. Whatever our experience with early or current relationships, we can create a restorative, reassuring home base within. Self-compassion breaks the cycle, fosters healing, and allows us to relate to others as our fullest, best self.

- *Help your partner help you.* Your partner may not always be able to come up with the right words to help you calm down, but perhaps there are other ways they can show their support that you can tell them you appreciate (sitting beside you/hugs and back rubs/cooking you a nice meal). And remember—each of you can practice being active listeners to each other to show appreciation and understanding.[24]

---

[24] While expressing appreciation works for everyone regardless of attachment style, it's especially effective for those with avoidant attachment styles, both in personal relationships and at work. We know that managers who say thank you motivate their employees. Gratitude can improve productivity, encouraging us to work harder and longer.

- *Ask for what you need.* "Your words always provide comfort for me. Could you share a few words of wisdom with me today? I'm having a hard day and your messages always cheer me up."
- *Write or recall a positive memory.* One in which you felt safe, regarded, loved.
- *Write a letter to your future secure self.* What do you hope for them? What do you want to be able to give to others? What needs to happen; what do you need to give yourself? What do you feel you deserve (rest, sleep, acknowledgment)? What patterns do you want to change? What isn't working (e.g., pulling away, pushing too much)?

While these exercises may provide a degree of comfort, reassuring, and soothing, exploring one's attachment style in therapy can help deepen your insights and sharpen your coping skills.

Cultivate an Aloneness Practice

An aloneness practice both teaches us and reminds us of our ability to give to ourselves. It's the deliberate, intentional state of enjoyment of our own company—giving ourselves positive strokes of the kind described in chapter 5. It allows us to fully recharge so we can be fully present for others, reaffirms our value to ourselves, and helps ensure that we and our relationships aren't suffering because we're avoiding our emotions, not facing challenges, or expecting others to fill a void inside. It reminds us that we are the source of our own joy.

For many, being alone can feel uncomfortable. One study found some people would rather give themselves an electric shock than be alone with nothing to do. The central fear of solitude stems from the misconception that joy comes from the outside world or from our sense of belonging. When we have fun in another's company, we may associate that fun with the other person, not realizing that the fun, joy, laughter, and ability to experience and express positive feelings that we experience in another's company was already ours, waiting within to be claimed. Stop waiting for other people to give you permission to enjoy your inner home. You—your own mind, your own body, your own spirit—are the source of your own joy and pleasure. While social rejection and isolation hurt (and belonging is a basic human need), our sense of meaning and belonging is ultimately limited by how comfortable we feel in our own skin.

Distraction-free alone time can reveal so much about our hopes, dreams, and behaviors. The brain creates connections it can make only during periods of rest and quiet focus. Aloneness helps us regulate our emotions (specifically allowing us to deactivate strong negative emotions), promotes self-awareness, frees up our thinking for more effective and creative problem-solving, recharges and resets our batteries so we can relate better to others, and furthers our empathy and understanding for them. Our focus, productivity, and creativity all increase when we balance joyful solitude with intentional togetherness. Even positive engagement with others can serve as a distraction from the important work our brain needs to do in a state of active mental rest, when we are alone. So while alone time feels more preferable to some (Liz) than to others, learning how to be alone meaningfully is an important skill and part of a well-balanced life.

The self-befriending prompts above might be part of your aloneness practice. But it needn't be a big, heavy thing. You can do your aloneness practice in any quiet place at home, or practice being solo among others on a park bench, on a ferry ride, or at a café. Don't look at your phone. See chapter 7, "Present," for activities that inspire awe, gratitude, savoring, play, present-mind awareness, and flow.

Aloneness practice reminds us that the ability to experience and express joy is within us, waiting to be claimed as part of treating ourselves as we would a treasured friend. Our sense of belonging belongs, first and foremost, to us.

PO Pearls
You are the source of your own joy.

New Beginnings

Liz was discharged eight weeks after her suicide attempt. "It took a lot of people and work to put me back together again, but I'm glad they did," Liz said with a bright smile I hadn't really seen until then.

One day some time after that, I got paged to the nursing desk. There the unit clerk handed me a beautiful white orchid with a note: "Thank you for our new beginning."

It was from Liz's daughter-in-law. Liz had spent the summer with one of her sons and his family in Boston. They'd come to New York to help Liz pack up and move to Massachusetts to be closer to her family. She'd also pursued her passion for teaching, taking a visiting professor role at her alma mater, facilitated by the college roommate/friend she'd sent her calligraphy card to. With time, continued psychotherapy, medication management, and working on connection and mindfulness, Liz was able to feel and accept her family's love—and, for the first time in her life, balance her need for connection with her desire for autonomy and competence.

Two decades have passed since my conversations with Liz. What I find so inspiring about her, then and now, is her intentionality. Here was a woman who'd felt so hopeless, depressed, and lonely that she jumped off a bridge, who found her way to sending cards to friends, leading book groups, and making plans to live closer to family and start a second career. Liz's journey was complex and nuanced—an amalgamation of early life stressors, her unique attachment style and worldview, her genetic predisposition to and personal history of depression, later-life losses, and loneliness. But it was also one of recovery, hope, and Practical Optimism (though I didn't know it as PO at the time). After a lifetime of emotional walls, Liz made the decision to be vulnerable and intentional in her relationships. While Liz was fortunate in having access to professionals and treatment to help "put the broken pieces together," the commitment she brought to the process reminded me that it's never too late to reconnect—to uncover, compassionately challenge, and navigate around limitations. It starts with understanding that we are and can be more than the sum total of what happens to us. That we have the agency to heal in the present and shape our future through making nurturing relationship choices—with others and with ourselves.

When we do, it changes everything.

To view the scientific references cited in this chapter,
please visit doctorsuevarma.com/book.

CHAPTER 9

Practicing Healthy Habits

Automating Good Daily Decisions

*We are what we repeatedly do. Excellence, then, is
not an act, but a habit.*

—WILL DURANT

"I know what I need to do. I just can't seem to do it."

Over the past year, Stan,[25] a forty-four-year-old father of three, had
been started on medication for elevated blood pressure and cholesterol
and had been told diabetes medications were next if he couldn't turn
things around through diet modification and exercise. "Ideally, I'd like

---

[25] What you are learning about Stan is a condensed version of his story. I am of necessity selecting aspects of his case and treatment relevant to the points in this chapter, which focuses on
the importance of developing and maintaining healthy habits. Each individual's journey is
unique. It's not my intention to suggest or attempt to present a comprehensive discussion of
depression, grief, and metabolic problems, medical illnesses and their risk factors, or available
mental health and/or medical treatments or lifestyle interventions (nor suggest that they are
widely available to all individuals, given the disparities in healthcare, and society in general).
It's important to discuss your unique concerns with your healthcare provider.

to see if I could get off these medications. And in general, I want to be healthy for my family and for myself. But I can't stick with it."

Stan had long been fit and prioritized his health, but now he'd gone from being active and optimistic to feeling helpless in battling myriad metabolic disorders. His internist had referred him to me, suspecting he might be experiencing symptoms of depression and hoping that I could help him with stress management.

Stan was grieving the loss of his father, who'd died of a heart attack the prior year after a long history of cardiovascular disease. While his father's death was a reminder and motivator to deal with this family health risk, Stan struggled with motivation, saying his mood, energy, and motivation all waned within a month of committing to a new diet and exercise regimen. Circumstances inevitably interfered: a flooded basement, his wife's recent diagnosis with an autoimmune illness, his youngest daughter's learning challenges at school. Not being able to follow through on key health habits demoralized Stan.

Work changes had also disrupted his health habits. Before his job went remote, Stan's commute involved a two-mile walk if he opted out of the subway. He frequently took the stairs between office floors, and his office building had a free gym, where he sometimes worked out with coworkers at lunchtime. On-site work had also put a hard stop to his workday, so he could be active with his kids (he used to coach their sports teams), unwind with a family meal, and get to bed on time. Remote work blurred that boundary. Stan was answering calls at all hours and on weekends.

I reflected back to Stan how committed and devoted he was, and how much pressure he was under. He was mourning his father, helping his wife deal with a chronic illness, and helping his daughter navigate neurodiversity in a school system that didn't always know how to accommodate her. We also talked about how Stan's symptoms of depression were contributing to his struggle in following through on his diet and exercise regimen. "When I feel down, I cancel my workout plans, eat junk, and stay up late. I don't see my friends and I'm cranky around the house. This isn't me."

Depression, grief, and stress all can diminish our interest, energy, and motivation, making it harder to meet our goals or do things we once enjoyed. But not being able to keep his promises to himself was exacerbating Stan's depression. Low mood and canceled plans atop loss, grief, and acute stressors only further undermined his self-efficacy, which worsened the depression. Stan needed not only mood-boosting activities, but also proficiency builders to break this shame/low proficiency/depression cycle.

That's why habits are so important. We benefit health-wise from the beneficial habits we establish and, equally important, they confer and confirm our identity as someone who can keep our commitments to ourselves: *I'm someone who [fill in the blank, e.g., gets things done, eats right].* Thus good habits deliver double positives: in health and in identity. Optimists are what optimists do.

Stan was showing signs of a mild depression, but he let me know that medications wouldn't be his first choice since he was on so many drugs already. Another patient might have wanted medications (another doctor might have even suggested them to Stan), and there are many situations when medications would be appropriate, lifesaving, and life-changing. I'm open to all possibilities, but most of all, I like to listen to what my patient is telling me.

Stan had well-honed coping skills that he'd lost touch with amid the past year's stressors, including the loss of his father. And like many of us, Stan had fallen into the habit of over-delivering to others and under-delivering to himself. While he felt demoralized about his health outcomes, he wanted to improve them, and his feelings weren't rooted in a pervasive sense of hopelessness.

Not only did Stan prefer to see what his options were for mental health treatment without medications, but he hoped to get off the other medications. We agreed we'd start our work together with a non-medication approach that would help him connect with his own habit-change capacities. I'd continue to monitor him closely and could quickly step in with additional treatment options should they be necessary. And as I always do with my patients, we discussed, and he denied, thoughts, plans, previous attempts, or a past history of suicide and self-harm.

"Some of the medical problems you're facing run in your family, so there's some genetic predisposition," I told him. "But believe it or not, you have a lot more control than you think."

Many of us struggle with healthy habits and goals, even without the challenges and losses Stan was facing. Perhaps, like Stan, you've yearned to achieve something and know what you need to do— but have struggled to do it.[26] You wouldn't be alone. More than 75 percent of the time, people know what needs to be done regarding recommendations and guidelines for sleep, exercise, and nutrition, yet still don't do it.

Maybe, like many, you berate yourself for your poor choices. But what if focusing on choices is part of the problem?

We tend to think living healthfully is about making good choices. True . . . to a point. Yet remember what we've said about decision fatigue? We make thousands of decisions daily, and two hundred of those are about food! Having too many choices and decisions can lead to poor choices or not choosing. This, plus emotions, life's ups and downs, and temptations and distractions, can derail our best-laid plans.

Practical Optimists understand they have the power and responsibility to make good choices as part of creating good health outcomes.

---

[26] Motivation also wanes in the context of anxiety and depression. If you feel less motivated in general, and have for some time, you might want to consider talking to a therapist.

Yet they realize they may not always have the bandwidth to make those choices (and sometimes, despite their best efforts and intentions, there might be other, larger systemic barriers and inequities outside their control at play).

So they stack the deck in their favor. They've learned it's sometimes better not to have to make choices at all. What often appear to be good choices are actually good habits.

Active, conscious choice requires a lot of deliberate effort and planning—called slow thinking. According to the dual process model of thinking, we have a fast, habit-based type of thinking and a slower analytic type. If we can learn to act from habit, we aren't constantly reinventing the wheel in deciding what to eat, when to exercise, etc. We're simply automating proven positive outcomes.

Habits are automated decisions, often responding to or preventing a problem. When a behavior bypasses conscious thought to the point where we do it without thinking much about it, it becomes a habit. Habits are more resistant to outside obstacles and forces, including low motivation, day-to-day variability, choice, mood—even other bad habits. With practice, healthy choices can become second nature so that thought, chance, whim, or obstacles that could get in the way don't stand a chance.

Practical Optimists know the good health golden rule: If you want a healthy behavior to last, make it a habit, not a choice. Optimists are more likely to exercise and eat fresh fruits and vegetables, and less likely to smoke. They regularly attend well medical visits and adhere to treatment plans. They're more likely to regularly wash their hands and brush their teeth. But even more important: they've automated these behaviors.

PO Pearls
Motivation is overrated. Automation is the key to success.

From dental health to mental health, optimists practice healthy habits as if their life depends on it. Because, well, it does. According to a 2019 study published in *PNAS*, optimism was associated with an 11 percent to 15 percent increase in lifespan. An optimistic outlook has been continuously linked to those with exceptional longevity (living past age eighty-five). But the key to flourishing isn't just our lifespan—how long we live—but also our health span: how long we live in good health.

Americans are living, on average, thirty years longer than a century ago. But our health span hasn't budged much from our parents' and grandparents' generations: we're spending more of those years managing pain or chronic illness (in fact, more than half of adults ages sixty-five and up are on four medications)—despite U.S. spending on healthcare surpassing that of other developed countries. And while Americans are living longer than in the past, the United States trails other high-income countries in life expectancy, with obesity and smoking being in part responsible for early deaths. Yet optimists are healthier, with exceptional longevity and longer health spans. Good genes, maybe?

Genetics is just one small part of the equation. A study of Danish twins determined that how long the average person lives is only about 20 percent influenced by genes. Lifestyle shapes around 80 percent. Studies in a National Research Council and Institute of Medicine review found that as many as half of premature deaths in the United States are preventable—including from habits such as poor diet, a sedentary lifestyle, and tobacco use. The study of epigenetics is uncovering how behavior and the environment interact with and modify gene expression. Biology isn't destiny. You have more power over your health than you know.

Even optimism doesn't depend on genetics. As I've mentioned, genetics accounts for only about 25 percent of optimists' sunny disposition. The other 75 percent comes from the same place as everyone else's: the environments they spend time in and the choices they make. Practical Optimism is a habit that makes the power of optimism available for everyone.

You've automated many good habits: brushing your teeth, doing your laundry, keeping a calendar, and walking your dog, among others.

Of course, bad habits also get automated: too many happy hours . . . fast-food takeout and wine after "bad days" . . . work marathons causing missed meals, workouts, and sleep.

In this chapter, I'll help you take steps to automate good habits and phase out bad ones. While you may have gotten off track with healthy habits for different reasons than Stan did, the advice I gave him still applies.

Sometimes getting healthy may feel insurmountable. Numerous obstacles and challenges come to mind: cost, time, energy, access, resources, practice, knowledge, to name some. Most people, including Stan, struggle, despite knowing the importance of good habits. But we need to dwell on the possibilities that *do* exist. Practical Optimists are always aware of limitations. But they also seek to say, "Given my constraints and challenges, what are my options and work-arounds to help me attain my goals and practice good habits?"

Not sure where to start with healthy habits? Later in this chapter, I'll share the four habits I recommend as my top picks because they lead to other good habits while providing joy, pleasure, and satisfaction.

If you've been practicing the tools I've shared in the other Pillars, you're already investing in good habits. This chapter will reinforce what you're doing. Or you can begin with this Pillar and apply it to the others or to any goals you have. I hope to help you feel more confident in your efforts to develop habits. We have more power, control, and choice in health decisions and outcomes than we may think. Believing the deck is stacked against you affects how you play your hand. Do you want to play it with intention and confidence or leave it to luck? If you're reading this, I think you know the answer.

From Intention to Automation: The Practical Optimist's Guide to Forming Habits That Last

We're more likely to stick with a routine long enough to automate it by making the behaviors:

- Convenient
- Interesting
- Accessible
- Fun

Some of the key steps involved in habit formation include intention, decision-making, action, and automation. I've developed key strategies that incorporate these steps along with the points above to help you narrow the "intention to automation" gap (the sinkhole into which good intentions drop).

Be Intentional

Intentionality isn't just about setting a goal. Intention is asking ourselves: *What do I need to do to reach my goal?* It's about uncovering positive trends, vulnerability points, and stressors so you can replicate what's working and revise what isn't. Intentionality helps you evade *I'm a failure* thinking by

- gathering actionable data about when, where, and why things go well or sideways,
- becoming less vulnerable to exploitation by others with different intentions for you, and
- reducing the odds of looking back on another year gone by without doing the things you'd hoped to do.

Exercise: Origins of Old Habits

Being intentional about habits starts with acknowledging where we are right now and how our current habits came into existence, whether months or many years ago. Nonjudgmental self-examination helps you begin separating yourself from what you've been doing and redirecting your energy toward where you want to go.

When trying to break old habits or promote good ones, consider:

- What did mealtime/eating, exercise, spending money, friendship, or [insert your own] look like in your family of origin?
- What habits or blueprints did you take away from those experiences?
- What worked? Didn't work?
- What are the mindset and the set of actions that create or perpetuate the habits that aren't serving you?

As mentioned, intention is also about adjusting our process along the way, as we learn what is (and isn't) working. Suppose your goal is to pursue further training or education, and you need to study for the entrance exam while working full time. You plan to study at home after work. But once you get home, you just want to have dinner and relax. You revise your plan to waking up early to study, but then your energy fizzles during your workday. Cramming in study during the weekend doesn't work, either. Finally you see the solve: stay an extra hour at work and study there. Once you're home, your reward is knowing your studying's done; it's time to relax. You refine the plan by packing a dinner salad or sandwich or picking something up at lunchtime, so hunger doesn't impede your concentration. This is a habit you can automate. You are achieving a goal you value, have addressed practical issues like hunger and your energy levels, have established milestones and deadlines (an hour or so a day for X months will get the job done), and have identified positive cues that support your goal:

WORKSPACE = POSITIVE CUE FOR PROFESSIONAL BEHAVIOR
AND TASK COMPLETION
HOME = POSITIVE CUE FOR RELAXATION AND REST

Exercise: Intentionality Inventory

Keep a detailed calendar for a week of how you're actually spending your time. Then in a nonjudgmental fashion, ask yourself:

- Does my use of time match with my desired habits, values, or goals?
- If not, what's interfering with my sticking to them?
- What did I do this week that aligns with my values and goals?
- What helped me achieve those steps?
- How can I revise my plan to make my new habits more likely to stick?

Get Granular

You can optimize your chances for habit automation by setting specific, realistic, compassionate goals. Too broad ("lose weight and get fit" or "declutter") and the lack of a clear plan can lead to overwhelm, procrastination, and failure. Too onerous a set of expectations ("Lose forty-five pounds in three months by walking six miles daily, doing weight work every other day, and swimming and practicing yoga on weekends"; "Spend an hour every evening tidying and make trips to donation centers on weekends"), and those high expectations can derail us. An uncompassionate framing—"Stop being a fat, undisciplined slob"—only undermines self-efficacy by reinforcing negative self-images.

If you're setting goals to "be more/do more," ask yourself if they're based on arbitrary standards in comparison with others. Without a clear connection to your personal values, these artificially inflated goals can lead to failure and more self-flagellation (see Integrate Identity, page 285).

The goal of the "get granular" phase is to create a framework specific enough to get you started, broad enough to let you find your pace, and compassionate and intentional enough to feel appealing and attainable: "I want to make a plan to lose weight, get more fit, and enjoy a tidier home over the coming year."

Exercise: New Habits, New Directions

Choose a habit you'd like to start or change. Then consider:

- How might you frame your desired new habit positively, compassionately, and realistically? [Example: Reframe "I want to stop eating fast-food takeout" as "I want to prepare and eat food that energizes and nourishes my body and brain."]
- How might you be more specific about your intentions and proposed solutions? [Example: "I want to limit fast-food takeout to one day per week, buy a cookbook on simple, healthy home cooking, and start a walking program, maybe with a friend."]

Write your habit goal in your journal. Remember you can revise it as you learn what helps you maintain healthy habits.

A key step in automaticity is to have an *activity plan*: deliberate decisions about what, where, when, and how to implement the new behavior. The activity plans most likely to make a habit stick are detailed and anticipate and plan around obstacles—known as coping planning—which helps us devise realistic habits; determine logistics, including alternatives and contingencies; and enlist supporting habits to serve as a scaffold for the bigger main habit.

Since Stan's transition to remote work had blurred the lines between his professional and personal lives, his contingencies included clearly setting availability boundaries with his colleagues: blocking his online calendar after certain hours to meetings or calls, and leaving out-of-office messages when he was with his family, was prepping meals, or needed to work out.

Exercise: The Devil Is in the Details: Your Activity Plan

Here are some questions to consider as you create your own activity plan:

- *What will you do?* Starting when? How often? Which days? What time? With whom? And by when? As long as it's not unrealistic, setting a deadline date can help you carve out time for something you want to do. A patient of mine who is a very talented artist was having difficulty finding time to work on her art because of her busy corporate job. She enjoyed creating art for friends, so I suggested she pick a friend's birthday and give a piece of her art as a gift.
  - Whenever possible, utilize your "power hour": to avoid hits to your sense of proficiency, don't attempt demanding tasks when you are not at your best. Try to plan them for when you're most focused and energetic and least distracted. For me, it's just after I've seen my patients and before my kids get home from school.
- *What tools and/or information will you need?* Equipment, supplies, apparel, or gear? Instruction? (See Who Can Help?, page 273.)

- *How could you start small?* Studies have found that people who exercise regularly (three or more times a week) but with limited intensity are happier than those who exercise intensely but just once a week. Start by doing what you can on a regular basis. Instead of taking the approach that you have to be in the gym for ninety minutes or it's not a real workout, go for fifteen minutes (if you do more, great!). Through a process called successive approximations, you arrive at your goal by reinforcing the cumulative steps that shape the final behavior. Resist the perfectionistic temptation to do a job to completion. Instead, for example, schedule a time to get out and move for just fifteen to twenty minutes. Afterward, do something fun/rewarding. Then schedule a time to repeat. Scheduling encourages automaticity by removing choice/decision. Rewards reinforce the schedule. Small wins set the stage for bigger ones by telling us it's safe to think big, that we have a good likelihood of achieving our aims.
- *How could you break your desired habit into small successive steps?* Enter your habit formation schedule into your calendar.

Take Accountability

Accountability helps set you up for success by identifying how you'll know if you're meeting your goals. Accountability can seem scary (read: shame/blame). Let's reframe: accountability is about being in control of your habits by setting up supportive systems to get going, keep going, see how it's going, and help it go better.

Exercise: Your Accountability Practices

How will you monitor the inner game of habit change? Accountability is also about monitoring your thoughts and feelings related to a habit. Most of us are prone to all-or-nothing thinking, believing we're doing worse (or maybe better) than we really are. The truth is likely somewhere in between. We boost proficiency when we can locate and plug the holes where old habits are trickling through.

- *How will you track your progress?* Not to punish yourself, but to figure out how close you are to your goals, and how to get closer. While I've discussed my reservations about technology earlier, I believe it's a useful tool for monitoring habit formation. Whatever your habit goal(s), there's probably an app for it. Or keep a spreadsheet, or jot in your journal. Look for patterns, especially with setbacks. What happened? What time of day or night was it? Where were you? Who were you with? Were strong emotions, stress, hunger, or fatigue involved? What kind of day had it been? etc. What could you modify for better results? Is some emotional processing needed (chapter 3, "Processing Emotions")? Could you reframe real-time situations and thought distortions, as explored in chapter 4, "Problem-Solving," and elsewhere?
- *Who can help?* There was a social experiment where participants were asked to gauge an incline's steepness. Those who did this task alone thought the incline was steeper than if they did the same task with a friend. And addiction programs have had better impact when recruiting people who are friends.
  - Practical Optimists don't persist alone. They often find mentors, activity partners, groups, clubs, or confidants to support their habit formation journey.
  - I define accountability partners broadly. They might be people you engage in your new habit with. Most of us don't want to let someone down by bailing on them. Stan involved his friends in his fitness goals, meeting them for basketball or jogging, ensuring he'd show up (and have fun). But accountability partners can provide information—for

example, a nutritionist, a trainer, an instructor, or a coach. Or medical support—your doctor, a therapist, or other health specialists. Or physical or emotional comfort—a massage therapist, trusted friends who offer encouragement by phone or text or hang with you, doing their work while you work. Or logistical support: Stan's mother planned special nights out with his daughters so Stan and his wife could have date nights as part of his goal to strengthen their relationship.

- *How will you systematize self-monitoring?* Record how you're feeling while engaging in the desired habit. Self-monitoring has been shown to be effective for people in various settings. Use the Flip the Script exercise (chapter 5) to practice reframing self-critical statements. A key question to ask is: *What is the utility of feeling or thinking as I do?*

  - Stan and I created a PO habits tracker as a way to journal about his journey, keep track of supporting habits, be aware of what he was feeling, and even help him clear his thoughts before bed so he could get a good night's sleep—another goal. Depression had significantly affected Stan's motivation level, but by tracking his emotional responses through the day in the PO habits tracker, he noticed his mood was often highest when he completed a task he'd avoided. He felt the pride and proficiency associated with completing a task and, most important, could see his progress through his own tracking method. Both helped Stan's motivation when he wanted to avoid tasks. Often when we're feeling down or overwhelmed, we avoid doing the things we know we should be doing, often the things that are likely to cheer us up. It feels like way too much effort. But when you put one foot in front of the other and just make a start, even though you weren't initially in the mood, you inevitably feel good afterward and are glad you did it. Particularly if dealing with depression, we have to take steps to do the things we found enjoyable and felt adept at. They may not feel enjoyable at first, but the positive reinforcement comes later. Stan was learning this firsthand. Habit-tracking journals abound, so feel free to create your very own PO habits tracker. You can start with the strategies in this chapter (Be Intentional, Get Granular, Take Accountability, and so on) and develop your customized way to track your emotions, evaluate your obstacles, forge your habits plan, and then see how it's unfolding: what's helping; what's getting in the way.

Feed the Good Wolf and Starve the Bad One

What inhibits automaticity? Well, life . . . the moon, the stars, Mercury in retrograde (we actually did work Mercury into our care plan for an astrology-focused patient of mine—though he let little else interfere with his habit of working on a successful nutrition and lifestyle blog at seven A.M.!).

No discussion of habit formation would be complete without talking about how to deal with obstacles and setbacks. Big-picture goal: you want to feed the "good wolf" (remember the fable of "The Two Wolves" from chapter 1?) by making good habits accessible, convenient, and approachable, and starve the "bad wolf"—i.e., bad habits—by reducing temptation, opportunity, and accessibility.

Suppose you're working from home. It's been a rough day—your boss reprimanded you; a project went badly. Sometimes your partner is there for comfort. Today the house is empty, but the fridge is full. It's right there when you need to stretch your legs, escape your screen, or refill your water bottle or your coffee cup. It's stocked with yummy (less-than-nutritious) snacks. You just ate lunch, but you find yourself grabbing something, well, not so healthy to eat, just because it's readily available and provides immediate gratification.

Harmless, right? Sure—if it's once in a while. But I've seen and personally experienced how our not-so-great-but-comforting habits can come back to haunt us.

Bad habits persist for myriad reasons: they're easy, pleasurable, convenient, and accessible—thus automatic.

Wait! These are all the things we want our *good* habits to be! Let's get them to swap places! Fortunately, we can use the same methodology to break bad habits that we do to create good ones.

To automate habits, the three things to remove from the picture are motivation, decision, and willpower. Since making choices requires mental energy, the brain often relies on heuristic or fast thinking to arrive at the quickest solution to a problem, particularly when we're emotionally or physically vulnerable—e.g., stressed, angry, anxious, tired, or hungry. If turning to food or other unhealthy behavior is the convenient route, that's what it'll want to do. It's up to us to lay down the tracks for the good behaviors in the brain, and then ride along (practice) them. The more we do this, the stronger those neural pathways become. The key to habit automation is engaging in the behavior with regularity. Consistency, especially in the face of obstacles, is essential.

In everyday terms, this means making it easy to see, access, and use the things connected to your new behaviors, thus reducing the entry barriers to healthy habits, and raising the barriers against unhealthy habits by making them hard to repeat and be reinforced in the brain. Common sense, you say? Yup. But what's happening in the brain is quite significant. You're actually unhooking your feel-good brain chemistry from one thing and tethering it to something else.

PO Pearls
Set low barriers for positive behaviors, high barriers for negative ones.

We crave what we're used to and exposed to. Dopamine, a brain chemical, is released when we experience something we associate with pleasure, whether new or familiar. The connection to the source of that pleasure becomes so strong that just the idea or anticipation of the pleasure-giving activity, or seeing things associated with it, increases dopamine. We see this in addiction: the people, places, and things associated with the substance—passing a favorite bar, seeing the paraphernalia—all increase dopamine. And just as we can get accustomed to something (for example, our customary flavor intake and preferences in food—how salty or sweet we may prefer something), these all can be altered over several weeks simply by changing what we are used to. We see that people can become accustomed to a reduction of dietary salt or sugar intake over time, without needing flavor substitutes. We are what we're used to—and we can change what we're used to. As I told Stan: "You have a lot more control than you think."

So, the next time you berate yourself for lacking the willpower to implement whatever good habit you're trying to adopt, remember this: You don't lack willpower. You just got used to something you need to unlearn/get unused to.

If we crave what we're used to, then let's get used to the good stuff by making healthy habits easily accessible. I love adapting the concept of mise en place—a culinary term referring to having all your recipe ingredients prepped and equipment assembled, so all you have to do is bang out that tasty recipe.

We naturally already do this—hanging keys, sunglasses, and umbrella by the door so we can grab and go; stowing dental floss next to the toothbrush; putting that book we want to finish on our nightstand. But science supports it. Leveraging the cues that trigger habits can be incredibly effective. For example, one study found that one way to increase recycling was to put recycling bins next to trash cans—which people were already using—versus just twelve feet away.

If your goal is healthier eating and regular exercise, accessibility means putting healthy foods and snacks in plain sight; having your gym bag packed and ready; positioning your sneakers by the door for a run and your free weights near the TV for workouts with a fitness video or a show; stashing playlists, podcasts, and audiobooks on your phone for your stationary bike session; setting up a standing calendar date to meet your friend for pickleball.

Lowering barriers to positive behaviors can range from methodically working through logistical details (joining a gym, getting equipment) to processing negative emotions (feeling overwhelmed, which can lead to inconsistency, a low sense of proficiency, and procrastination).

The more positive experiences you have with your new habits, the more you'll reinforce the associated pleasure chemistry—one more reason to celebrate successes. Taking advantage of this dopamine system is why we will talk about adding small rewards later in this chapter.

Tracking your progress (see Take Accountability, page 272) helps get the dopamine response of anticipation going—pleasure at just the thought of the reward: You'll see yourself gaining on your goal and visualize the day it will happen—how great it'll feel.

You can prevent obstacles and setbacks by being prepared with contingency plans and an if-then mindset. Suppose you're trying to drink less alcohol. If you have to go to a business dinner or are invited to a happy hour with friends, you'll make sure you have a contingency plan in place before you go—for example: a one drink maximum, leaving early, or (in the case of the nonobligatory happy hour) deciding not to go and/or offering a daytime workaround where there's likely to be less alcohol involved. (If you think these sound like situation selection and modification from chapter 4, you'd be right!)

Conversely, remove or make it inconvenient to access or even see reminders of the habit you're trying to extinguish. Again, commonsensical but effective: even with a habit as entrenched as smoking, one important way to curb cigarette purchases is by reducing the visibility of cigarette packs in stores.

In our sample goal of healthier eating and regular exercise, raising the barrier for negative behaviors might mean: Keep unhealthy snacks and foods out of sight, available in limited portions, or (mostly) not in the house. Plan your menus, make a grocery list, and look for and buy only those items. Yoke together good behaviors: when you hydrate, take your vitamins. Uncouple behaviors that don't serve your goals (offering a daytime alternative to happy hour, as noted above, is one example). If binge-watching preempts your workout, disrupt that pattern—maybe set a TV reminder on your phone and watch only when it pings.

Why We Get Stuck

Understanding Procrastination

It can be upsetting and confusing when we don't start, stick to, or complete things we want or need to do. What's going on?

People procrastinate not because they're lazy or disorganized, but because they don't believe their desired outcome is possible. Procrastination is more about self-management than time management.

Procrastination happens when we overestimate a task's magnitude and underestimate our ability to execute it. We assume it is too complex or arduous, is above our skill level, will overwhelm us, will demand more than we can offer, or will have a negative result. Intimidated and thinking we can't rise to the challenge, we give up, avoid, or don't initiate.

Overestimate Task Magnitude + Underestimate Proficiency = Procrastination

Another factor: if you have perfectionist or maximizer tendencies (try the quiz for the latter in chapter 4), you believe there's just one right method that can be found only through a comprehensive analysis. Lacking time for that analysis, you don't make a decision.[27]

Excessive worry can paralyze us. Sometimes we're aware of it, but sometimes we're not: we think, *I haven't had a chance to schedule*

---

[27] Remember, too, humans' tendency toward choice overload when facing too many choices (chapter 7).

my mammogram because I've just been so busy with XYZ, when the real reason is worry powered by unprocessed emotions: *What if I have breast cancer like Mom?*

Brain studies show small amounts of pressure can be helpful for learning and memory, but large amounts can be debilitating. The root of procrastination is seeing the task in its entirety—and that's too daunting.

The solution: Use the strategies in this chapter to downsize the magnitude of the task; upsize your sense of proficiency. As you chip away at things and start seeing results, you narrow the attainability gap between the task and you. You start seeing yourself as someone capable of achieving those results. This is the core philosophy behind my approach to implementing and practicing healthy habits.

Troubleshooting Tips

The first step in troubleshooting obstacles and setbacks in habits is recognizing that they show up in all sorts of forms, including avoidance, procrastination, lack of accountability, and quitting, and they often appear in the midst of stressful events leading to emotional upheaval—as in the case of Stan, who was dealing with grief and loss. Coping skills can be compromised and overwhelmed by distressing emotions and depression. They can also show up as new or chronic medical illnesses as a result of difficulty adhering to key lifestyle interventions.

Asking self-compassionate questions can help ensure that you're feeding the good wolf and not the bad one when such obstacles appear and setbacks happen.

Can I Be Kind and Curious About Setbacks?

No one ever automated a habit while grumbling about what a failure they are. We need to be kind to ourselves when the brain's working hard to adopt new behaviors and let go of old ones. Offer TLC as you would for a friend.

Stan needed to stop beating himself up.[28] Research shows that self-compassion exercises can lead to a more optimistic mindset, resilience, a growth mentality (using failure as an opportunity to learn and grow), and intrinsic motivation—i.e., wanting to learn or improve at something for its own sake. Self-compassion helps us take responsibility without shaming self-judgment, which cripples proficiency by telling us we're inadequate. Thus it supports us in reframing failure, seeking help, and trying again. Better yet, it appears to motivate health-related behaviors that pose challenges for many of us, such as sticking to a diet, quitting smoking, or starting a fitness regimen. When setbacks happen, what's important is getting back in the saddle. The key: Bolster your sense of self-worth and proficiency, which take a hit when we can't uphold promises to ourselves. Otherwise the bad habit may snowball. Suppose you have a shopping habit you know is interfering with your financial security. But the more you do it, the less confident you feel about your ability to stop—so you shop more to comfort yourself. Snowballing happens to everyone at times. Blaming yourself, your situation, or others won't help. Self-compassion is associated with a greater desire to improve in the face of setbacks.

Owning setbacks involves acknowledging reality and learning from it. As a Practical Optimist, you don't look at failure as permanent. Instead:

- *Stay present. Here I am. It is what it is.*
- *Channel compassion.* What would you say to a friend going through this?

---

[28] Feelings of worthlessness, guilt, and shame are typical symptoms in depression. Ruminations about the self, but ruminative thoughts in general, are associated with severity and relapse in depression—which is why we want to combat them early, including getting help when needed.

- *Take back the reins with some caring but direct questions. What am I craving? What am I missing? What do I really need?* Remember that questioning yourself—forcing yourself to engage in an active, conscious, deliberate inquiry—is a form of slow thinking. In this situation we want to slow things down so your brain doesn't default to the old habit.

- *Find gratitude for whatever you learned or what went right.* Maybe you stuck with things longer, found a useful app, or made a schedule versus winging it (see Your Activity Plan, page 271). Or perhaps you've learned some takeaways that you can implement in adjusting your plan.

- *Boost your motivation by recalling your previous successes.* Reminders of navigating past challenges can help manage your perspective and give you confidence. For Stan, this meant recalling habits he'd incorporated at other times when he was better able to manage his metabolic systems through a healthier lifestyle and when he was physically able to coach his kids' sports teams or ride bikes as a family. What skills, abilities, or habits have you drawn on in the past?

- *Pause, don't quit. If I'm tired after fifteen minutes at the gym, I can leave and take a nap.* If you feel overwhelmed, pause the experience and reschedule. Pausing is self-compassionate, helping you regroup rather than quit. If you're tempted by a "bad wolf" habit, take a ten-minute pause. Ask: *Is this going to make me feel better now? What about tomorrow?*

- *Gently challenge feelings, thoughts, and beliefs.* I've heard my patients say things like "I hate/am disgusted with myself for being unhealthy and out of shape," or "I've let myself down." Negative thoughts and emotions interfere with habit formation, invoking pessimistic thinking by reinforcing the perception that any setback is permanent, pervasive, and personal: *It will never get better, I'm failing, it's all my fault/I'm a disaster.* Pessimism makes us passive: *I can't do this. I might as well give*

up. I'll just have to wait for the right conditions/more motivation.
Reframing feelings and thought distortions using ABCDE, as
you practiced in previous chapters, helps open you to possibilities.

- Stan used his PO habits tracker to monitor his progress.
  He acknowledged when he was having a hard time and
  reminded himself that anyone in his position would feel
  the same. Self-compassion accepts emotions—*I know what
  this situation stirs up/brings up for me. This is hard*—while
  reminding us that emotions aren't facts.[29]

- ***Deploy harm reduction.*** Accept that a setback is in progress
  and act to limit the damage. Headed for a cookie coma? Reserve an individual portion and put the whole package out of
  sight—no visible temptation. Better yet, bag portions in advance. Workout not happening? Do some yard work or take a
  walk in your neighborhood. Didn't listen to your language lesson? Tune in to online radio in that language. Get back on the
  horse tomorrow.

- ***Include breaks.*** Not receiving satisfaction from a behavior is a
  setup for setbacks. We'll disengage, not sticking with it long
  enough to automate it. We must be rewarded. This positive
  reinforcement confirms our belief that the decision to change
  our behavior was worthwhile. Particularly if setbacks are frequent, build in periodic down days, rest days, "cheat days," or
  "cheat meals," when you give yourself some flexibility or a
  limited time off from the habit-formation process. Consider
  them rewards for how you've been doing, plus setback prevention, all rolled into one. And add them to your PO habits
  tracker.

---

[29] There was a time when I was shy, believing people wouldn't be interested in what I had to
say. If I'd held on to that belief, I wouldn't have the pleasure of talking to you today, one
Practical Optimist to another.

Are My Goals Realistic, or Do I Need to Reassess?
My dad used to share this example: You have a bunch of pencils rubber-banded together. Someone tells you to break them all. You look at the bunch and say, "No way can I do that." But . . . no one said you couldn't break them one at a time.

Optimists experience less pressure and more self-compassion when they don't try to meet rigid, arbitrary, or strict standards. Make sure your goal is realistic for *you*—not your friend or sibling, an influencer or celebrity, or the "you" you were before you had kids, broke your leg skiing, or were doing the jobs of two people.

Not a morning person? Then going from 0 to 100 mph by signing up for a six A.M. hot yoga class requiring you to go to bed earlier than you'd like, get up at five, wolf down a protein bar, tug on your fancy yoga pants, commute to meet your early-bird friend for class, then rush home to shower, dress, and be bright-eyed at your desk for your first meeting of the day is a prescription for failure. Personally, if I have to change five habits to adopt one new one, it probably won't happen.

I'm not saying don't push yourself. But an inflexible approach that doesn't honor your current situation isn't humane and risks habit failure. With a more gradual route, you might come to enjoy that sunrise class.

- *Are your goals and standards compassionate?* Are they harsh, critical, rigid, idealistic standards that belong perhaps to somebody else (if so, to whom)? If things aren't working, reassess. Do you need to add breaks? Celebrate smaller wins?
- *Recognize the triggers for bad habits.* Do long, stressful workdays lead to mindless scrolling/eating/missed workouts? When you understand what triggers negative habits, you're better able to devise a plan to thwart them.
- *Uncouple cues from the habitual reward by choosing an alternative.* Instead of moseying to the kitchen after stressful work events, put a yoga mat next to your desk and drop down there

for a stretch or a five-minute meditation audio, until that becomes your go-to.

- *Spot permission-giving statements.* Bad habits sneak through when we lower the bar with permission-giving statements. Like those times you stay up late scrolling—colloquially known as revenge bedtime procrastination—trying to reclaim lost time in a day spent serving/taking care of others (*I had a long day; I deserve fun*) or not working on the project you're trying to get done (*I won't be productive anyway*). Then the next morning you skip your morning workout class—even though you paid for it in advance—and sleep in: "I need to be on my game at work." A PO habits tracker can help you track setback triggers. Stan learned to recognize permission-giving statements about not needing to hit the gym when they popped up, to acknowledge them, and to redirect his thoughts toward his ultimate goal of living a healthier life for his family.

By de-escalating emotions, recognizing your triggers, controlling your environmental cues, and detecting permission-giving statements, you're catching bad behaviors before they snowball, or exerting damage control and stockpiling future prevention tactics if they do.

Integrate Identity

Practical Optimists use habits to reach their goals and create goals to stick to good habits. That first part seems obvious. But what about the second?

Practical Optimists connect their goals to their deeper values. When you do this, your why and your why not—why you can't go without pursuing it—become highly compelling. It's called goal-congruent behavior: behavior tied to a larger theme or purpose. We're more likely to follow through with goal-congruent behavior because

our purpose serves as headlight and engine, illuminating our direction
while powering the journey. When your goal connects to your identity
and values—not arbitrary measures of success/external validation—
it's non-negotiable. So, by extension, are the habits needed to meet it.
One way to set up goal-congruent habits: make your goal part of your
identity. You know who runs regularly? Runners. Seeing ourselves as
"someone who is a _____" makes a desired habit much more
likely to automate.

Complete this sentence:

I WANT TO SEE MYSELF AS _____

_____.

Some fill-in ideas might be:

. . . someone who cooks/is organized/is fit/takes care of their
    health.
. . . a calm, poised public speaker.
. . . a certified practitioner of [fill in the blank].
. . . a reader.
. . . a community contributor.

Stan wanted to take charge of his health to be there to support and
provide for his family. I asked Stan to set long- and short-term goals
that would influence his habits.

Stan's long-term goals: To eventually get his blood pressure and
    cholesterol levels under control to the point where he could
    successfully wean himself off medication under his doctor's
    supervision. He also had a longer-term goal to run a marathon
    one day.
Stan's short-term goals: To coach his children's sports games with-
    out tiring or losing his breath. He added a bonus short-term

goal to run a 5K within the year—a feasible goal to work toward as a short-term indicator of his success in adhering to his daily healthy habits. Many of my patients use races to motivate themselves toward daily health behaviors. I'm open to whatever works for you!

To reach his goals, Stan committed to working with his doctors, a nutritionist, and a trainer if needed to improve his blood pressure, cholesterol, and blood sugar levels. Not everyone has the resources for or necessarily needs a trainer, for example, to meet their goals. Take a look at your options and your needs, and see what makes sense for you.

If you see yourself as a community contributor, you might spend internet time searching for a local project to be involved with instead of scrolling social media. If you're bound to be someone who cooks, you might swing by the grocery for salad ingredients and fish to grill instead of the drive-through nearby. The more your goals fit with things you value, the more likely you are to persist in the habits required to attain them, despite setbacks.

Jump-Start with Fun

We're often so focused on productivity that we feel self-indulgent if we're having fun. Remember: Positive emotions associated with a habit help us to feel stimulated, relaxed, rewarded, satisfied, and proud. Such emotions inspire us to persist and lower the entry barrier to automaticity. It was very important for Stan to prioritize fun in taking better care of his physical and emotional health. He created a fun-based health habit of jogging or playing basketball with friends two to four times weekly. Seeing his buddies while burning calories was a highly motivating win-win (it added accountability, too).

Celebrate small victories and mini milestones. Will it be every five pounds lost? Power walking the hill without stopping? Reading a book for thirty minutes a day for a week?[30] Completing a test-prep chapter? Your celebration or reward might be a quiet mental high five (I like to actually say to myself, *You've come so far*), an exuberant text to a friend or an accountability partner, admiring your progress on a tracking app or smart watch, or a small treat that makes the day feel special. Make sure your reward supports your goal (if you're trying to lose weight, your reward shouldn't be eating a whole chocolate cake in one sitting). Pick something different—maybe a massage. For bigger milestones, enjoy bigger rewards. When Stan reached the halfway point on his weight-loss journey, he treated himself to new golf clubs. He wasn't accustomed to spending on himself, so this reward was a sign of self-compassion and self-commitment.

Celebrating wins along the way boosts confidence, our sense of proficiency, and our pride by affirming that our efforts are making a difference and prevents the harsh thinking that says we're a failure if we don't attain the Big End Goal. Maybe we haven't lost all the pounds we'd hoped to by our class reunion, but we can rejoice that we've started exercising regularly and relish the results.

PO Pearls
Never minimize the small wins, for they beget the big ones.

When we first undertake a new habit, we often associate pleasure with reaching milestones or goals. When anticipation *of the activity itself* causes excitement or pleasure, you're well on your way to habitualization. The more joy you can find in the journey, the easier it'll be

---

[30] Did you know that reading books might lengthen your life? One study found that reading books provided a twenty-three-month survival advantage (and a 20 percent reduction in mortality), thanks to its beneficial effects on cognition (and not because of participants' already having higher cognition—the researchers adjusted for that). The magic number to get this benefit? Just thirty minutes daily. Reading improves vocabulary, concentration, empathy, social and emotional intelligence, problem-solving skills, critical thinking, and deep reasoning. Join a book club and you're also decreasing isolation, which has its own cognitive benefit.

to stick to your habits. If, like Stan, being social energizes you, your "I am someone who cooks" statement (using identity to form a habit) will feel even more fulfilling when you cook with friends. Inspired by nature? Try an exercise class in a beautiful setting. If your goal is to contribute to the community, choose an activity you'll enjoy, not just be good at. An accountant could certainly volunteer to do pro bono work—but if that accountant is a passionate weekend gardener, volunteering in a community garden might bring enormous joy and satisfaction. One study found that the mortality risk of participants who volunteered one hundred or more hours per year was reduced by 44 percent—an incentive to attach your habits to a volunteer activity if there ever was one!

Activities that meet the criteria for flow—somewhat challenging but involving, fun, or fulfilling—also optimize habit formation. One friend who would die of boredom in the gym found forty years of fitness in studying dance, where the music and the chance for artistic expression and technical precision fed her mind and soul while keeping her body in shape.

Sometimes we just have to push through something we don't like doing. Build in fun by redeploying your attention or planning a reward for yourself when you reach your goal. Maybe you don't love stretching but don't mind doing it while watching your favorite TV show. Or schedule that annual mammogram you've been postponing, followed by fun with a friend or your kids.

How could you make your chosen habits or goals more interesting, fulfilling, and fun? What will your milestones be? What will you do to celebrate them?

The 4 Ms of Mental Health

After listening to Stan, speaking to his primary care physician, and reviewing his labs and patient questionnaires, I believed Stan's depression was situational and mild—and, one could argue, a normal reaction to the overwhelming events in his life. While I support the use of medications in conjunction with psychotherapy for the treatment of depression, I didn't think a traditional prescription was appropriate for him. I believed that in therapy, we could address his self-limiting beliefs and distressing emotions, optimize his coping skills, and talk about transitions at home and in the workplace, including the blow he took when he became someone who "lost his way a bit." We continued to process the grief around all that had happened in his life (including distressing world events) in recent years. Stan came to feel that through all his challenges, he was able to gain a broader perspective on what really mattered—something I often hear from my patients who've gone through extreme stress. Interestingly, it would be the challenges that ultimately bolstered his optimism in life. Stan was an optimist who under the weight of his obstacles experienced pessimism and depression, and then, I would say, built a lasting optimistic outlook based on intention, skills, and practice—the essence of PO as a mindset, skill set, and action set. Some optimists are born; some are made. And some are a combination of both! Stan was able to tap into his new, well-honed coping skills, confident they would last.

Stan and I worked on many of the skills you've been reading about in the 8 Pillars of Practical Optimism. We pulled from some of my favorite CBT techniques, including behavioral activation—putting the cart before the horse by activity planning—doing an activity that previously brought you pleasure and is good for you, even when you don't feel like it. This improved Stan's mood, increasing his leisure time. Importantly, the more time he made for rest and fun, the more he practiced self-compassion; and the more he practiced the 5 Rs of Emotional Regulation and Real-World Problem-Solving (chapter 4), the more productive he became. It wasn't work productivity, he told me. He was always productive at work even at the height of his depression— a phenomenon colloquially known as high-functioning depression, where, in the grip of our depression, we exhaust ourselves trying to continue to meet important social and role obligations in our life. But now he was leaning in more at home instead of engaging in emotional avoidance. He found the 5 Rs particularly useful in navigating real-time problem-solving with his wife: "I realized she isn't looking to me to fix it. She just needs to feel like we're in this together—a team." Lara, Stan's wife, joined us several times, and they practiced using the XYZ technique (chapter 8) to discuss her feelings of needing Stan's help. Lara told me she was happy to have "happy Stan" back again. Stan wasn't the same, though, he would tell me. How could he be? So much of the world wasn't the same. It was a sentiment I could understand and relate to. But pressure builds diamonds, my dad would tell me. (My hope is that we find ways to build diamonds without extreme circumstances.)

Stan also worked on activating his inner caregiver (chapters 5 and 8). He realized his dad's death brought about many feelings, including guilt that their relationship had become distant: "I was so busy at the end, I didn't make time for my dad as much as I wish I had." Stan isn't much different from other people—regret, remorse, shame, and inadequacy can all become louder when our lives are already noisy. There was no one technique that helped Stan get better, but rather a comprehensive approach involving many of the battle-tested approaches to mental health treatment in this book.

However, there are other habits—which can be pursued independently or in conjunction with therapy—that have proven benefits in the prevention and treatment of depression. Some can be as beneficial as medication, in mild to moderate cases. And they're wonderfully helpful to any of us grappling with twenty-first-century life. We have touched on these ideas in other chapters, but these habits distill those lessons down to their core. If there's one change I'd implore everyone I see to incorporate into their life, it is the 4 Ms of Mental Health.

The 4 Ms are natural, free, and backed by tons of evidence—and the benefits are exponential. Plus they lead to other good habits. Furthermore, they bring tremendous gratification in and of themselves.

I posted the 4 Ms on social media and in the mainstream media during the pandemic. I also shared them on an international live televised event with Global Citizen hosted by the United Nations, where I was honored to appear alongside people I admired and was asked to offer a sixty-second mental health message. I was surprised and inspired by how many people responded to them. I believe this is because they offer hope and courage, while also helping counter major life and health challenges we face, including burnout, our sedentary lifestyle, ubiquitous loneliness in a culture focused on autonomy, and the uses and distractions of technology.

Mastery
Through dedication to improvement, we shape our sense of meaning and purpose.

Movement
Through movement, we can elevate mood, sharpen and calm the mind, and support countless aspects of physical health.

Meaningful Engagement
Through our unique presence, actions, and words, we connect with others.

Mindfulness
Through gently directing our attention, we open a gateway to compassion for ourselves and others, and appreciation for life.

The 4 Ms lengthen life and improve its quality. They're the core of Practical Optimism. If you take one "prescription" from me through this book, I hope it is the inspiration to prioritize them in your life.

Mastery

Learn, improve, or get better at something! Ideally it's
something that "strengthens" you and that you care about.
It could be job-related or personal. Try, revive, or deepen a
hobby or skill: cooking, gardening, learning a new language.

What makes you feel happy, productive, creative, challenged? Go do that! You needn't become an expert to experience mastery. It's more about consistently improving your skill at something and feeding your sense of fulfillment. Always be learning and investing in yourself. Seeing your progress builds proficiency (aka competency—which, with autonomy and belonging, is considered one of our three basic needs). For older adults, proactive technology use (computer games, communicating in group chats) can preserve and promote memory and concentration and delay certain signs of aging. Research shows that for older adults, one hour of computer activity and fewer than two hours of TV per day, as well as engaging in physical activity, can reduce the risk of dementia.

Attending to this M can be as simple as incorporating fifteen minutes a day of learning through purposeful reading, practicing a new skill, starting a class, taking up a hobby, or reviving an old one. Not sure where to start? Explore the "purpose in motion" ideas in chapter 2, including tapping into flow. Flow states linked together can help boost confidence and can help build mastery when applied toward a particular skill or hobby. Need ideas for what brings you flow? Pick a task you enjoy—perhaps something you're already good at or are learning, liking, and want to get better at. Make time and space . . . let yourself immerse.

Flow needn't take hours or result in something substantial. You can write a page or a tome; plant a window box or a garden—and experience flow. Many people find flow in cooking, gardening, playing music, dancing, rewarding work, supporting a cause they believe in, or helping others.

For those living with depression, mastery can be a hard M to prioritize. One of the toughest parts of depression is that it can decrease our pleasure in things we once loved—a phenomenon called anhedonia. I asked Stan to focus on engaging in an activity that was stimulating and slightly challenging, and to have fun while doing it. He built playing sports with his friends into his activity plan. Try sparking motivation through behavioral activation: engage in a behavior first, and often the associated motivation and pleasure follow. I often ask my patients to rank things that bring them joy on a scale of 1 to 10 and suggest that they prioritize those activities, as the behavioral activation associated with them is all but guaranteed.

Learning changes the brain, causing new neuronal activity. Short, regular bursts of learning can be better than marathon sessions, giving the brain time to consolidate and subsequently retrieve the information. If you decide you really want to excel in a given area, see chapter 6 for proficiency-building info and strategies.

Movement

Get moving! Exercise or just go outside for a walk. Staying
active eases symptoms of stress, depression, and anxiety.
Take a couple of ten- to fifteen-minute fitness breaks and
enjoy a short walk, a bike ride, some yoga, or some stretches.

Our bodies weren't made for sitting all day. The body rewards us for moving. Besides helping you look stellar, exercise reduces inflammation, thought to be a main culprit behind countless medical illnesses. It also:

- releases endorphins, which reduce pain perception and activate the brain's reward centers, circulating higher levels of dopamine, serotonin, and endocannabinoids (our body's own cannabis-like substance) and generally making us feel happy and motivated;

- increases cerebral blood flow and regulates our autonomic nervous system and hypothalamic-pituitary-adrenal (HPA) axis, all thought to improve depression symptoms;
- supports nerve cell growth in the hippocampus, the part of the brain responsible for mood, learning, and memory;
- can help us combat genetic predispositions toward anxiety, mood disorders, Alzheimer's, and PTSD by regulating/increasing levels of an important protein in the brain called brain-derived neurotrophic factor (BDNF), facilitating healthy brain growth and learning.

How much exercise is needed to garner these brain-boosting benefits? According to a 2018 *Lancet Psychiatry* cross-sectional study of 1.2 million people, approximately 45 minutes, three to five times a week, is ideal.[31] But even a single exercise episode can positively impact cognitive-emotional processes such as mood, rumination, and attention, and can increase BDNF. Small amounts of exercise, even 20 minutes per day (split into 10-minute increments if need be), can have a big impact on mental and physical health. According to the *Lancet* study, regular exercise can help reduce poor mental health days by 43.2 percent.

I recommend moving for at least 15 to 30 minutes daily at whatever you enjoy. Hike, walk, swim, garden, dance while doing the dishes . . . just move! While the *Lancet* study found that team sports, mostly because of their social component, showed the greatest benefit, what's most important is finding activities you like and will do consistently. Nor is it about being athletic: a 2017 study found that light exercise, like walking, was actually more beneficial to mental

---

[31] Current physical activity guidelines for Americans, according to the U.S. Department of Health and Human Services, is 150 minutes per week (a combination of moderate-intensity aerobic and strength training). According to the Centers for Disease Control and Prevention (CDC), less than 30 percent of people in the U.S. meet the recommendations.

health than vigorous exercise.[32] And according to a 2014 Stanford study, walking boosted creative output by 60 percent when compared with sitting.

How inventive can you be at squeezing 15 to 30 minutes of activity into your day? Walk around your workspace during phone calls, break into a light jog while walking the dog. Plus errands, chores, yard work. Every bit adds up!

Meaningful Engagement

Humans need to connect. Remember your community; think about your connections, your friends, workmates, and family. Volunteer, reach out to a friend, share a joke.

Meaningful engagement isn't about how many friends we have or how social we are. It's about making sure our life contains vitalizing sparks of connection with others. We are each other's anchors in ways we don't even realize.

Who we spend time with matters. Peers predict health habits more than parents, genes, even our spouse. Our brains evolved to be highly sensitive to how others behave toward us—in fact, we have mirror neurons predisposing us to imitate what "our" group is doing, presumably to be accepted and survive. Surround yourself with people who have good habits—because they will influence you. True social support is about giving and receiving encouragement toward healthy goals and habits.

---

[32] Ever wondered why we sometimes pace when we're thinking hard, or find that taking a walk clears our mind? Our cognitive powers and our ability to walk erect evolved in tandem. Walking speed seems linked with our inner state: faster when we're excited or upset. Walking more slowly can actually reduce tension. Optic flow, which is the word for the natural orienting movement of the eyes during walking, was the basis for the development of EMDR (Eye Movement Desensitization and Reprocessing), a treatment for PTSD and anxiety disorders developed by psychologist Francine Shapiro, PhD, after she noticed its calming effect.

Cultivating meaningful engagement is especially important for those of us who live alone (a third of the people in Western countries do). Living alone increases the risk for social isolation, which increases our risk for a number of medical illnesses, including cardiovascular disease, stroke, and premature mortality. A recent study showed living alone increases the risk of depression by 42 percent.

There's something vulnerable about eating with someone. Generally, we eat with people who matter to us. And, at least for family dinners, the health benefits of this single habit boggle the mind.[33] But don't feel guilty if you can't do family dinners regularly. Try to spend a total of 20 to 30 minutes of device-free quiet time per day with kids. It's the intentional attention that matters. That goes for grown-ups breaking bread, too. If you live alone, regularly meet friends or invite them over for coffee or a bite to eat, or takeout and watching the game. It needn't be fancy. It's about connecting and being intentionally together.

Stan's favorite pastimes included family barbecues, riding bikes with his kids, and date nights with his wife. Define what feels meaningful to you. A quiet walk or sitting with a friend . . . watching a movie with your kids . . . coaching youth sports . . . reading to retirement-home residents. Engaging needn't be a big effort. Nod hello. Ask people how they are and really listen to their answer. Share an article or photo you think someone would like. Use the habit formation strategies in this chapter, coupled with the ideas in chapter 8, "People," to set up a connection habit!

---

[33] Regular family dinners are associated with lower rates of depression, anxiety, substance abuse (marijuana, tobacco, and alcohol), eating disorders, and early teenage pregnancy; greater resilience, pride, and proficiency; improved emotional processing, problem-solving, grades, and literacy; deeper conversations, improved family ties, and stronger trust with others—in essence, family dinners are a way to promote Practical Optimism in our kids.

Mindfulness

You can practice being present to your mind during any routine activity—sewing, washing your hands, playing an instrument, mowing the lawn, cooking, cleaning, and more. Practice 10 to 15 minutes of deep breathing, express gratitude, and appreciate nature.

Take a slow, deep breath. Then exhale.

Great. You're a natural.

Practicing mindfulness is about cultivating deliberate, compassionate, accepting, present-moment awareness of reality. You can direct your attention to your breath, your thoughts (even the less-than-great ones), observation, or action (doing things single-mindedly, with intention and focus).

Stan was intrigued by meditation, so I shared a quick overview of the benefits of mindfulness meditation based on research. Regular meditation creates structural changes in the brain, reducing volume in the amygdala, that part of the brain responsible for emotions such as stress, fear, and anxiety, while increasing the cortical thickness (gray matter concentration) of the hippocampus, the region involved in memory and regulating emotions. Meditation results in improved attention and concentration, and decreased mind wandering. Mindfulness-based meditation, specifically, can help alleviate symptoms of depression alone or in combination with more traditional treatments such as medication and therapy. Meditation can slow or stall the cognitive decline associated with aging. Many people report decreased stress and overall increased well-being—a greater sense of control over their emotions and life.

Stan decided to use mindfulness exercises when he felt stressed, instead of turning to food. Luckily, there are abundant resources to help us cultivate a mindfulness practice, and a good number are free. Experiment with downloading apps to your phone or tablet. Or go old-school by taking 1 to 10 minutes a day to simply sit, breathe deeply, check in with yourself, and do a body scan meditation (try the Befriending Your Breath and Befriending Your Body exercises in chapter 3).

Some people practice meditation formally in groups, trainings, and retreats, and many spiritual traditions incorporate meditative practices. These also afford community with others. But you can practice at home or anywhere—after all, your mind goes wherever you do!

I hope you'll incorporate mindfulness into your life on a regular basis. Take small doses of mindfulness throughout your day—a few minutes in your backyard or in a quiet room in the morning, on a park bench on your lunch break, or before you go to bed.

Flourishing

I woke to the giggles of my cousins, sisters not much older than I, holding candles and tickling my legs.

"*Utho!*" (Get up!) one of my cousins said.

It was 4:30 A.M. I'd had many novel experiences during our family's two-year stay in India, but never this early.

"*Chalo, chalo!*" (Let's go!) "We want to show you something."

In the misty morning air, dewdrops dotted the moonlit flowers. An aroma, majestic and heavenly, enveloped us. "*Raat ki rani,*" said my cousin. Queen of the Night—or night-blooming jasmine, I later learned. A fitting name.

The neighborhood was already starting to bustle, with street vendors pushing large rolling carts. Our elderly neighbors, in their seventies and eighties, were all coming out of their homes, dressed in traditional garb from different parts of India. Some had turbans, some had canes.

"Hello. Good morning."

"*Namaste.*"

"*Ram-Ram.*"

"*Sat sri akal ji.*"

"*Salaam.*"

I could understand their greetings in Hindi, English, Urdu, and Punjabi as we walked together—Hindu, Sikh, Muslim, Christian—all chatting, all apparently headed in the same direction. "*Guten Tag*"— there was even the German expat. I'd lived here for months, but who knew so many people started their days at this hour? Apparently, this was what everyone did, more or less, every morning.

And why were we all going into the park? Was there some kind of holiday or festival? Then as we turned the corner, beyond the cows, goats, and street dogs, I saw it: row upon row of people, of all shapes and sizes, doing sun salutations as the sun rose.

My cousins pulled me into the crowd. "Wait! I can't do those poses," I said, seeing someone do a handstand, like that was totally normal to do in a park at dawn surrounded by a thousand strangers. "I don't have a mat."

"Neither does anyone. Come on!"

So I did. I even attempted the pretzel pose. Mid-contortion, I heard someone say, "*Beta, bahut accha.*" (Very good, good job, child.) My grandmother's best friend had come over to encourage me. She'd been practicing yoga since she was my age, she said. "*Mere ghar aana, me tumhe bahut badiya bhojan khiloungi.*" (Come to my place later; I will feed you a lot of delicious food.)

"*Aunty-ji, namaste,*" I said. "*Main zaroor aaungee.*" (I will definitely come.)

Heading back to our grandmother's house, we could smell the scents of cardamom and cinnamon. Back home, the aromas of chai and chapati filled the air.

"Do you want to help me?" asked my aunt.

"Yes, please!" I said and got to work with the new wooden *belan* (rolling pin) they had gotten me to perfect my rotis.

I laughed, I moved, I ate with my family. When I look back at that time, these daily practices of mindfulness, meaningful engagement with family and community, and the mastery of learning new skills laid the early foundations of the 4 Ms of mental health, which have since become my lifelong habits, the cornerstone of everything I do. These were routine behaviors I observed in my home daily. I grew up seeing my dad meditating, writing academic papers, teaching medical students, volunteering, and presenting workshop panels in psychiatry. Now in his eighties, he still reads voraciously. His yoga mat travels with him. Nothing keeps him from his stretching, strength training, and daily three- to five-mile walk. And every single morning he talks to me. It might be a very brief conversation. But it's a non-negotiable habit. I'm certain my dad's daily habits are a major reason for his extraordinary health and longevity—not to mention that big old smile on his face.

Stan's story had a happy ending. After a full year of committing to his habits, including many basketball games with friends, bike rides with his family, and date nights with his wife and a commitment to journaling and a meditation app, as well as regular medical check-ins with his primary care physician and nutritionist, not to mention his sessions with me, Stan had lost twenty-five pounds of mostly fat, gained muscle, and lowered his blood pressure. His fasting glucose level, total cholesterol, and LDL cholesterol were the best they'd ever been. He had successfully reversed many of his heart disease risk factors (sedentary lifestyle, processed foods, poor sleep habits, excessive unmanaged stress) and was weaning himself off the myriad medications he'd been prescribed under his primary care doctor's observation and supervision.

At our final session, I sat in awe of all he'd done in a year's time by creating and sticking to better habits through short-circuiting negative feedback loops in the face of extreme stress. Through therapy, Stan gained insights into how his emotions impacted his choices, habits, interpersonal relationships, and thought processes—and how all of this affected his proficiency and ability to reestablish a healthy baseline. Whether you are recommitting to healthy habits you once practiced or attempting to develop new ones, it's important to know how our emotions and thought patterns either help or hinder us. At the end of our work together, Stan shared that he was no longer depressed, which he was grateful for. But the work he did also brought about something it seems he hadn't been expecting.

"Dr. Varma, my positive outlook . . . it's back," he told me. "I thought it was gone. I'm so grateful for that."

"Whether the glass is half full or half empty matters less and less with time," I said. "I think it's more important to know that it's always refillable. You took the time to fill your glass."

We want more than to fix what's broken, replace what's lost—we want to go far beyond that. How can our traumas and tragedies be opportunities for a type of growth that can only come through hard knocks and the humility, stillness, and vulnerability they bring?

For a long time now, my goal for myself, as well as for my patients, has been not just to withstand adversity, but to thrive in the face of it. My dream is that we create a culture that promotes exceptional emotional health and flourishing for all people. Until that day comes—and indeed, in hopes of doing our part to bring it about—we can create our own personal culture of well-being through the habits we pursue. We can't always control our circumstances, but we have control over our attitudes and behavior—what we do for our minds and bodies, and then in the world. May our habits be acts of kindness and beneficence toward ourselves and others. May Practical Optimism and the 4 Ms be a life prescription we write ourselves in quest of a lifetime of flourishing.

To view the scientific references cited in this chapter,
please visit doctorsuevarma.com/book.

EPILOGUE

*Even if the world was going to pieces, I would still
plant my apple tree.*

—UNKNOWN

After my mom passed, we decided to take a family trip to India. It was
the first time I had brought my own family. My husband and I watched
from behind as my father held my school-age son's hand, both gazing
up at the Taj Mahal.

"*Nana-ji*," said my son, looking up adoringly at my father.[34]

"Yes, *beta*."[35]

"I miss *Nani Maa*."[36]

"I miss her, too," my dad said, looking at my son. "She loved you
all so much," he said, turning to my husband and me.

"I miss her, too," I said to my son.

The last time I was at the Taj Mahal, I was holding my mother's
hand. How I missed those beautiful, warm, strong hands. Soft but
textured, with a firm grip reflecting her clarity of purpose and self-
assurance. She radiated wisdom, depth, and experience even when
she couldn't speak in her final days. Her signature laugh and her

---

[34] *Nana-ji: Nana* means maternal grandfather in Hindi; *-ji* is an honorific.

[35] *Beta* means son, but is also a term of endearment for a grandson or an affectionate term for
a child who could be the age of one's child or grandchild.

[36] *Nani Maa* means maternal grandmother.

savant-like ability to grasp the complexity of any situation and advise accordingly are among the things I miss the most. And, too, the delicious aloo parathas, pakoras, and chapatis—comfort foods she made for me even when she barely had the strength to stand. And when she couldn't stand, she pulled up a chair and gave my dad step-by-step instructions so I could be greeted with my favorite foods when I came home.

"Be the light in the darkness" were some of my mother's first words to me. They would also be some of her last. Sudeepta, my name, means beautiful light in Hindi. My mother was always the light for me, for my family, and for so many people in the communities she dedicated her life to helping. "Be the light in a dark room," she'd say to me.

We erect monuments in honor of the people and principles we hold dear, just as Shah Jahan did for his beloved wife when creating the Taj Mahal. I realized that what my mother gave me had the potential to live on—through the lives of my children, my patients, my community and media work, and my passions. Why couldn't I continue my mother's legacy in my own way?

We each have our own legacy to offer. These last few years, world events have challenged us all. Now more than ever, we're collectively looking to emerge from a stressful period equipped with the skills to protect and safeguard our health, happiness, and capacity for resiliency. Practical Optimism can help us not only develop our ability to tolerate and withstand stress, but also incorporate our challenges into an ever-evolving self that becomes—like the kintsugi vases with their gold-veined cracks in my dad's house and in Dr. L's office—uniquely more complex, beautiful, and inspiring.

Maintaining your mental and physical health is not selfish. It's a vital act of personal and public service. As our world becomes increasingly interconnected and our effects on one another increasingly far-reaching, our well-being and the world's well-being become ever more intimately and immediately entwined. We cannot be at our best for ourselves or others when our cup is empty (due to physical/emotional exhaustion) or when we perceive it as such (due to pessimistic thinking). The more each and every one of us can flourish, the better our world can flourish as each of us lives, loves, works, and contributes as only we can.

Practical Optimism isn't magical thinking or flowery language, but rather a tangible and concrete philosophy rooted in best practices and scientific evidence. It improves with practice, being put into use to meet your needs day by day. Give yourself time and grace to acclimate to the Pillars. Try applying them to specific goals or challenges. If you're not one for self-care routines or simply haven't found the time to create a practice for yourself, you might use PO to help you incorporate a different mindset and those routines you've been meaning to integrate into your life. Or it may support you in your decision to seek out therapy.

Practicing Practical Optimism in my own life has helped me to take chances, persist in the face of obstacles, and enjoy successes I didn't think were possible for me. As a result, I've been fortunate to be able to share PO principles with many more people than I'd dared to hope.

I've been thinking about Practical Optimism in some shape or form for over twenty years, though I didn't always have a name for it. And though I didn't know it growing up, the shadowy beginnings of these principles were there. They've been my footprints in the sand, the ever-present support and belief system that has been there for me through my journeys.

———

"*Nana-ji?*" my son said, looking at my dad.

"*Ha, beta.*"

"How old was Mom when you all moved here?" my son asked, referring to our two-year stay in my parents' homeland.

"She was about your age."

"Really?!" my son said excitedly, turning back and smiling at me.

"Yes." My dad looked at him with curiosity. He is a child psychiatrist, after all.

"*Nana-ji?*"

"*Ha, beta.*"

"Can you tell me more about the story of Mom and the cockroaches?"

My dad and I looked at each other and smiled. It was hard to believe I was really here, after all these years, this time with my own child, remembering that morning monsoon shortly after our arrival in what felt to me at first like an alien land, when we killed what seemed like ten thousand cockroaches invading our home—and I had my first lesson in Practical Optimism: accept the situation, persevere, do the best you can.

———————

Acceptance is perhaps the hardest part of the Practical Optimism practices—at least it has been for me at times. How do we balance a can-do attitude with one that asks us to accept with grace the things we cannot change? In my case, the push/pull of that duality was embodied in the cultural tenets I learned growing up in the West and those I absorbed from the East through my family. But the push-pull of conflicting emotions, ideas, goals, or relationships can happen in anyone's life. Mine aren't the same as yours. But the key in life and in good mental health is having a wide variety of flexible coping mechanisms—and then knowing which ones to use, depending on what life throws at you. Bending helps us not break. But when we break, the golden glue of joinery, Practical Optimism, can help make us that much stronger and more beautiful.

My inner battles ultimately helped me understand people in all their complexity, how nuanced and unique we are, and that there's rarely a black-and-white answer. It's okay to struggle. We all do—whether it's wanting to be a good parent, worker, or partner or feeling like we don't measure up. We want to be seen, recognized, valued, appreciated. We want to love, learn, and grow. Most important, we're all trying to leave a legacy, to pass on something positive. This is a basic human need.

Practical Optimism is ultimately about making your mark in the world as only you can, through small thoughtful, kind, and effective acts. It's about improving yourself and helping the lives of others around you—even when presented with challenging situations or limited options. As Practical Optimists, we're on a journey to sharpen the lens we look at our life with, to see the beauty that is there, to recognize the trials and traumas we experience as part of our journey, to draw from ourselves abilities lying deep within from the wholeness we already are, and to manifest our best in the world.

Although we may never meet, I hope that through this book you'll feel me as a friendly presence, practicing PO right alongside you. And while disappointment is the cost of doing business as a human, and even the most optimistic among us will experience disappointment from time to time, I hope that Practical Optimism will offer you the strength and conviction that your mind and body are worth investing in and fighting for, will help sustain you in your times of need, and will make the good times even more wonderful.

What is the essence of being a Practical Optimist? It is one and the same with my wish for you. It is that each day, no matter how imperfectly, you show up:

To confront the day with energy and enthusiasm.
To respond to challenges thoughtfully and proactively and persevere in the face of obstacles.
To cultivate a sense of purpose by pursuing your passions.
To find meaning in everyday joys and sorrows.
To create belonging with people, nature, and the universe at large.

*To be able to see the beauty in your imperfections and give grace to
   yourself for them.*
To hope for the best so that you can get the best.
To find gratitude amid the grief.
*To be able to refill your glass so much that it runneth over with abun-
   dant love, laughter, kindness, and compassion shared with others.*
*To have a deep sense of knowing that, fundamentally, we are all
   connected—that each of us is home, in this body, in this mind, that
   we've been given. And that we have always been home.*

This is my wish for you—to realize all these wonders residing in
you, waiting to be expressed in the world. For this is what it means to
have lived authentically, my friend the Practical Optimist.

———

My son was looking up at my dad expectantly. My dad—who is to me
a living example of Practical Optimism, my daily dose of inspiration
in his compassionate yet indomitable agency in his life and his tireless
dedication to helping others achieve the same. My dad—who, with a
wise smile, embraces the fact that we can't stop the waves of life, but
we can learn to surf.

My dad and I glanced at each other one more time. Then he took
my son's hand and said, "Sure, come with me. I will tell you the roach
story again."

———

Thank you for sharing my journey with me, and for allowing me to
accompany you on yours.

Let's stay in touch—on social @DoctorSueVarma (Instagram,
Twitter, Facebook), on LinkedIn (Sue Varma, M.D., P.C., DFAPA), or
via my website, doctorsuevarma.com.

Acknowledgments

As a Practical Optimist, I believe that when we are deeply moved to accomplish something and the timing is right, the universe conspires to help us. To that end, I want to thank all of my coconspirators, starting with my amazing team at Avery, Penguin Random House. Lucia Watson, thank you for treating this manuscript with the utmost dedication, decisiveness, and clarity of vision, and for your friendship. It's been a true delight working with you. Megan Newman, for believing in this book's potential. Suzy Swartz, for all your hard work moving every stage of the book along. Lindsay Gordon, Casey Maloney, Farin Schlussel, Anne Kosmoski, and Maya Ono, for bringing this book into the world. Sally Knapp, Laura Corless, Patrice Sheridan, Nellys Liang, and Nancy Inglis, for your work on production and design, as well as the author development team, Alison Rich, Zehra Kayi, Rachael Perriello, and Stephanie Bowen. I say that the entire Avery team had me at hello!

I want to give a special thanks to Toni Sciarra Poynter for all your help in editing and reweaving with such commitment and dedication. I will always treasure the conversations we had, the priority you gave me and this book. You are a gem.

To Kimberly Rae Miller—I'm so thankful that you believed there was a book in me. I once joked with you, okay, so how do we get this book out of me? Your unwavering belief in me, support, expertise as an editor, commitment to this work, dedication, and now friendship are incomparable. I'm so grateful to you for helping me get this book out into the world. Thank you for all you do.

With gratitude to my team at CAA—Andy Elkin, David Larabell, Alison Pepper, Emily Westcott, Zoe Willis, Claire Nozieres, Christine Lancman, and Shannon Moran—thank you for all your help in getting this book out into the world.

Dr. Eric Manheimer, author of *Twelve Patients* (adapted to the screen as *New Amsterdam*) and respected physician, mentor, and friend of twenty years, thank you so much for inspiring and encouraging me to write my own book. I will cherish and continue to use the beautiful blank leather-bound notebooks you and Diana gave me for my birthday some years ago to nudge me to write my own book. They came in handy and were just another sign I needed from the universe! Dr. Anita Sacks—I cherish our friendship, your wisdom, and your help with this book. Dr. Laura Clarke—we've been friends for years. Your dedication, time, and support for this book were invaluable to me. I'm forever grateful.

Juliana Himawan, thank you for your dedication, hard work, and continued support for this work—you are such a pleasure to work with. Dr. Ramaswamy Viswanathan, thank you for your belief in me since the very beginning.

Thank you for your support and belief in me, for amplifying my work, and for the inspirational work you do: Dr. Len Adler, Safia Samee Ali, Dr. Tal Ben-Shahar, Dr. Carol Bernstein, Sara Blanchard, Michael Bociurkiw, Caroline Bologna, Dr. Grant Brenner, Dr. Gregory Brown, Hannah Chubb, Dr. Jessica Clemons, Erin Connors, Dr. Lisa Damour, Dr. Saumya Dave, Dr. Ken Duckworth, Stephanie Essenfeld, Dr. Jeff Friedman, Dr. Deepti Gandhi, Dr. Nerina Garcia-Arcement, Dr. Jen Genuardi, Keri Glassman, Dr. Jessi Gold, Dr. Jake Goodman, Dr. Sasha Hamdani, Dr. Peter Haugen, Angela Haupt, Donna Hill Howes, Tricia Himawan, Dr. Sireesha Jathavedam, Dr. Dilip Jeste, Dr. Judith Joseph, Jeff Kreisler, Dr. Monica Krishnan, Dr. Pooja Lakshmin, Asia Lee, Tara

Lipinski, Dr. Scarlett Magda, Dr. Vania Manipod, Dr. Charles Marmar, David Moin, Jenny Mollen, Alicia Muñoz, Dr. Uma Naidoo, Dr. Vivian Pender, Dr. Molly Poag, Michelle Poler, Dr. Rachelle Ramos, Dr. Drew Ramsey, Dr. Joan Reibman, Dr. Stephanie Rosen, Gretchen Rubin, Dr. Laurie Santos, Anu Sehgal, Dr. Ian Smith, Anne Teutschel, Dr. Vatsal Thakkar, Joey Thurman, Ginnie Titterton, Dr. Jasdeep Virdi, Colleen Wachob, Dr. Greg Wilde, Susan Zinn, and Dr. Jaime Zuckerman.

To NBC, CBS, ABC, and other media networks that have given me and my work a regular platform for many powerful mental health discussions over the years. At NBC: Jenna Bush Hager, Carson Daly, Dylan Dreyer, Cecilia Fang, Willie Geist, Savannah Guthrie, Lester Holt, Chris Jansing, Sheinelle Jones, Hoda Kotb, Allie Markowitz, Jill Martin, Craig Melvin, Vicky Nguyen, Talia Parkinson-Jones, Al Roker, Gadi Schwartz, Savannah Sellers, Stephanie Siegel, and Dr. John Torres; at CBS: Nate Burleson, Tony Dokoupil, Jericka Duncan, Vladimir Duthiers, Chandler Gould, Gayle King, Dr. Jon LaPook, Norah O'Donnell, and Caitlin Pawson. Thank you for bringing mental health to the forefront years ago, when it wasn't talked about as much on TV.

Thank you to the American Psychiatric Association for your support and leadership. I'm grateful to NYU Langone Health for the opportunities I received to both learn and also give back. To my friends at NYCPS and the IAPA, thank you for recognizing my work.

Thank you to Sharecare and MedCircle—we've created award-winning mental health content together over the years. Thank you for getting this important work out into the world!

My patients—thank you for trusting me with your health and allowing me to be a coconspirator with you in your journey to exceptional wellness.

I'm indebted to all those who inspire me, giants in the field, named and unnamed.

To my family—you are the light and love of my universe. Thank you for your love, support, and guidance every step of the way.

Index

Note: Italicized page numbers indicate material in tables.

ABCDE techniques of cognitive
    restructuring, 102–3, 138–43, 170,
    245–46, 283
absolutist (all-or-nothing) thinking,
    104, 140
acceptance, 244, 306
accessibility, 275–76, 277, 278
accountability, 272–75
acknowledgment of choices, 53–55
"act" element of supportive listening,
    240–41
action plans, creating, *97*
activity planning, 270–72, 290
adaptability, 177
addiction programs, 273
adolescents, 51
adrenaline, 75
adversity, 6, 23
agency, 23, 78, 102, 106. *See also* control,
    sense of
AIM pathways
    acknowledgment of choices, 53–55
    identifying what is (or is not) working,
        54, 57–59
    moving forward, 54, 59–63
Ainsworth, Mary, 228
alcohol consumption, 278
alienation, 126
all-or-nothing thinking, 104, 140
aloneness, 256–57
alternative perspectives, seeing, 141

altruism, 62–63, 126
Alzheimer's, 295
amygdala, 82, 109, 115, 298
anger, 91, 209, 251
anhedonia, 294
antidepressant use, 12, 12n
anxiety
    addressing, with PO, 10
    and behavioral activation, 175
    and comparisons, 201
    impact of exercise on, 295
    impact on motivation, 263n
    languishing as related to, 30
    and leisure practice, 208
    and overestimation of threats, 74
    and passivity, 77–78
    pessimists' risks of, 24
    as product of unprocessed emotions, 147
    and rumination, 31
    self-compassion as buffer against, 147
    and worry journals, 89–90
apologies, 250
approval, 177, 230, 233
arrhythmia, 226
assessment, personal, 31–36
assumptions, challenging, 110
astrology, 275
atherosclerosis, 24
attachment styles, 128, 227–34, 228n, 255n
attention, 219, 233, 298
attraction of good people/opportunities, 31

autoimmune disorders, 127
automaticity
  and fun-based health habits, 287
  and "get granular" phase of habit
    formation, 269–72
  and goal-congruent behavior, 286
  and good wolf/bad wolf paradigm,
    275–76, 280, 283
  and habit formation process, 264, 266, 267
  and scheduling, 272
autonomic nervous system, 295
autonomy, 252
avoidance, 21, 44, 81, 163
awe, connecting with, 61, 213–14, 257

Bandura, Albert, 166, 179
Baucells, Manel, 79–80
Beck, Aaron T., 102n
befriending exercises, 88–89, 255–57
behavioral activation, 61, 175,
    290, 294
behavior reinforcement, 243
benefit of the doubt, extending, 135–36
Berne, Eric, 128, 228
Beyond Boredom and Anxiety
    (Csikszentmihalyi), 49n
biases, cognitive, x, 102n, 103–4
bigger-picture thinking, 63–64
blame/blaming, 97, 140, 250
blind spots, identifying, 36
blood pressure, 248, 260, 287, 301
blood sugar levels, 287
body image, 247
body scan meditation, 299
bonding, 227–28, 248, 249. See also
    attachment styles
boredom, 44
boundaries, 251–55, 271
Bowlby, John, 227
brain-derived neurotrophic factor
    (BDNF), 295
brain physiology and function, 21, 72, 225,
    294–95, 296, 298
breaks, 283
breathing practices, 86
broken heart syndrome, 226
brokenness, inner feelings of, 160
Buddhism, 168, 195
budget constraints, 254

burnout, 44, 54, 56–57, 61
Burns, David D., 102n

cardiovascular disease, 225, 229, 297
caregivers and caregiving
  and attachment styles, 227–28,
    231, 234
  and habits of good mental health, 291
  influence of our early, 128, 138
  and self-compassion, 255
catastrophizing, 140, 171, 199
Centers for Disease Control and Prevention
    (CDC), 295n
cerebral cortex, 72
challenges, 10, 61, 169
Chisholm, Shirley, 179
choices
  acknowledgment of, 55
  and cultivating healthy habits, 263–64
  overload in, 279
  paradox of, 196–97
cholesterol, 225, 260, 301
Churchill, Winston, 113
civic engagement, 224
cognitive behavioral therapy (CBT)
  about, 25–26, 25n
  author's initial experience with, 3, 4
  buffering effects of stress, depression, and
    anxiety, 24
  and cognitive restructuring, 102
  and Mindfulness-Based Cognitive
    Therapy, 87, 87n
cognitive dissonance, 78–80
cognitive distortions, 102n, 103–4, 186
cognitive flexibility, 240
cognitive powers, 296n
cognitive restructuring, 102–3, 138–43, 170
collaboration, 116, 253
communication, openness in, 254
community engagement, 226
commuters, 243–44
comparisons
  consequences of, 201
  evading, with self-compassion, 147
  frequency of, 129–30
  and healthy/unhealthy pride, 126–27
  purpose as buffer against, 44
  and sleep deprivation, 206
  trapped in, 200–201

unfair, 141
and vicarious experiences, 176–77
compassion
and boundaries, 253
four steps to living with, 147–50
and healthy/unhealthy pride, 124
pausing as act of, 284
practicing, 92
and reframing emotions, 90
and taking responsibility, 281
and ultimate goal of PO, 153
See also self-compassion
computer activity, 293
conclusions, jumping to, 199
conditioning/messaging from youth, 128–32
confidence, 163, 186, 288
conflict/conflict resolution, 226, 233, 242–43
consistency, 276
contingencies, 271
control, sense of, 23, 78
convenience, 267, 275–76, 278
cooperation, 253
coping strategies/mechanisms, 29, 85–86, 97, 152, 164
cortisol, 24, 51–52, 127, 226
COVID-19 pandemic, 12, 28, 46, 56–57, 223, 292
creativity, 253, 257
criticism, 116, 128
Csikszentmihalyi, Mihaly, 43
cultural roots, 46–47, 58, 129
curiosity, 61, 177, 280–81
cynicism, 44, 56, 147

Darwin, Charles, 71
death, 12, 21, 50–51, 225, 265, 297
decentering practice, 86–87
decision fatigue, 109, 196–97, 263
deficits model of health, 5, 31
dementia, 52, 293
denial, 19, 22
Dennett, Daniel, 65
depression
addressing, with PO, 10
and attachment styles, 229–30, 231
and automating habits, 280
chronic, 230
and comparisons, 201
and effects of loneliness, 227
and 4 Ms of mental health, 290–91, 294–95, 297, 297n, 298
and healthy pride, 127
impact on healthy habits, 261–62
impact on motivation, 263n, 274
and lack of purpose, 44, 45–46
languishing as related to, 30, 42
as leading cause of ill health/disability, 12, 28
and learned helplessness, 78
and leisure practice, 208
neural basis in brain for, 21
and overestimation of threats, 74
oxytocin's connection with, 23
pessimists' struggles with, 24
as product of unprocessed emotions, 147
rise in rates of, 12n
and risk of early death, 12
and rumination, 31, 202n, 281n
and self-compassion, 147
and sense of helplessness, 45
and shame, 45, 126, 147, 281n
and social media use, 194
and suicide risk, 221
symptoms of, 281n
and uncontrolled stress, 75
and value of social connection, 225
destructive behaviors, 81
"detect" element of supportive listening, 239
dharma, 47, 129, 136, 154
diabetes, 260
dietary habits, 275, 277, 278
discrimination, x
distorted thoughts, 102n, 103–4, 169–71, 186
distractions, 44, 97, 115, 197, 257
divorce, 221, 242
dopamine, 196, 211, 218, 276–77, 278
dorsal raphe nucleus (DRN), 78
doubt, feelings of, 44
drinking too much, 81
Durant, Will, 260
Dweck, Carol, 169

early life/environments, 230, 234
economic instability, 11
eight pillars. *See* Pillars of Practical Optimism

Ekman, Paul, 71
Ellis, Albert, 151
EMDR, 25n, 296n
emotional processing, 66–93
about, 9, 38, 69
claiming emotions, 84–85
disrupting unhealthy patterns, 85–86
emotional regulation as related to, 69
and exerting a positive influence, 70
and four steps to self-awareness, 81–92
and iceberg effect, 70
and management of one's mind, 70
naming emotions, 82–84
and purpose of emotions, 70–73
reframing emotions, 90–92
and rumination, 76–77
sleep's role in, 109
taming emotions, 85–90
and unprocessed emotions, 73–80
emotional reasoning, 104, 140
emotional regulation
about, 69
and attachment styles, 227
of author, 29
defined, 95
elements of, 245
emotional processing as related to, 69
emotional recognition as essential to, 95
five Rs of, 105–15
goal of, 105
reappraising situations, 113–15
reassessing situations, 105–8
and recognition/validation of
emotions, 111
redeployment (distraction) from, 115
refueling, 108–10
reminding yourself of positives, 112
requesting input, 110–12
and suppression/inhibition of
emotions, 95
emotions
being in touch with, 70
as biological/physical experiences, 71, 82
etymology of word, 70
as feedback signals, 69, 121
fleeting nature of, 73
gaining clarity on, 185
impact of, on behavior, 121
masking of, 72

naming, 82–84, 95
persistence of negative, 73
prolonged experiences with (moods), 71
purpose of, 70–73
reading others' expressions of, 125–26
recognition of, 95
suppression/inhibition of, 81, 82, 95
underlying, 98
See also emotional processing; emotional
regulation
empathy
and action, 241
extending, 92
and guilt, 126–27
intentionality in, 193
and oxytocin, 23
and reframing emotions, 90
and self-compassion, 153–54
and sleep deprivation, 206
and technology usage, 191, 192–93
employment and workplaces
burnout in, 44, 54, 56–57
connections in, 226
dread of, 44
finding meaning in, 43
and quiet quitting, 165
and salary gap, 68
self-compassion mindset in, 174
and self-efficacy, 163–64
and sense of purpose, 48–49, 49n,
52–53, 62
and work-life balance, 127
workplace accidents, 226
endorphins, 225
energy levels and burnout, 56
Engineering Happiness (Sarin and
Baucells), 79
envy, 44, 201
epigenetics, 229, 265
epinephrine, 24, 51–52, 75
escape behaviors, 44
evolution, 244, 296, 296n
exercise and movement, 13, 63, 64, 86, 194,
195, 272, 292, 294–96
exhaustion, physical and mental, 44
expectations
managing, 79–80, 93
of other people, 92
of positive outcomes, 102

and problem-solving skills, 116
responses to, 151
and social media use, 200–201
experience and empowerment, 175–77
exposure therapy, 90
external locus of control, 164

failures as learning opportunities, 177–78
false equivalents, 141
family
dinners, 297, 297n
impact of, on sense of purpose, 46–47, 58
and maintaining traditions, 108
medical history of, 261
fatigue, 11, 167, 174–75, 229, 231
feedback, 179–82, 187, 243
Festinger, Leon, 176–77
five-year views, 141
fixed mindsets, 169
flexibility, 167, 168–74, 177, 254
flourishing, 6, 30, 42, 299–302
flow state, 43, 58, 61, 211–13, 257, 293
focus, power of, 38. See also present,
remaining
FOMO (fear of missing out), 44, 201–2, 210,
216, 218
forgiveness, 250–51
Frankl, Viktor, 65, 94
Fredrickson, Barbara, 133, 236, 237
friendships. See people and relationships
friendship styles, 235–39
Friesen, Wallace, 71
fun in habit formation, 272, 273, 285, 287–89
future, 24, 171, 199

Gandhi, Mohandas, 129
genetics, 22, 23, 226–27, 226n, 229–30, 263,
265, 295
glass ceilings, self-imposed, 169
Global Citizen, 292
Global Emotions report (Gallup), 11–12
goals, 62, 119n, 162, 171–73, 284, 285–87
Google Calendar, 248
Gottman, John M., 116, 243
grace, 132–33, 135, 210–11
grandiosity, 137
gratitude, 133–36
benefits of, 134, 255n
and coping with setbacks, 282

extending grace through, 210
and FOMO (fear of missing out), 210
and grief, 59
grounding effect of, 209–11
intention required by, 135
mantras for, 211
practice of, 154
reinforcement of positive behaviors
with, 243
for things you no longer want, 59
Gretzky, Wayne, 121
grief, 59, 251, 261, 262
growth mindset, 169, 178, 179
guided imagery, 183
guilt, 45, 125–26, 137, 147, 281n, 297

happiness
and dopamine hits from technology, 196
and leisure practice, 207–8
and managing expectations, 79
and purpose, 42
and self-efficacy, 163
survival prioritized over, 72
United States' ranking in, 28
harm reduction, 283
headaches, 11
healing, taking responsibility for, 188
Health and Retirement Study, 51, 64
health and well-being, 21, 22
healthy habits, 260–302
about, 10, 39
and accountability, 272–75
challenges, 263–66
and flourishing, 299–302
and 4 Ms of mental health, 289–99
and fun, 287–89
and goal setting, 269–72
and good wolf/bad wolf paradigm,
275–85
and healthy pride, 127
and integrating identity, 285–87
and intentionality, 267–69
heart attacks, 225n, 226, 261, 301
helplessness, sense of, 45, 126, 167–68
help-seeking, 230, 233, 247
Heraclitus, 168–74
Hinduism, 47
hippocampus, 74–75, 295, 298
hobbies, 48, 49, 213

home life, developing a meaningful, 60
hopelessness, 45
Horney, Karen, 151
humanity, common, 92, 147, 149
humor, 113, 221
hurt, acknowledging, 92
hygge practices, 108
hypothalamic-pituitary-adrenal
    (HPA) axis, 295

illness and value of social connection, 225
immune function, 225–26, 248
imperfection, accepting, 143–46
impermanence of life, 168
inadequacy, feelings of, 155
indecision, 97, 199
India and Indian culture, 122–23, 299–300
Indian Cultural Institute, 47, 50
inequity, x
inflammation, 24, 127, 225, 294
insomnia, 11, 81, 152, 199, 202
Institute of Medicine, 265
intentionality
    and attachment styles, 231
    and cultivating aloneness, 256–57
    and cultivating healthy habits, 264
    and cultivating meaningful engagement,
        239–40
    and cultivating relationships, 222, 225, 235
    and elements of mental health, 290,
        297, 298
    and forming healthy habits, 267–69, 270
    and friendship styles, 238
    and habit formation process, 266
    and healthy boundaries, 253
internal locus of control, 164
irritability, 44, 81, 231

Japanese culture, 72
jealousy, 127
JOMO (joy of missing out), 210
journaling
    and conditioning/messaging from youth,
        131–32
    and negative self-talk, 170
    and personal assessment, 31–36
    to regain calm, 86
    and regrets about losses, 209
    and releasing worry, 208

worry journals, 89–90
    and wound healing, 89n
joy, 42, 43, 59, 63, 133
judgment focus, 140

Kabat-Zinn, Jon, 87n
kindness, 125, 132, 147, 280–81
kintsugi, 16, 157, 188, 304
Konrath, Sara H., 192

labeling, 140
languishing, 30, 42, 46, 56, 61
learned helplessness, 77–78, 162, 163, 165
learning, 177–82, 187, 295
legacies, 304
leisure, 207–8
life expectancy, 265, 301
lifestyle, 265
listening, 211, 239–42
locus of control, 164–65
loneliness, 28, 223–27
longevity, 51, 64, 265
love as ultimate goal of Practical
    Optimism, 153

magical thinking, 31, 305
Maier, Steven F., 77, 78
Mandela, Nelson, 113
Man's Search for Meaning (Frankl), 65
masking emotions, 72
mastery, 292, 293–94, 300–301
maximizers vs. satisficers, 98–100
meaning, sense of, 59. See also purpose
medications, 29, 258, 260–61, 262, 290
meditation, 52, 86, 298–99, 301
memory, 75, 295
mental fatigue, 206–9
mental filtering, 140
mental health
    4 Ms of, 289–99
    gratitude's impact on, 134
    and OXTR gene, 24
    and peripartum disorders, 68
    prevalence of mental health
        conditions, 12
    purpose as protective of, 46
    struggles with, as leading cause of ill
        health/disability, 28
    WHO's definition of, 28

mental ruts, 119
mentors and mentorship, 61–62
message registering, 240
milestones, 287–88
Milgram, Stanley, 197n
Mindfulness-Based Cognitive Therapy
    (MBCT), 87, 87n
mindfulness/mindfulness practices, 86, 87n,
    147–50, 258, 292, 298–99
The Mindful Way Through Depression
    (Williams, Teasdale, Segal, and
    Kabat-Zinn), 87n
mind-reading, 140
mindsets, growth vs. fixed, 169
"mise en place" concept, 277
mistakes, normalizing, 149
monkey mind, 195–97, 203–4
mood disorders, 295
moods, 71, 290, 295. *See also* emotions
mortality risk, 289, 297
motherhood, 76–77, 79–80
motivation
    and anxiety, 263n
    and automating habits, 276, 281–83,
        287, 294
    and cultivating healthy habits,
        261–62, 264
    and depression, 263n, 274
    impact of stress on, 75
mysig practices, 108

National Research Council, 265
nature, time in, 63, 86, 213–14
Neff, Kristin, 147
negative events, personalizing, 137
negative filtering, 103, 140, 171
negative thoughts and emotions,
    78, 282
nervousness, 11
networking groups, 62
neurobiology, 234
neurodiversity, 261
neurogenesis, 74–75
neurological conditions, 12
neuronal activity, 294–95
nonattachment, 250
nonverbal communication, 237
norepinephrine, 24, 75, 211
novelty bias, 196

obesity, 51, 265
obstacles, 275
online shopping, 224
opiate-use disorder, 28
optic flow, 296n
optimism and optimists
    advantages enjoyed by, 21–22
    attitudes of, 20
    characteristics of, 20–21
    coexistence of pessimism with, 26–27
    coping strategies of, 20
    and denial, 19, 22
    genetic component of, 22, 23
    and healthy habits, 265–66
    as an intervention, 22
    neural basis in brain for, 21
    overly optimistic people, *96–98*
    pessimism and realism compared to, 19
    and PO mindset, 290
    and self-compassion, 127
    stress withstood by, 20–21
Ostrich Optimists, *96–98*
outside-the-box problem-solving, 116
overgeneralization, 171
overly optimistic people, *96–98*
Overmier, J. Bruce, 77
overwhelm, feelings of, 168–74, 215
oxytocin, 23–24, 127, 225

pain, 62–63, 93, 229, 231
paradox of choice, 196–97
parents, 128, 170–71, 193, 229, 252
passivity, 21, 77–78, *97*, 132
past, being trapped in, 198–99
pausing, 282
people and relationships, 220–59
    about, 10, 39
    and attachment styles, 227–34
    and befriending yourself, 255–57
    benefits of, 220
    competing agendas in, 251
    declining quality of, 12
    definition of friends, 222n
    ending, 255
    friendship styles, 235–39
    guide to meaningful engagement, 239–55
    and healthy boundaries, 251–55
    impact of technology on, 191–95
    lapsed, 248–49

people and relationships (*cont.*)
  and liking gap, 245
  and loneliness epidemic, 223–27
  and meaningful engagement, 292, 296–97
  of optimists, 22
  oxytocin's connection with, 23
  and "people practice," 222–23
  of pessimists, 24
  and purpose, 43
  releasing unhealthy, 58
  role of emotions in, 71
  self-compassion's impact on, 154
  and sense of purpose, 48
  and shallowing hypothesis, 191–92
  and social-emotional rest, 206–7
  and suicide risk, 220–22, 258–59
  and types of friendships, 235–39
perception/perceptions, 110–11, 169–71,
    185–86, 230, 243–50
perfection/perfectionism, 99, 143–46,
    151–52, 170, 200
peripartum mental health disorders, 68
persistence, 177–78
personal/direct experiences, 166
persuasion, verbal, 166
pessimism and pessimists
  coexistence of optimism with, 26–27
  culture of, 28
  and fixed mindsets, 169
  health consequences of, 24, 202n
  impact of PO on, 23–24
  and low proficiency, 163
  and negative self-talk, 282
  neural basis in brain for, 21
  optimism and realism compared to, 19
  and passivity, 77–78
  and personalizing negative events, 137
  problem-solving practices of, *96–98*
  reactions to adverse events, 23
  relationships of, 24
  and shame, 126
physical symptoms
  of author, 1–2, 4, 73, 152
  exhaustion, 44
  found in Stress in American Survey, 11
  and optimists, 22
  as product of unprocessed emotions, 147
  and self-compassion, 147
physical trauma, 221

physiological feedback, 166
Pillars of Practical Optimism, 9–10
  about, 37–39
  acclimating to, 305
  and neurophysiology of optimism, 21
  and personal assessment, 36
  rooted in evidence-based techniques,
    26, 31
  synergistic interactions of, 36
  transformative power of, 13
  See also healthy habits; people and
    relationships; present, remaining; pride
    and sense of self-worth; problem-
    solving; processing emotions;
    proficiency and self-efficacy; purpose
play, 257
plural pronouns, 153
political divisiveness, 11
positive emotional responses (PER), 163
positive/negative strokes, 128, 131, 154
positive psychology, 23
positivity
  positive behaviors, 243
  positive memories, 256
  positive outlook, 244, 302
  positive reinforcement, 283
  positivity resonance, 236
possibility, dwelling in, 31
Practical Optimism
  author's father as personification of, 7–8
  as a daily practice, 39–40
  goals of, 153
  and kintsugi, 16
  origins of, 4–6
  power of, 31–32
  as proactive approach, 29
  rooted in evidence-based techniques,
    26, 31
  transformative power of, 40
  See also Pillars of Practical Optimism
praise, 181–82, 230
prefrontal cortex, 195–96, 203
present, remaining, 189–219
  about, 10, 38
  and awe/nature, 213–14
  cultivating present-moment awareness,
    203–5
  and flow state, 211–13
  and FOMO (fear of missing out), 201–2

and gratitude, 209–11

and monkey mind, 195–97, 203–4, 214

and overcoming mental fatigue, 206–9

and owning setbacks, 281

and starlight, 218–19

and taking back your time, 214–18

technology's impact on, 191–95

and three cognitive traps, 198–203

present-mind awareness, 257, 298

present-moment awareness (PMA), 203–5

Prevention and Relationship Enhancement
Program (PREP), 242n

pride and sense of self-worth, 122–57

and ABCDE techniques of cognitive
restructuring, 138–43

about, 9, 38

and accepting imperfection, 143–46

and art of healing, 155–57

and compassion, 124

and cultivating kindness, 132

and empathy for others, 153–54

factors that influence, 128–32

four components of, 124–27

and GRACE, 132–33

and gratitude, 133–36

and kintsugi, 157

and leisure practice, 136

and living mindfully/compassionately,
148–50

and oxytocin, 23, 127

and realistic attribution, 137–38

relationships promoted by, 126–27

rooted in self-assurance, 124

and self-compassion, 146–53

self-esteem compared to, 125

problem-solving, 94–121

about, 9, 38

acknowledgment/denial of problem, 96

and activation of "hope circuitry," 78

and cognitive restructuring, 102

and decision fatigue, 109

embracing what you cannot control,
104–5

feeling alone in, 111–12

and feeling stuck, 119–21

5 Rs of, 105–15, 170, 245, 291

and mastering your mind, 101–5

and maximizers vs. satisficers, 98–100

minimizing/magnifying problems, 97

with others, 115–17

practices of different personas, 96–98

and sleep, 109

in a therapist's hour, 117–19

processing emotions. See emotional
processing

procrastination

at bedtime, 285

exercise as antidote to, 64

and lack of purpose, 44, 46

and low proficiency, 163

in problem-solving, 97

understanding, 279–80

productivity, 130–31, 224, 257, 290

proficiency and self-efficacy, 158–88

about, 9, 38

and barriers/limitations, 161–62, 167–75

benefits associated with, 160–61, 163–64

and coping with setbacks, 281

definition of, 160

developing clarity on, 185–87

and embracing positive emotions, 183–84

and empowerment through experience,
175–77

and feedback, 179–82, 187

and growth mindset, 181–82

as a journey, 161

lack of, 44

and learned helplessness, 162, 163, 165

and learning, 177–82, 187

as a mindset, 162–63

pathways to, 163, 166

and procrastination, 279–80

two active states of, 164

visualization's role in, 182–83, 187

projection, 96

psychotherapy, 3, 4, 258, 290

PTSD, 295

purpose, 41–65

about, 9, 37

of author's parents, 47–48, 50

benefits of, 43–44, 50–53

and bigger-picture thinking, 63–64

and burnout, 56–57

changing of, over time, 50

connecting goals to, 171–73

creating, 37

defining, 43

and depression, 44, 45–46

purpose (*cont.*)
  experience of having joy and, 43
  feeling disconnected from, 42
  and flourishing, 42
  gaining clarity on, 186
  as good for business, 52–53
  happiness without, 42
  impact of family/cultural roots on, 46–47
  and joy, 42, 43
  key question for finding, 46
  lack of, 42, 44, 46
  misconceptions about, 48–50
  movement's connection with, 63, 64
  as reclaiming what is important, 63
  three pathways to reigniting, 53–63
  as universal longing, 42

quiet quitting, 165

racial climate and racism, x, 11
radical acceptance, 250
reading and books, 192, 193, 217, 218, 288n
realism, optimism and pessimism compared
    to, 19. *See also* Practical Optimism
reality TV, 192
Real-World Problem-Solving, 245
reappraising/reassessing situations, 105–8,
    113–15
recognition of others' efforts, 57
reestablishing social connections, 248–49
"reflect" element of supportive listening,
    240–41
reframing, 90–92, 134, 274
refueling, importance of, 108–10
regret orientation, 141
regrets, 54, 58, 199, 209
reinforcement of boundaries, 254
rejection, 113, 202, 230
relationships. *See* people and relationships
relaxing, 108–9
remote work, 271
researching problems, 97
resentment, 251
resilience, 6, 8, 20, 24, 30, 156
responsibilities, 97, 98, 126, 137
rest, importance of, 257
revenge bedtime procrastination, 285
rewards, 288
Rogers, Fred, 66

role models, 192
role play, 182–83
roles, releasing unproductive, 58
Roosevelt, Eleanor, 122
Rotary clubs, 62
Rumi, 81
rumination
  as being trapped in the past, 198–99
  CBT's interruption of, 87n
  and depression, 31, 202n, 281n
  as emotional loop, 76–77
  learning to sidestep, 31
  pessimists' struggles with, 24
  in problem-solving, 97
  releasing, 208–9
  self-compassion as buffer against, 147
  and self-referential thinking, 202
  and shame, 126

sadness, 73
salary gap, 68
Sarin, Rakesh, 79–80
satisficers vs. maximizers, 98–100
scheduling, 272
Segal, Zindel, 87n
self-acceptance, *144–45*
self-awareness, 29, 81–92
self-blame, 93, 137
self-care, 13, 155, 174, 254, 304–5
self-commitment, 288
self-comparison, 247
self-compassion, 146–53
  and attachment styles, 231
  of author, 29
  and befriending yourself, 255–57
  benefits of, 127
  as catalyst for hopeful future, 132–33
  and empathy, 153–54
  and feedback, 181
  flexibility paired with, 170
  and healthy pride, 125, 127
  and impact of early caregivers, 128
  and improving relationships, 154
  and inner critic, 144
  and learning/asking for help, 174
  as most important tool in PO, 147
  in problem-solving, 97
  and resilience, 156
  self-care as expression of, 155

and self-criticism, 155
and self-support, 174
and social connectedness, 153
three key elements of, 147
and "The Two Wolves" parable, 280
self-consciousness, 247
self-criticism, 87n, 126, 127, 143–44,
 144–45, 155
self-disclosure, 240
self-doubt, 230
self-efficacy. See proficiency and self-efficacy
self-esteem, 125, 144
self-judgment, 281
self-monitoring, 274
self-referential thinking, 202
self-reliance, 228, 230, 232–33
self-soothing, 227–28, 233
self-support, exercising, 167, 174–75
self-talk, 169–70
self-worth. See pride and sense of
 self-worth
Seligman, Martin, 23, 77, 132
Seneca, 41
September 11, 2001, terrorist attacks, 4–5,
 158–60, 167–68, 171, 175
serotonin, 211
service, 58, 62–63
setbacks, 177–78, 275, 281
Seven Principles for Making Marriage Work,
 The (Gottman), 116
sexism, x
shallowing hypothesis, 191–92
shame
 and criticism/self-blame, 138
 and depression, 45, 126, 147, 281n
 pride as protective against, 126–27
 in problem-solving, 97
 self-compassion as antidote to, 147
 and severe self-criticism, 126
 and stress hormones, 127
 unprocessed feelings of, 147
Shapiro, Francine, 296n
should statements, 104, 141, 150–53
skills/skill building, 61, 293–94
sleep
 and mental wellness, 13
 of optimists, 21
 and problem-solving, 109
 and sense of purpose, 52

sleep deprivation, 109, 110, 206
 and social media use, 194
slowing down, 63
smoking, 265, 278
snacking, 275, 277, 278
snap decisions, 97
social anxiety, 127
social bonds/connections, 248, 258. See also
 people and relationships
social comparison theory, 176–77
social-emotional rest, 206–7
social experiments, 273
social isolation/withdrawal, 126, 127, 202,
 223–27, 297
social media, 193, 194, 195, 200–201,
 215–16, 224, 287, 292
social skills, 24
social snacking, 237
solitude, 256–57
stagnation and lack of purpose, 46
standards, 79, 127
starlight, 218–19
State of the American Workplace report,
 52–53
stigma around mental health, 7
Stoics, 219
strengths-based model of health, 5–6, 31
stress
 addressing, with PO, 10
 of author, 2, 73, 123
 chronic, 75
 consequences of, 52
 and learned helplessness, 78
 and leisure practice, 208
 neurogenesis as impacted by, 74–75
 optimists' ability to withstand, 20–21
 and OXTR gene, 24
 perceptions of, 75
 pervasiveness of, in America, 11–12
 PO's power to help with, 31
 prevalence of, 28
 and reassessing situations, 106–7
 and shame, 126
 in small quantities, 74–75
 and technology usage, 205
 and value of social connection, 225
stress hormones, 24, 51–52, 127, 170, 248.
 See also cortisol; epinephrine;
 norepinephrine

Stress in America Survey, 11, 28
strokes, 225n, 297
stuck, feeling, 167, 168–74
subway commuters, 243–44
success, 70
successive approximations, 272
suicides/suicide risk
    attempts, 220–22, 230, 258–59
    and lack of purpose, 44–45
    and learned helplessness, 78
    rise in rates of, 28
    and self-reliance, 228
    Suicide and Crisis Lifeline, xi
supportive listening, 239–42
support to others, offering, 51
Survey Center on American Life, 223
systems, broken/flawed, x

task crafting, 62
Teasdale, John, 87n
technology, personal
    and comparisons, 201
    and dementia risks, 293
    and empathy, 191, 192–93
    impacts of, 191–95
    managing, 207
    prescriptions for, 216–18
    reliance on, 189–90
    social media, 193, 194, 195, 200–201,
        215–16
    texting, 205
    time/attention dedicated to, 191
    tracking progress with, 273
television, 293
telomeres, 52
texting, 205
therapy, 29, 117–19, 232, 290, 291
Thích, Nhất Hanh, 211
thought distortions, 102n, 103–4, 186
threats, overestimating, 74
threat system, overactive, 234
time famine/affluence, 130
to-do lists, 208
tracking progress, 273–75, 278,
    283, 285
tragedies, 302
transactional analysis (TA), 128

traumatic experiences, 128–32
    expressing gratitude following, 134
    and feelings of inner brokenness, 160
    as opportunity for growth, 302
    and recognizing what is out of our
        control, 164–65
    September 11, 2001, terrorist attacks, 4–5,
        158–60, 167–68, 171, 175
    talking/writing about, 82
triggers, 220, 232, 277, 284–85
trust, 23
tuning problems out, 97
"Two Wolves" parable, 27, 28, 30, 275–85

uncertainty, feelings of, 44
United States, 28, 265

validation, 167–68
values, 59, 80, 171–73, 285–87
venting, 111
ventromedial prefrontal cortex (vmPFC), 78
vicarious experiences, 166, 176–77
violence, 11
Virgil, 158
visualization, 63, 182–83, 187
volunteering/volunteerism, 51, 289
vulnerability, 36, 258

Ward, William Arthur, 19
weight loss, 269–70, 288, 301
Weil, Simone, 189, 219
wellness, 4, 59
what-ifs, 104, 141, 199
Whillans, Ashley, 130
Williams, Mark, 87n
Williams, Robin, 224
withdrawal, 98
women, 12, 68
World Happiness Index, 28
World Health Organization (WHO), 12, 28
World Trade Center Mental Health Program
    (WTCMHP), 5, 6, 62–63, 173–74, 178
worrying, 72, 97, 163, 208–9

XYZ technique, 242–43, 291

yoga, 300–301